GUYANA
FRAGILE F

Loggers, Miners a

Marcus Colchester

LATIN AMERICA BUREAU

WORLD RAINFOREST MOVEMENT

IAN RANDLE PUBLISHERS

This is the fourth in a series of reports by the author on the political ecology of tropical forest exploitation. *Pirates, Squatters and Poachers: the Political Ecology of Dispossession of the Native Peoples of Sarawak* was published by Survival International and INSAN in Petaling Jaya, Malaysia (1989). *Slave and Enclave: the Political Ecology of Equatorial Africa* was published by the World Rainforest Movement in Penang, Malaysia (1994). *Forest Politics in Suriname* was published by International Books, Amsterdam (1995). These case studies complement a general overview of the deforestation crisis published by Zed Books, the Ecologist and the World Rainforest Movement, *The Struggle for Land and the Fate of the Forests*, edited by Marcus Colchester and Larry Lohmann (1993).

© Marcus Colchester 1997

First published in Great Britain in 1997 by

Latin America Bureau
 (Research and Action Ltd)
1 Amwell Street
London EC1R 1UL

Published in Jamaica by
Ian Randle Publishers
PO Box 686
206 Old Hope Road
Kingston 6

World Rainforest Movement
Forest Peoples Programme
1c Fosseway Business Centre,
Stratford Road,
Moreton-in Marsh,
Gloucestershire GL56 9NQ

A CIP catalogue record for this book is available from the British Library
A catalogue record for this book is available from the National Library of Jamaica

ISBN: 1 899365 02 8 (UK)
ISBN: 976 8123 22 2 (Jamaica)
ISBN: 0 85345 971 1 (USA)
Cover photo: Fiona Watson, Survival International
Cover design: Andy Dark
Maps: The Drawing Office, Geography Department, University College London
Printed and bound: Page Bros, Norfolk NR6 6SA
Trade distribution in the UK by: Central Books, 99 Wallis Road, London E9 5LN
Distribution in North America by: Monthly Review Press, 122 West 27th Street, New York, NY 10001

Nico Colchester
In memoriam

CONTENTS

Foreword..vii
Guyana in Brief ix
Chronology... x
Map of Guyana... xii

Introduction.. 1
1. From Trading Allies to Colonial Subjects............................... 5
2. Plantation Politics.. 25
3. Development Domination.. 36
4. Roads and Ranches.. 45
5. Undermining the Interior... 61
6. Forests for Sale.. 96
7. Amerindian Survival 127
8. Future Options.. 141

Useful Addresses.. 158
References and Bibliography.. 159
Index.. 167

Maps
1. Vegetation 6
2. General Distribution of Amerindian Peoples.............................. 8
3. Dutch Trading Posts 11
4. Disputed New River Area 59
5. Location of Mines 63
6. Logging Concessions 108

Boxes
The Venezuelan Connection 30
The New River Controversy with Suriname 59
Suriname: Golden Star and the Maroons 87
Venezuela: Mining Madness 91
The Scourge of Tropical Forest Logging 100
Timber Pirates 104
NGO Statement to the Caribbean Group for Cooperation in Economic Development... 112
International Norms regarding Natural Forest Logging 115
Logging Amerindian Land 123
Indigenous Rights in International Law 127
The Curious Case of the 'Amerindia Nation' 152

Table 1: Major Forestry Concessions in Guyana 109

ACKNOWLEDGEMENTS

This essay draws on the efforts of many people. My attention was first focused on Guyana by Audrey Butt Colson to whom I owe an enormous debt of gratitude for years of encouragement and support, and who has acted as a mine of information. As Projects Director of Survival International during the 1980s, I had responsibility for the organization's work on Guyana, which included tracking the progress of road-building and mining in the interior and pressuring the international aid agencies to respect indigenous rights. This work led to a fertile collaboration with the Guyana Human Rights Association one of the only non-governmental organizations in Guyana promoting the rights of Amerindians during those years and I am particularly grateful to Mike McCormack and Merle Mendonca for their help and hospitality in Georgetown. My move to set up the World Rainforest Movement's Forest Peoples Programme in the early 1990s coincided with the emergence of the Amerindian Peoples Association, while at the same time the Guyanese government was liberally handing out logging concessions to foreign companies. These circumstances led to an energetic collaboration, particular with the APA's Programmes Administrator, Jean La Rose.

In preparing this text and previous articles about Guyana, I am in particular grateful for the contributions of Audrey Butt Colson, Roger Moody, Francis Sullivan, Gordon Bennett, Jean La Rose, Merle Mendonca, Mike McCormack, Dominic Hogg, Phil Hazelton, Rachel Crossley, Jannette Forte, John Dorman, John Hemming, Mike Eden and Stuart Wilson. Audrey Butt Colson offered invaluable comments on draft chapters as they emerged from the word-processor. I would also like to thank Peter Poole, Nick Hilyard, Saskia Ozinga and Ricardo Carrere for helpful criticism of the penultimate draft. Louise Henson provided calm administrative back-up and helped me organize the bibliography. None of these, of course, is responsible for the interpretation of events given in this book. Funding for the research and publication have come from a Pew Conservation Fellowship, Novib and the IUCN-Netherlands. Finally I would like to thank James Ferguson of the Latin America Bureau both for asking me to write the book and seeing it into print.

FOREWORD

In describing Guyana's interior as a 'fragile frontier', Marcus Colchester aptly encapsulates the country's present-day predicament after a decade of developments in the hinterland. In shifting from 'cooperative socialism' to free-market capitalism, recent governments have seen the need to invite in foreign investment – investment which is chiefly aimed at exploiting the country's natural resources.

Guyana was until recently among the few remaining countries in the world whose forests had survived intact after centuries of destruction elsewhere. Prior to the mid-1980s, the interior had remained virtually untouched, but with the advent of a new development model based on logging and mining, this situation is rapidly changing. The invitations to foreign companies issued by the administrations of Desmond Hoyte and Cheddi Jagan have set in train a process through which, as Colchester puts it, 'the interior of Guyana is now under threat as never before.' A change for the worse is inevitable if the timber and mining companies which are clamouring to operate in Guyana are allowed to do so without regulation and supervision. Problems and conflicts cannot be avoided if roads are built through communities and if land is given away without consulting the people who live on and off that same land.

This book shows how most activities in Guyana's interior, whether under way or in the pipeline, take place without any consultation with its majority population, the Amerindians. In the case of the road linking Guyana with Brazil, for instance, the possible benefits of the project are outweighed by doubts over its long-term effects. The government policy of non-disclosure and the fact that recommendations concerning the road have been ignored cannot augur well for the Amerindian communities which stand to lose most from a road driven through their land. For vulnerable indigenous peoples who are already facing an onslaught from concessions to mining and timber multinationals, the further opening-up of their territory by road networks poses yet more dangers.

The search for investment takes place within the context of servicing a vast national debt, but such economic imperatives are likely to take little account of the Amerindians and their traditional culture. They have been accustomed to living as one with the forests for centuries and have managed to maintain and preserve a way of life which cannot be replaced by modern technology or foreign ideologies. Through this unique relationship with their environment the Amerindians have helped to protect the interior, surviving and adapting because they conserve the forests even as they live off them.

Yet, as Marcus Colchester reveals, the environmental impact of widescale mining has already left its negative mark on the traditional Amerindian economy with a resulting breakdown in indigenous society as well. This damage is even more dramatic than the devastation inflicted by the timber sector, where there is also plenty of evidence of harm inflicted on the environment and Amerindian communities. Any increase in these activities could shatter the *fragile frontier* beyond repair.

Guyana's Amerindians have been quick to realize the extent of the threat that faces them and have been insistent in calls to government and those in positions of power to ensure that their various rights, especially their right to land, are guaranteed and that their right to self-determination is respected as a matter of policy. The issue of self-determination is increasingly being raised by the Amerindians themselves as they become aware of the urgency of their plight and point to the international legislation which stipulates their legal ownership of ancestral lands and their right to decide on their use. Having been ignored in their demands for land rights and protection, the Amerindians have decided to move a step further and call for sub-surface rights to their land.

Fragile Frontier makes clear that the Amerindians occupy and have always occupied vast areas of Guyana's interior. It shows how during the country's period of colonial control the Amerindian presence was vital to the export economy and local survival. Yet just as the rights of the Amerindians were only recognized when it was expedient to the British, so today they are taken seriously only when it suits those in power or, in practical terms, when election time comes around. Beyond such intermittent concern, the Amerindians are largely ignored and marginalized.

Colchester concludes that ' a favourable outcome will only come about if the Guyanese people have the strength and courage to assert their own destiny and face down these foreign impositions.' The odds are heavily stacked against the Guyanese people as a whole and even more so against the Amerindians as a distinct group, since history and geography have limited their strength to slow the advance of the multinationals and government. Many Amerindians, even some in positions in responsibility, are largely unaware of the implications of opening up the interior to the logging and mining companies. Many are still unaware that short-term employment does not spell long-term benefit, especially when the income generated by interior development is not put back into Amerindian communities themselves.

The struggle for Amerindian rights is still at an embryonic stage, and international support is needed if it is to advance and succeed. The Amerindians themselves are willing to fight for their rights, but limited resources and experience mean that they are far from winning a battle which could end in their extinction as a people. Marcus Colchester is among the supporters of indigenous rights and I hope that this much-needed book will go a long way in making the issues clearer and assisting Guyana's Amerindians in their goal of survival.

Jean La Rose – Amerindian Peoples Association, Guyana

GUYANA IN BRIEF

Statistics

Geography	National territory	21.5 million hectares
	Forests	16.1 million hectares
	State Forests	9.1 million hectares
	Deforestation (1992)	0.1% per annum
Population	Total number	750,000 (1996)
	Growth rate	0.7% per annum
	Population density	4 persons/square kilometre
People	East Indians	49%
	Afro-Guyanese	36%
	Mixed	7%
	Amerindian (nine peoples)	7%
	Chinese and Portuguese	1%
	Other	1%
Religion	Christian	46%
	Hindu	37%
	Muslim	8%
	Not Stated	9%
Health	Infant mortality	47 per 1,000 live births
	Life expectancy	65.4 years
	Population per doctor	6,809
Economy	GDP (1996)	US$420 million
	GDP per capita (1996)	US$560
	GDP growth	7.9% (1996); 5% (1995); 8.5% (1994); 8.3% (1993)
	Inflation	4.5% (1996); 8.1% (1995); 16.1% (1994)
	Exports (1996)	US$565 million
	Imports (1996)	US$589 million
	Foreign Debt	US$1,500 million (1996); US$2,050 million (1995); US$1,950 million (1994)
Principal towns	Georgetown	180-250,000
	Linden	35,000
	New Amsterdam	25,000
Government	Elected President. Single-chamber National Assembly with 65 seats. 53 by proportional representation and 12 from regional and local authorities. Five-year terms.	

CHRONOLOGY

1580   Dutch make contact with Carib Indians.

1621   Dutch West India Company takes control of Essequibo trading posts.

1651   Berbice under Dutch control.

1665   British attempts to drive out Dutch fail.

1678   Shipment of African slaves to British Guiana to work on the sugar plantations.

1708   French fail to drive out Dutch.

1814   Territory ceded to Britain by Treaty of London.

1831   Three counties of Essequibo, Berbice and Demerara merged into British Guiana.

1838   Abolition of slavery in British territories.

1841   Portuguese immigrants arrive.

1851   Indentured Indian labourers brought in to replace slaves.

1853   Chinese immigrants arrive.

1860   Gold boom begins.

1917   End of indentured immigration.

1919   British Guiana Labour Union formed - the first trade union in the Caribbean.

1939   Moyne Commission established to investigate social unrest in British Caribbean colonies.

1950   PPP formed under leadership of Dr Cheddi Jagan.

1953   First elections under universal adult suffrage. Constitution suspended after 135 days.

1955   PNC formed from split in PPP led by Forbes Burnham.

1957   PPP wins general election.

1961   PPP wins general election.

1963   80-day general strike led by civil service, financed by the CIA. Firms lock their workers out, leading to rioting.

1963/4 Racial violence, murder, arson, hundreds killed as PNC and UF supporters denounce PPP government as communist. Britain refuses to grant independence to British Guiana under PPP rule.

1964   Elections under new proportional representation system. Despite increasing its share of the vote, PPP wins only 24 seats. The PNC wins 22 seats and the UF seven. PNC asked by Governor General to form a government in coalition with UF. Geneva Agreement reached on Venezuelan border dispute.

1966   Independence from Britain. Name changed from British Guiana to Guyana.

1968   Elections massively rigged by introduction of 'overseas vote'. PNC wins majority, drops UF from coalition.

1969   Rupununi rebellion. Relations with Venezuela reach all time low.

1970   Guyana declared a 'Co-operative Republic'. Governor-General replaced
        by non-executive President.
        Protocol of Port-of-Spain freezes Venezuelan border dispute for twelve years.
        Nationalization of bauxite industry from the Demerara Bauxite Company.

1970-6 Nationalization of all major foreign economic assets except banks and
        insurance companies.

1972   Diplomatic relations established with Cuba.

1973   Elections massively rigged. Ballot boxes seized at close of polling by the
        army. Released after 24 hours, when PNC declared to have won a two-
        thirds majority.

1975   Doctrine of the 'paramountcy of the party' enunciated in the Declaration
        of Sophia in which all state institutions including government institutions
        are declared to be arms of the ruling party. All private schools taken over by
        the state.

1978   Referendum to allow a two-thirds majority to change any provision of the
        constitution. Aimed at postponing elections, government claims a 71 per
        cent turn-out and a 97.7 per cent 'yes' vote. Civic groups claim a 14 per
        cent turn-out and PPP claims 12 per cent. A two-year extension of the life
        of parliament follows.

1979   Formation of WPA: multi-racial independent Marxist party.

1980   Assassination of Dr Walter Rodney, leader of WPA, allegedly by government
        agent.

1980   New constitution promulgated. Executive presidency introduced with
        'virtual imperial powers'.
        General elections denounced as fraudulent by International Observer Team.

1981   Government spending cuts cause major redundancies in the civil service.
        Widespread food shortages and breakdown of public and social services occur.

1982   Food shortages broaden, flour imports stopped, production and exports
        reduced.

1983   Bauxite industry in crisis, strikes in sugar and bauxite industries.

1984   Golden Star Resources Ltd commences prospecting.

1985   Death of Forbes Burnham.

1986   Desmond Hoyte assumes presidency, start of liberalization policies.
        Establishment of Guyana Natural Resources Agency.

1988   Economic Recovery Program begins under IMF and World Bank supervision.

1989   National Forestry Action Plan, carried out by CIDA, approved.

1991   Timber deals with Lord Beaverbrook and Barama Company Ltd; Omai
        mining agreement reached; Amerindian Peoples Association formed.

1992   PPP election victory; Cheddi Jagan assumes presidency.

1995   Omai mine disaster.
        Agreement to ODA-funded Forestry Support Project.

1997   Death of Cheddi Jagan.

GUYANA

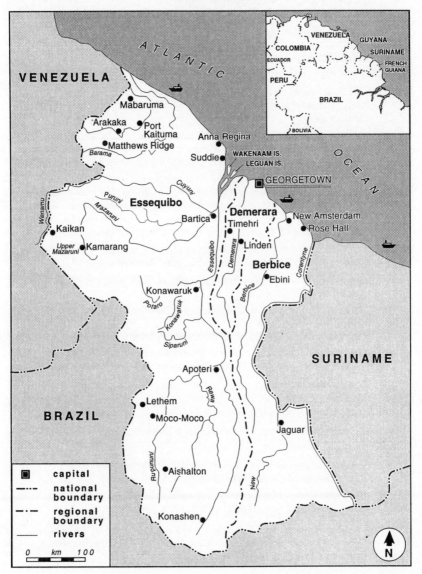

INTRODUCTION

'Decisions are being taken with regard to our forests, rivers and natural resources which will change the way of life of our Amerindian communities forever... We are therefore at a cross-roads... We can choose the path of making fast profits at the cost of destroying both the environment and Amerindian communities, or alternatively, we can take the path of using our resources in caring and renewable ways, ways which recognise that vigorous Amerindian communities are the best form of conservation.'
Bishop Randolph George, Speech to the Amerindian Peoples Association 11 April 1991.

The interior of Guyana is now under threat as never before. Nearly nine million hectares of rainforest, an area the size of Portugal, have been handed out to foreign logging companies, many with disturbing track records overseas. Another area the size of the Netherlands is currently under negotiation. A mining bonanza is also underway, with a host of foreign companies energetically searching the interior for gold, diamonds and other minerals. Guyana now has the dubious distinction of playing host to one of South America's largest gold mines, which in August 1995 suffered a massive tailings dam burst, pouring three million cubic metres of cyanide-laced waste into the country's main river. It was a tragedy that Cheddi Jagan, the country's president, called 'a national environmental disaster'.

At the same time, under heavy pressure from Brazilian interests, an all-weather laterite road is being constructed across the forested interior to link the northern Brazilian cities of Boa Vista and Manaus with a proposed deep-sea container port near Guyana's capital, Georgetown. The interior of the country has become an enclave for overseas business interests, a situation reminiscent of the colonial age, when the country was dominated by foreign-owned sugar and mining companies.

Those most affected by these developments are the country's 60,000 Amazonian Indians, Guyana's indigenous peoples referred to locally as Amerindians. They make up the majority population in the interior, yet are being marginalized by the 'development' process. Denied adequate land rights and control over decision-making in their own territories, they see their environments despoiled, their millennial cultures undermined and their labour exploited by foreign companies in league with politicians in the capital.

1

The critical situation has generated fierce national controversy and international condemnation, some of it spurred by the World Rainforest Movement. A host of voices have spoken out ranging from Congressmen to Malaysian environmental organizations, warning the Guyanese government not to repeat the mistakes made in other parts of the world, where short-term profit-seeking has led to long-term loss and human rights abuse. Apart from putting the Amerindians' futures in jeopardy and irreparably damaging the environment, it has emerged that many of the deals with these foreign businesses make very little profit for Guyana. Hints of shady deals between barely accountable politicians and transnationals have sharpened fears that the country's very democracy is in peril. The government has been urged by national and international non-governmental organizations (NGOs) to freeze the hand-out of logging and mining concessions until it is able both to regulate these invading industries and extract better profits for the national exchequer. With considerable effect, Guyanese NGOs have appealed to the aid agencies to curb further funding for interior development until these conditions are agreed to by the government.

These debates have not ignored the wider context in which the government has made apparently reckless decisions to open up the interior. Guyana, which at independence was heralded as 'the jewel of the Caribbean', with one of the continent's highest per capita incomes, is just emerging from three decades of one-party dictatorship. These years of sorrow left the country bankrupt, massively indebted and with a wasted infrastructure. Food shortages, low wages and chronic unemployment led to living conditions reminiscent of the nineteenth century, when British colonial planters had extracted their wealth by exploiting black slaves and indentured labourers from India. Denied further credit and with growing domestic pressure for reform, change was inevitable.

In the 1980s, the Guyanese government reluctantly turned its back on 'Co-operative Socialism' under heavy pressure from the international development agencies to liberalize the economy and carry out structural adjustment. A central part of the World Bank and International Monetary Fund's formula for economic recovery was to promote 'non-traditional exports', gold and timber. The pillage of the interior was launched.

Guyana was one of the world's first countries to receive structural adjustment lending from the World Bank and is now hailed as a model of effective reform. The economy has begun to perform better and wealth is beginning to trickle down to some, though further hardships have been imposed on others. Foreign investment has begun to pour in, but what is unique about Guyana's situation is the extent to which the invading companies are themselves from the 'South' – logging companies from South East Asia and Korea, flush with fresh capital from the new Asian stock exchanges – bringing with them new forms of patronage, corruption and political control, different from the familiar manipulations of northern businesses.

This book is an attempt to detail this story. It reaches back to the very beginnings of the colony to try to trace the origins of the social injustices being played out today. Previous social critiques of the history of Guyana have looked at the country from the point of view of the slaves and plantation workers whose labour provided the foundation of the country's wealth. However, this book focuses on the country's hinterland where the majority of the population are Amerindians, descendants of the indigenous peoples who inhabited the area before European colonization. Once crucial allies of the first colonists, these peoples gradually became marginal to coastal history as the wealth of the plantations grew. After two centuries of uneasy alliances with the Dutch, they were absorbed as lowly colonial subjects and were written out of the country's history, forgotten in the interior and derided as 'backward natives', 'primitive tribes' and 'bucks'.

Today, however, with the plantation economy stagnant on the coast, it is the country's interior resources that foreign companies and development agencies have their eyes on. With attention now focused on lucrative timber and mineral resources, the Amerindians once more find themselves on a new frontier, locked in an unequal struggle with transnational companies and coastal interests. The history of Guyana at the close of the twentieth century is thus one of internal colonialism and southward expansion. Once again, the indigenous peoples are at the receiving end and, once again, they are resisting the takeover of their lands and natural resources. New organizations representing indigenous communities are springing up and the Amerindians have found renewed strength to voice their concerns and demand that future development should respect their rights and accommodate their interests.

This essay is then explicitly partisan. It looks at what is happening in Guyana today from the point of view of the Amerindian communities of the interior. It takes as its point of departure norms established in international law: that the Amerindians are the lawful owners of their ancestral domains and may rightfully demand a decisive voice in what happens in the interior. Encouragingly, there are today many Guyanese on the coast who not only sympathize with the Amerindians' demands but share many of their aspirations: to have more control over development, to evolve a participatory democracy, to use resources rationally for the long-term benefit of the country and not the short-term profit of foreign enterprises and a national elite. Happily too, there are many in government who express similar aspirations. But the forces within and outside their country with other priorities are also very powerful.

3

How this complex struggle resolves itself only future histories will relate. What Guyana's history already teaches us is that the forces of the market are very strong and where allowed 'free' play easily overcome local alternatives. The pressure from foreign development advisers to open up Guyana to foreign investment and cash in on the country's natural wealth has thus to be resisted, but debt, lack of local industry and domestic capital, and the short-term imperative of relieving the conditions of the poor do not allow the government much room to manoeuvre.

A favourable outcome will only come about if the Guyanese people have the strength and courage to assert their own destiny and face down these foreign impositions. They are, however, not entirely alone in confronting this challenge. All around the tropics, debt-strapped 'third world' countries are being offered the same package of reforms by the international financial institutions – structural adjustment, foreign direct investment, economic liberalization – part of the leaping acceleration in the globalization of world trade – and many are also resisting this pressure. Even in the 'North', Guyana is not without allies, citizens' groups of many kinds, not only environmental and human rights organizations, share a view that the present trend towards a tariff-barrier-free global market dominated by unregulated, overpowerful and unaccountable transnational companies threatens their own homes, jobs, environments and futures.

Above all, this book argues, the future course of development in the interior of Guyana should be determined by the people who live there, the Amerindians. They are the ones who have evolved unique ways of life attuned to the difficult conditions of tropical forests; they are the ones who suffer the impacts of the extractive industries; they are the ones who will have to rebuild their lives in their despoiled forests once the foreign companies have made their profits and left. The present pattern of development which denies their rights and excludes them from decision-making is neither just nor prudent and Guyana can only benefit if this is changed.

As one Amerindian from the Upper Mazaruni told the author:

> Development is a big word which needs defining more clearly. Even though we may not have big buildings we are also developed. You cannot look at only one aspect. You can destroy both the culture and the environment by just focusing on money and that is what we are trying to avoid.
>
> This territory is rich but we need to develop it carefully. If we get rights to this land, we can develop it by ourselves. We have to go ahead and develop our own community. It is not that we are selfish, we are self-employed and believe development means becoming self-sufficent.

CHAPTER 1
FROM TRADING ALLIES TO COLONIAL SUBJECTS

'These laws were made by Colonial people in a language not fully understood by the Amerindians. As Amerindians learnt the English language, they realised that certain laws were not suited to Amerindian needs. Some of these laws make our living in our homelands very uncomfortable.'
Captain Lawrence Anselmo, Arekuna from Paruima[1]

Approached from the sea, the coast of Guyana is not obviously welcoming. Muddy beaches extend along the forested coast where powerful silty rivers debouch through slack tidal mudflats. Westward the coast is heavily covered by mangrove swamps, behind which flooded wet savannahs and coastal forests are cut through by a maze of narrow channels as sluggish waters from the interior meander seawards. Protected only by the mangroves and beaches, the extensive inland forests and swamps are for much of the time below sea-level and for long were considered uncultivable wastelands. Inland from the swampy coastal forests, the interior is more open. Patches of savannah on famously infertile white sands alternate with forests whose tannin-rich leaves stain the clear river waters a brackish brown. Further inland again the ground rises slightly and here extensive rainforests cover the entire width of the country, stretching away in an almost continuous carpet to the Brazilian frontier 650 kilometres due south.

Yet it is only after travelling some 150 kilometres inland that the relief changes. Travellers voyaging up the lower rivers sooner or later run up against spectacular falls, where the rain-charged rivers spill over the outer edges of the Guiana Highlands. These are the outermost defences of the country's mountainous interior, a vast eroded tableland established on ancient rocks dating back to the continent's creation. Known by geologists as the Guiana Shield, the Pre-Cambrian crystalline rocks that underlie the hinterland are still capped in places by Cretaceous sandstones, the eroded remnants of which stand as spectacular mesas – huge cliff-edged massifs that rise into the clouds. Greatest of these, tucked into the corner of the country, is Mount Roraima, which at 2,700 metres is one of the continent's highest mountains east of the Andes and whose inaccessible heights gave rise to Sir Arthur Conan Doyle's vision of the 'Lost World'.

Vegetation

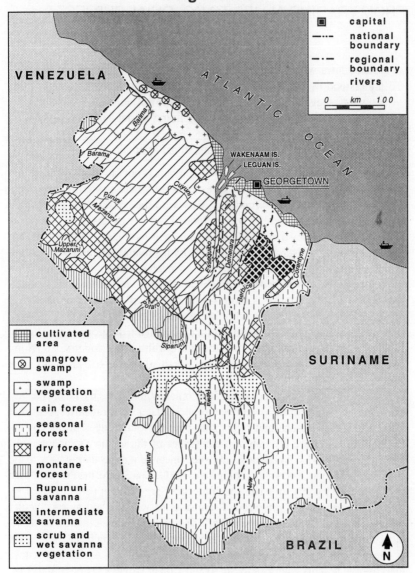

Here, on the Brazilian and Venezuelan border, are large swathes of grassland which extend from the Gran Sabana in Venezuela, around the Pakaraima mountains, east into the Rupununi savannahs and south down to the Rio Branco in Brazil. Under a wide sky and across rolling hills and plains, the landscape offers sweeping vistas interrupted near and far by forested watercourses that wend their way down to the Amazon and the high sandstone mesas that tower over all.

When the Spanish sailor Vincente Yáñez Pinzón, blown off course on his way around Africa, first sighted the Guyana coast in 1500, almost nothing was known in Europe of this New World. But for all its wild and untamed aspect, the area was far from uninhabited.[2] Indeed, recent estimates suggest that there were as many as 160,000 Amerindians living along the Guyana coast in the countries now known as French Guiana, Suriname and Guyana.[3]

The Amerindian peoples were not only numerous, they were also diverse. The widely differing environments had stimulated the emergence of societies finely adapted to make the most of local resources. In the mangrove and swamp forests along the coast, the Warao nation had developed an economic and social order based on fishing and seafood, palm starch and tuber cultivation. Master boat-builders – their name means 'Boat People' – the Warao used to make adzes without metal and still today have an elaborate ritual and material culture. Much of their life is spent afloat in their dugouts, moving between their fisheries and the stands of palms which provide their daily bread. Little involved in agriculture, the Warao have traditionally relied principally on foraging and fishing and exploit their forests for fruits, palm cabbage, wild pineapples, honey and herbs as well as larvae, snails, crabs and the eggs of turtles and iguana.[4]

Where the Warao have learnt to live from the flooded swamp forests, their neighbours, the Arawaks, favour the higher ground along the rivers flowing to the sea. Fragmentary archaeological finds suggest that the Arawaks have long practised agriculture based on cassava or manioc, a starchy and acidic tuber that grows well on the region's poor and sandy soils. Over the millenia the Amerindians have selected increasingly productive, yet toxic, varieties that require careful processing to eliminate their cyanide-bearing glucosides. But cassava is but one of a huge range of Amazonian crops that they cultivate, while their diet is balanced with the fish that come from the rivers. It seems likely that it was the ancestors of today's Arawak people who established elaborate raised fields in the interior lowlands, remains of an intensive form of agriculture that is no longer recalled today.

Further inland, are the territories of the Akawaio and Patamona nations, who live especially on the middle and upper reaches of the Mazaruni, Potaro and Ireng rivers, in the Pakaraima mountains and whose name for themselves, *kapon*,

General Distribution of Amerindian Peoples

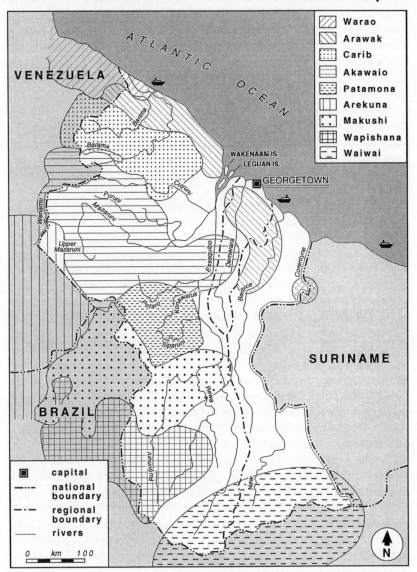

may mean appropriately 'sky people'. The Akawaio were renowned as traders, notably of cassava graters, laboriously made by inland tribes by hammering narrow chips of jasper into a wooden board. They also specialize in making 'wood-skins', delicate river craft made by cutting off the strong, curved bark of the 'purpleheart' tree. Heavier than water and thus perilous to the inexperienced if they ship water, the little boats are ideal for navigating the narrow creeks of their mountain territory. Akawaio also live down stream, at one time populating the upper reaches of the Berbice, Demerara and Cuyuni as well as the Middle Essequibo.[5]

South, in the Rupununi savannahs, live the Carib-speaking Makushi, an eastern arm of the Pemon nation, whose other branch in Guyana, the Arekuna, live along the western border. Widely dispersed in small homesteads across an area sparse in resources, the Pemon peoples are renowned for their strongly egalitarian traditions.[6] Still further south live the Wapishana, another Arawak people highly skilled in agriculture, fishing and hunting, and producing an abundance of cotton hammocks, while in the extreme south where only the forest-dwelling Wai Wai remain today, a number of groups once lived from trade in forest products and hunting.[7]

All these societies were, and still are, woven together by an intimate network of trading alliances, in which foodstuffs, tools, poisons, drugs, resins, dyes and magical objects and a whole host of other forest products were exchanged. Communications were maintained along the maze of waterways and across portages, around falls and rapids and over low watersheds, which reached right up into the highlands. Where water connections became impossible they were complemented by an intricate network of forest trails.[8]

By the time Europeans arrived, much of this trading economy on the coast was dominated by the Caribs, a vigorous hunting and fishing people who may have been relative newcomers to the region, part of a wave of peoples that had moved north from the Amazon over the previous centuries.[9] The Caribs were widely spread out along the coast from just north of the mouth of the Amazon to the north coast of Venezuela and out across the Antilles. They were famous and feared by their neighbours for their abilities as warriors, raiding for women and food.

Whereas today all these Amerindian peoples are remarkable for their egalitarian structures and individualism,[10] in the past the authority of chiefs may have been somewhat greater. Along the Amazon and Orinoco, archaeologists have revealed the existence of well-ordered and technologically complex hierarchical societies based on intensive agriculture and fishing.[11]

Some of this cultural diversity has been lost today. One or two groups like the Atorai and Taruma in the south seem to have been wiped out in the wars and by epidemics,[12] unless their descendants have mixed with surviving peoples further south in Brazil. Others, in the north, have almost forgotten their original languages. Economic changes resulting from contact have also served to homogenize the Amerindian world. Environmentally-honed economic strategies adapted to the regional trading networks have been lost as more lucrative trades with newcomers took over.

European Arrival

When the Europeans burst into this dynamic and self-sufficient world, they were viewed at first with amazement but then also with awe. Apart from the strangeness of their skin and body hair, their weird garb and outlandish values, they were above all prized as trading partners for their metal goods. The Amerindians found that with a metal axe or cutlass they could cut wood ten times more efficiently than with their stone axes. The huge saving in labour that these tools represented in making canoes, clearing forests and constructing houses was to have a radical effect on the history of the continent.

The trading opportunities and natural resources were equally attractive to the newcomers. While avaricious dreams of gold, silver and gems may have motivated the early adventurers, actual profits were made by bartering industrial goods for forest products. The economy of the first colonials thus fitted into a dynamic local trading system that it first complemented and only dominated much later.[13]

Guyana was made most famous in Europe by the publication of Sir Walter Raleigh's account of the *Discoverie of the Large, Rich and Bewtiful Empire of Guiana*, which recounted in glowing terms his failure in 1595 to establish an English presence near the mouth of the Orinoco.[14] The less vainglorious Dutch efforts to establish colonies proved more successful. Following several decades in which occasional landings were made for the purposes of trade, the Dutch established their first permanent settlement in 1616 at the confluence of the Cuyuni and Essequibo rivers.[15] Little more than a wooden palisaded fort, the settlement at Kykoveral was to provide a model for the early Dutch presence along the coast. Heavily outnumbered by the Amerindians and almost entirely reliant on these indigenous neighbours for food, the settlers could only secure profits through trading alliances. Conquest was out of the question, though the military superiority of European firearms was soon proven and conflicts were frequent in the early years.[16]

The Dutch presence on the Essequibo and Berbice was not formalized until 1621 when the first land grant was secured by the Dutch West India Company.[17] Berbice was formally established six years later by sixty or eighty male colonists with their six African slaves.[18]

10

Dutch Trading Posts

Source: Whitehead 1988:152.

11

Although from the outset the colonists planned to establish plantations of tropical crops – sugar, coffee and cocoa – for trade with Europe, the first settlements were chronically limited by lack of capital and labour. In the absence of the necessary machinery, slaves, shipping and port facilities to embark immediately on cash cropping, the initial trade from the region revolved around forest products derived from Amerindian labour.[19]

The main commodities were timbers and dyes, but the early settlements also relied on the Amerindians for food – cassava, maize, salted fish and wild meats. The Arawaks supplied most food, while the Warao traded fish and canoes. The first Dutch settlements were dependent on their Amerindian allies having access to the Orinoco fisheries, although this area was notionally controlled by the Spanish.[20] However, the early Spanish settlements on the lower Orinoco were so cut off from the administrative centre on Isla Margarita and so deprived of Amerindian allies that they were forced to trade with the Dutch just to survive.[21]

In the early years, easily the most important trade item was a red dye called annatto, derived from a cultivated shrub (*Bixa orellana*). Extraction and preparation of the dye was labour-intensive as the fruits had to be cultivated and harvested and the red pulp around the seeds then scraped out by hand and rendered down into a thick paste through sieving and boiling. Crab wood oil was required to preserve the paste in vats. To augment their own labour the Amerindians used slaves captured from interior groups. Letterwood and balsam copaiba were other important forest products then in demand in Europe.[22]

In order to promote the growing trade with the Amerindians, the Dutch established a network of posts throughout the interior and along the coast where the Amerindians could come in their canoes to trade their foods, pottery, woods, dyes and other forest products for European goods. Metal axes, choppers, knives, adzes, razors, scissors, hooks, pins, pots and pans, combs, mirrors and beads soon became essential to the Amerindians' economies. The Dutch even produced metal arrowheads especially for trade with the Amerindians in the fort at Kykoveral.[23] Boasted one early Dutch historian, 'we carry on with them [Amerindians] a great trade... and receive from them many services in return for trifling presents.'[24]

There has been much argument about the extent to which slavery resulted from the European presence or was already practised by the Amerindians. The Spanish, eager for an excuse to capture slaves for their own use, readily exaggerated the Amerindians' alleged ferocity and lack of morality. Very early on, they established the norm that Caribs, whom they called Cannibals, could be enslaved on the grounds that they not only raided the Spaniards' allies, the Arawaks, for slaves but also ate their prisoners.

12

What does seem true is that the dominant Amerindian nations did exploit the labour of less powerful or bellicose peoples. In recognition of the service that these peoples rendered, the Caribs referred to them as their 'sons-in-law' (*poitos*).[25] In the Upper Orinoco and Rio Negro these exploited groups were also referred to as Macu or Witoto. By the eighteenth century, the term *poitos* was used throughout the Guianas to refer to the 'red slaves' captured by Amerindians for sale to the Europeans.[26]

This transformation in inter-ethnic relations, whereby sub-dominant groups who rendered labour services to neighbouring Amerindians were turned into slaves, was brought about by the demand for cheap labour in the coastal settlements but was equally determined by the Amerindians' unquenchable thirst for European goods. Slaves were hence always a part of the early European settlements. Amerindian slave-labour was particularly in demand to produce food supplies for the forts and visiting ships. When plantations for export crops began to be established in earnest in the 1640s, black slaves began to be brought over from Africa.[27]

Allies and Enemies

In contrast with the policy of the Spaniards, who declared the Caribs their enemies and sought to submit the Amerindians of the Orinoco to the *encomienda* system of forced labour,[28] the Dutch forged fraternal alliances with the Caribs and even entered into formal treaties with them. As in Suriname to the east, the Dutch in the three Guyana colonies of Essequibo, Demerara and Berbice recognized that without Carib support their toeholds on the continent were untenable.[29] A written treaty in the form of a legal contract was signed with the Caribs in 1672. A treaty with the Arawaks followed in the early eighteenth century, and in 1769 renewed treaties were signed with both them and the Warao and Akawaio.[30]

Through these treaties and negotiations with Amerindian leaders, the Dutch encouraged slave-raiding as well as guerrilla actions against the Spanish settlements on the lower Orinoco. The Caribs increasingly exchanged the slaves they captured for European firearms, which they used in their raids on forest communities in the interior. Armed, the eastern Caribs became indispensable to the Dutch in maintaining the regional balance of power with the Spanish.[31] To secure these alliances, the Dutch established the custom of making annual presents of trade goods from their posts, which were the responsibility of 'postholders' who acted as local representatives of the Dutch administration.[32] At the same time, a handful of black traders were issued permits to ply the lower rivers to encourage the annatto trade.[33]

In a bid to limit the anarchy of the spreading slave wars which multiplied through the interior to serve the European market, the Dutch also formally announced in both Suriname, Berbice and then their other colonies that certain Amerindian peoples were 'free nations' and could not be subjected to slavery. In Suriname, those so defined were the Arawaks, Warao, Caribs and the Akurio. In Guyana, the four 'free nations' were the Warao, Arawaks, Akawaio and Caribs. As Anna Benjamin points out, 'technically, any member of a nation other than the above-mentioned could be legally held in slavery in the Guyana colonies.'[34] Moreover, since in Suriname the Akawaio were not recognized as 'free', they became fair game for the Caribs who raided deep into the highlands and brought them down to the main market for 'red slaves' on the Suriname coast.[35]

Despite intensifying trade, the West India Company was not financially secure. Bankruptcy was followed by recapitalization with increased Dutch government involvement, and in 1675 the New West India Company was refloated with a fresh emphasis on the build-up of plantations. Sugar estates were developed on the Lower Mazaruni and Cuyuni, and British planters from Barbados established new plantations on the Demerara. While 'red slaves' continued to be popular as farm labourers for producing food and to operate trading canoes, slave labour on the estates was increasingly drawn from Africa.

The gradual expansion of the plantation economy provided a new role for the Amerindian allies of the Dutch. Black slaves brought over from Africa, familiar with forest living and resentful of their miserable treatment on the estates, fled into the interior. Referred to as 'Maroons', after the Spanish term *cimarrón* used to describe feral cattle in Hispaniola, the runaway slaves established themselves as a new force in the interior. The Dutch rewarded their Amerindian allies when they recaptured Maroons and brought them back to the plantations and the Amerindians' policing of the interior gradually became an essential function in the regional economy.

By 1713, when the signing of the Treaty of Utrecht with Spain consolidated Dutch gains, the plantation economy was in a phase of rapid expansion and gradually began to eclipse trade with the Amerindians and the raiding of Spanish possessions as the main economic activities.[36] Nevertheless, trade was still intensive. According to the available records, between 1700 and 1742 some 335 tons of annatto were traded with the Amerindians in exchange for 200,000 cutlasses, while during the same period the total number of 'red slaves' being traded along the whole coast has been estimated at exceeding 500 annually.[37]

The Spanish presence on the Orinoco also began to strengthen. Between 1729 and 1740 the Caribs found themselves increasingly at war with Jesuit missionaries who relied on their own Amerindian militias to curb the slave trade

14

along the Middle Orinoco. Moreover, by the 1730s, as trade with Amerindians declined relative to the growing plantation economy, the Dutch became less enthusiastic about the Caribs' anti-Spanish activities. Not only did they fear Spanish counter-attacks, but they depended on trade with the Spanish for plantation mules.[38] Realizing that Carib power had become a serious threat to the fledgling plantation economy, the new Director-General sent out by the New West Indies Company, the magnificently named Storm van 'S Gravesande, tried to restrain the Caribs' anti-Spanish raiding and prevent the sale of firearms to Amerindians. He was unsuccessful in imposing this embargo, however, because of the numerous private traders who did not see the strategic needs of Guyana in the same way.[39]

For the Caribs, an alliance with the Dutch was crucial, and as the ability of the Spanish to control the Orinoco basin grew, they depended increasingly on Dutch suport. Carib raids on Capuchin and Jesuits mission on the Orinoco intensified,[40] sometimes in alliance with English privateers who raided Spanish settlements along the Orinoco and Caroni repeatedly between 1740 and 1742.[41]

The solution for both the Dutch and the Caribs was to shift slave raiding away from the banks of the Orinoco up into the highlands. Slaves continued to be exchanged for guns, powder and shot. As Anna Benjamin has noted, 'the slave trade allowed the Caribs to become virtually the sole distributing agents for European goods among the interior nations.'[42] To evade Spanish control, the Caribs developed new lines of commerce in the interior, looping around behind the frontier forts through the Upper Cuyuni, Mazaruni rivers and up the Essequibo and through the Rupununi savannahs. Caribs pushed south into the Rio Branco in Brazil and raided up the Caura and over into the Ventuari in the Upper Orinoco in the Venezuelan Amazon.[43] By the 1740s, Dutch and Spanish sources were both reporting that the sole source of livelihood for the Caribs appeared to be the slave trade.[44]

Spanish Expansion

The Spanish, however, were investing heavily in securing their area of influence. They had been alarmed by the report of a missionary, who in 1740 had travelled to the Upper Orinoco from the Lower Orinoco, perhaps the first European to do so. He had discovered Portuguese slavers who had entered along the river Casiquiare, going about their business in what the Spanish considered their territory. To head off the Portuguese from what they still hoped was the site of El Dorado and in order to crush the Caribs, the Spanish mounted a seven year-long *Real Expedicion des Limites* in 1754.[45] Their aim was to reinforce their southern frontier by establishing a line of forts right across the Guiana highlands linking the Lower Orinoco with its headwaters, while at the same time crushing

15

Carib resistance and reducing the Amerindians to subservient status at the missions. They recruited Maroons and Arawaks to help them in their war against the Caribs. The Caribs, however, regrouped in the Caroni, Aro and Caura,[46] while the forts in the Upper Orinoco were soon overthrown by another Carib-speaking people, the Ye'kuana.

Meanwhile, the Spanish missions began to push south of the Orinoco. Rejecting the Dutch policy of trading with free Amerindian allies, the Spanish strategy was to establish *reducciones*, whereby they forced the Amerindians to relocate into large centralized villages and subjected them to mission control.[47] In 1758 Spanish raids reached as far east as Waini and Pomeroon. Capuchin missionaries allied with Arawaks advanced towards the Guyana border deeper into the Sierra Imataca, into the Upper Cuyuni basin and towards the Essequibo forests, all the time contested by Caribs who nevertheless withdrew east and south to the Barima, Cuyuni, Mazaruni, Essequibo, Maikoni and Rupununi. To secure their missions, the Capuchins recruited into their militia the Caribs' enemies, the Akawaio, who remembered how the Caribs had sold them into slavery in Suriname.[48]

Squeezed from the north and west, the slave trade shifted south again. In 1753, the Caribs temporarily subdued the Wapishana for the Dutch, who opened up trade with the Amazon along the Rio Branco.[49] The consequence was not entirely to the Caribs' immediate advantage, for the Dutch now began trading with another famous Amerindian slaving people, the Manao, who had established pre-eminence in the 'red slave' trade with the Portuguese. The Caribs were jealous of these contacts and fierce fighting between the Caribs in southern Guyana and the Manao in Brazil ensued, all fuelled by the Dutch market. The bitter war between the Caribs and the Manao reached its peak in 1763.[50]

The Dutch-Carib penetration south had also brought them into an area that the Portuguese had long considered their sphere of influence. Indeed, Portuguese traders had extended into the Rupununi by 1660 and the area had become a regular trade point from that time on. Provoked by Dutch and Spanish incursions, the Portuguese moved to affirm their control of the Upper Rio Branco from 1776 by intensifying their programme of *aldeias* (the Portuguese version of *reducciones*). Despite revolts in 1784, 1790 and 1798, in which many Amerindians were massacred or transported to settlements thousands of kilometres to the south, the Brazilian claims were secured and they populated the Rio Branco and Rupununi savannahs with cattle to provide food for the forts and missions.[51]

Direct confrontation between the colonial powers was in no-one's interest. The Brazilians feared that the Dutch aimed to take over the Rio Branco and Rio Negro headwaters, while the Dutch, accepting the need to avoid clashes with the Portuguese and avoid confrontations with their Carib allies, decided to forego further trade with the Manao. However, the escalating 'red slave' trade led to serious disturbances in the interior. In 1750, the Akawaio rose in revolt against depredations on their villages, and they and other tribes increasingly began to take up the Carib practice of raiding for slaves. Within a few decades the annatto trade was all but abandoned.[52]

By the 1760s the new pattern of Guyana's economy was clear. In the interior the Amerindians were heavily involved in slaving, both to capture 'red slaves' and to recapture escaped blacks. Meanwhile, the Dutch and British occupied themselves with their estates and shipping. The plantocracy had become the dominant political force in Guyana.[53] The numbers involved were not great. In 1762, for instance, the total population for all the Essequibo consisted of 346 whites, 244 red slaves and 3,833 black slaves.[54] The Amerindians must have outnumbered them ten to one.

One year later the crucial role of the Amerindians in the survival of the Guyana colonies was again proven. An uprising of black slaves on the plantations, known as the 1763 Berbice Slave Rebellion, 'threatened Dutch hegemony throughout the Guianas'.[55] The Amerindians realized that their own interests were equally at risk and readily accepted the offer of Dutch arms to help put down the rebellion. The result was a mass mobilization of Amerindians to suppress the rebellious black slaves. Caribs, Arawaks and Akawaio flocked to the Dutch flag and succeeded in curbing the uprising, an action that the Amerindians had to repeat in 1772.[56]

As Director-General Storm van 'S Gravesande reported:

> Our Caribs, both from these rivers and even from Barima, have loyally done their best and are yet doing it, constantly roving about between the two colonies and having, through the Lord's blessing been so successful in all their expeditions as to have lost none of their own people, thus making them bold and beyond belief and expectation enterprising, and even reckless; and these occurrences cause a great embitterment between the blacks and them, which, if well and reasonably stimulated, cannot fail to be of much use and service in the future of the Colonies.[57]

Indeed, at times the Caribs became quite truculent with the Dutch, who had trouble controlling them. They cheerfully exploited the planters' reliance on them to find escaped slaves in order to drive hard bargains about payments and the terms under which they would support the Dutch.[58] In an attempt to regularize these relations, the Dutch administration gave particular status to the leaders with whom they chose to do business by giving them the title of 'Owls' and providing them with silver-headed sticks as symbols of their authority.[59]

As the importance of the plantations grew, disturbances in the interior caused by raiding for 'red slaves' increasingly troubled the Dutch. The steady supply of black slaves from Africa made the 'red slave' trade superfluous to the Dutch, who felt that the Amerindians were better employed policing the forests for black runaways. Accordingly, the Amerindian slave trade was abolished in 1793.[60]. The role of the Amerindians as trade partners crucial to the Dutch colonies was at an end.

The Spanish war against the Caribs meanwhile continued. The Caura Caribs were conquered by the new Governor of Angostura, Centurion, in 1771.[61] The Capuchin missions extended their hegemony by monopolizing all commerce between the Amerindians and the Spanish settlements. Meat, hides and agricultural produce, the results of Amerindian labour, were the main mission products. By 1779, eighty per cent of all the cultivated land in Venezuelan Guyana was under mission control.[62]

The Caribs gave way inch by inch. As one missionary wrote of a notable *cacique*, Oraparena, of the Caroni:

[He] did not want to give up his Kingship and go into a state of misery in the Mission, where he could not have authority, wives, freedom to capture *poitos* or to trade with his friends the Dutch, who provide him with cotton goods, axes, cutlasses, dyewoods and whatever he requires. To these reasons he added many others in favour of uncivilized life, and so he remains obstinately attached to that sort of existence.[63]

Gradually the resistance crumbled. Epidemics continued to sweep through Amerindian communities and the Spanish used arms from time to time to force Indians into the missions. As one missionary admitted, 'The voice of the Gospel is heard only when the Indians have also heard the sound of firearms.'[64] The Caribs finally succumbed, yet only decades later the loyalist Capuchin missionaries and their Amerindian allies were totally overcome by the forces of Venezuelan independence. As Neil Whitehead, the chronicler of the Carib wars concludes, if the Caribs had only held out, their fate and that of southern Venezuela might have been quite different.

British Guiana

As a consequence of shifts in the balance of power in Europe, the three Dutch colonies of Essequibo, Demerara and Berbice passed into British hands in 1803. British sovereignty was confirmed under the Treaty of London of 1814 and the three colonies were united in 1831 as 'British Guiana', but none of this meant much change at the local level. The Act of Capitulation to the British enshrined the power of the planters, who were confirmed in their rights and privileges; no laws or usages changed, only the flag. Power was shared in an awkward triangle between the plantocracy represented through the Combined Court, which controlled local revenues within the colony, the British Treasury, which controlled the British contribution to the administrative budget, and the Governor, appointed by London.[65]

The interior trade with the Amerindians continued to decline. The selling of 'red slaves' had already ended and the marginal profitability of forest products meant that, as far as the colonial state was concerned, the only important function of the Amerindians was to act as a 'bush police'. The British began to close down the interior trading posts and the custom of present-giving also gradually declined.[66] The British did, however, continue to recruit Amerindians to undertake 'bush expeditions' to recapture 'bucks' and harass runaway communities. Under the control of the 'Quarter-Master General of the Indians', arrangements were made whereby several hundred armed Amerindians could be mustered within a few days of the outbreak of any civil disturbance. On more than one occasion the Amerindians were deployed alongside regular troops to exterminate settlements of Maroons. So long as the colony continued to be based on black slave labour, Amerindian allies remained crucial to its survival. In 1811, for instance, the colony was comprised of only 2,000 whites, who lived off the backs of 60,000 blacks.[67]

The situation was soon to change, however. Despite the vehement objections of the planters, slavery was abolished by the British in 1833 and all slaves were freed. A startling example of the degree of Amerindian dependence on the capture of slaves and runaways is recounted by historian Mary Noel Menezes. When they heard that the British had abolished slavery, the Caribs were dismayed and one of their chiefs, Maharnava, stormed into the capital demanding to be told what he should do with his captives. He indicated that since he had no use for them, he had no choice but to have them put to death. To give credence to his threat the chief dashed out the brains of one slave when the British Governor refused to accept charge of the slaves.[68]

The Amerindians' economy entered into a precipitous decline. By 1830, gift-giving to the Amerindians had already fallen to one-sixth of its 1820 level. By the 1840s the colonial government entirely ended the practice on the grounds that it did not want to perpetuate an 'idle, parasitic community of natives'. To fierce objections from the Amerindians, an interior militia was created to replace the 'bush police'.[69]

By the 1840s, most of those on the coast considered the interior an area of 'risk, discomfort and no profit'.[70] The Amerindians gradually withdrew inland

19

once they were no longer required to maintain the balance of power and as they were eased off their coastal territories by the expansion of the plantations.[71] The Warao, in particular, suffered territorial loss as the plantations expanded into the swampy lowlands with the use of organized drainage systems.[72] Impoverished and suffering continued epidemics, Amerindian numbers sunk to an all-time low until by the end of the 1840s there were scarcely 6,000-8,000 survivors, a mere four per cent of the colony's population.[73] As Vincent Roth noted:

> There being no more runaway slaves to be caught and no further fear of rebellion of the serfs, their police and military usefulness came to an end and the Amerindians, from being a useful and necessary part of the body politic gradually deteriorated to the position of the merely curious and interesting people, useful only as hunters, porters and boatmen to parties having business in the interior and as providing cheap labour for the slowly developing forest industries.[74]

With the ending of the 'red slave' trade and the termination of gift-giving, the role of the 'postholders' was also gradually phased out. The previously important position of 'Protector of the Amerindians', by then a virtual sinecure held by one of the senior planters who lived in town on the coast and cared little for the Amerindians, was abolished and his few remaining duties were assumed by newly created Superintendents of Rivers and Creeks.[75]

This shift in emphasis corresponded to a new change in the interior's economy. Trade with the Amerindians in forest products gave way to an expanding timber industry. The Superintendents were given charge of the interior's forests and their main job was to generate revenue for the colony from those granted licences to exploit forests, rivers and creeks. By the 1870s, the Superintendents' notional responsibility for the Indians was almost entirely dropped.[76]

The British continued the Dutch policy of indirect rule through village leaders who were designated as 'Captains'. By the end of the Dutch period, the process of naming the 'Captains' was increasingly subject to colonial control, with the Governor providing the Amerindians with a list of names from which they could select their leaders.[77] The British perpetuated this practice but the policy of indirect rule led to perplexity in the courts. Were the Amerindians subject to British law or did their own customs, administered by the recognized 'Captains', obtain? After several trial cases, it was decided that the Amerindians were subject to British law, but since *de facto* British jurisdiction extended only along the coast and up the lower reaches of the larger rivers, in the interior customary law continued to prevail.[78]

Boundary Issues

The Amerindians in the interior were largely forgotten and their rights only asserted when the British needed to defend the colony's boundaries against others.[79] The vexed question of where indeed the colony's boundaries lay began to exercise the minds of the British administrators. The eastern boundary, it was agreed, lay along the Corentyne and the matter only came into dispute with Suriname in the twentieth century as a result of conflicting surveys identifying different headwater streams as the real Corentyne.

The border to the west was far less clear. Dutch trading posts had certainly been established far up into the hills now known as the Sierra Imataca, but as Spanish power had grown and trade with the Caribs had shifted inland the Capuchin missionaries had moved in. These mission stations had in turn collapsed during Venezuela's Wars of Independence and many of the Amerindians had moved east to make the most of British protection and trading opportunities. In an attempt to settle the matter, the British government offered the coast in 1844 to the newly independent state of Greater Colombia as far east as Moruca on condition that Amerindian rights were protected. Receiving no reply and having discovered gold in the area, the British then decided instead to assert a line recently surveyed by the colonial geographers, Robert and Richard Schomburgk,[80] who had trudged and canoed their way along virtually the whole frontier between 1839 and 1842. The decision remains contentious, however, and Venezuela continues to claim all of Guyana up to the Essequibo river.

Responsibility for the Amerindians of the interior was increasingly considered the duty of the Christian missions. As Governor Light wrote in the 1830s, 'The only chance of making the rising generation of Aborigines permanently useful to the colony is by religious and moral instruction.'[81]

The Dutch, who had at first been highly suspicious of missionaries, had later allowed them to take over some of the duties of the 'postholders' in certain areas. Moravian missions, first founded in Suriname in 1735, had been opened on the Berbice, Corentyne and at Hope between 1738 and 1821 but moved back to Suriname with the transfer of power. The first Anglican missionaries started to operate in Bartica in 1831 and gradually expanded to include the Berbice, Waraputa, the Pomeroon, Moruca and Demerara by the 1860s. A Roman Catholic mission was allowed to establish itself in Santa Rosa in Moruca 1837, to cater for the Amerindian fugitives from Venezuela who had fled the collapse of loyalist missions during the the the Wars of Independence.

The expansion of British missionary efforts into the Rupununi savannahs also led to the definition of the southern frontier with Brazil. In 1838 a zealous young missionary originally stationed at Bartica had moved by stages, and without official authorization, to a recently established Brazilian mission at Pirara on the Upper Rupununi. The Brazilian authorities strenuously objected to his presence there and this, combined with reports of continued Brazilian slaving raids across the Tacutu, embroiled a reluctant British government in the dispute.

As anthroplogist Peter Rivière has documented, the plantocracy in Guyana gave very low priority to the frontier. They refused to allocate local revenues either for mapping and demarcating the border or for the establishment of religious missions. And once the Governor decided that the British would have to assert control of the frontier and rescue the mission, they likewise refused to fund the necessary military expedition.[82]

After protracted negotiations, mutual denunciations and flag waving at the frontier, the Brazilian government, fearful that the British might use the incident as an excuse to expand their claim south to the Amazon, acceded to British demands and the present line of the frontier, only formally agreed in 1904, was defined.

All these frontier agreements were made without any reference to the indigenous peoples. As Audrey Butt Colson has pointed out:

> From the point of view of the indigenous occupants of these territories, the treaties represent an international carve up, in that national sovereignty was assigned in distant capitals of the world, principally in other continents, and boundaries were created without reference to the traditional rights of the occupants. These superimpositions could make no sense in terms of local structures, for they cut across and divided geographical, ecological, social and cultural unities, placing in separate political areas populations which conceived themselves to have been in possession of the land 'from the beginning of time' and as being far more closely interrelated amongst themselves than the peoples and cultures of the nation states which were engulfing them.[83]

The 1840s also saw a change in colonial policy towards the Amerindians. The previous British policy of encouraging them to seek civilization and British protection on the lower rivers changed to a strategy of defining the frontiers under the pretext of protecting the rights of Amerindian subjects.[84] The growing significance of mineral and timber resources in the economy encouraged this change.[85] Repeated reports of slaving incursions from Brazil, which continued until 1857 and where slavery was not outlawed until 1888, provided the basis for such expressions of concern. The Dutch policy of alliance with the Amerindians to ensure trade in goods and slaves was thus substituted with a policy of making alliances with the Amerindians to assert claims to their territories.[86]

Implicit in this assertion was the idea that the Amerindians were indeed the ancestral owners of these lands which could be rightfully claimed by the colony once they had become British subjects. Humanitarian arguments – protecting the rights of 'poor Indians' – were used to justify British annexation of the Amerindians' territories, which were then administered as Crown lands.[87] From being independent nations allied through trade with the Europeans, the Amerindians had been stealthily transformed into colonial subjects.

[1] Cited in Forte 1994:13
[2] Menezes 1977:1
[3] Whitehead 1988; Benjamin 1992
[4] Wilbert 1972; 1993. It may be from the Warao that Guyana got its name. In Warao *wayana* means 'without canoe', a term by which they referred to the peoples of the Imataca mountains south of them.
[5] Butt Colson 1983
[6] Thomas 1982
[7] Guppy 1958; Yde 1965
[8] Coppens 1971; Thomas 1972; Butt Colson 1973
[9] Lathrap 1970
[10] Rivière 1984
[11] Carneiro 1961, 1995; Roosevelt 1980, 1991
[12] Butt Colson and Morton 1965
[13] The similarities to the early North American colonies are striking, cf Jennings 1975, 1984
[14] Raleigh 1596
[15] Benjamin (1992) mentions an unsuccessful settlement on the Corentyne in 1613.
[16] Benjamin 1992; ARU nd (c)
[17] Whitehead 1988:93-94
[18] Benjamin 1992:1

[19] Menezes 1977:2
[20] Benjamin 1992:2-3
[21] Whitehead 1988:99
[22] Whitehead 1988:160; Benjamin 1992:4
[23] Benjamin 1992:3
[24] ARU nd (c)
[25] Saignes 1961; Rivière 1964:81; Kaplan 1977
[26] Gilij 1780
[27] Menezes 1977:1
[28] Whitehead 1988:99
[29] Buve 1975; de Groot 1977
[30] Menezes 1977:46
[31] Whitehead 1988:95,159
[32] Menezes 1977:45
[33] Benjamin 1992:9
[34] Benjamin 1992:9
[35] Whitehead 1988:128; Benjamin 1992:10
[36] Whitehead 1988: 153
[37] Whitehead 1988:186-7. Benjamin argues, however, that in Berbice in the 1680s and in Essequibo somewhat later, the annatto trade was gradually eclipsed by the 'red slave' trade.
[38] Whitehead 1988: 154
[39] Whitehead 1988:155, 165
[40] Benjamin 1992:10
[41] Whitehead 1988:124

[42] Benjamin 1992:100
[43] Caulin 1778
[44] Benjamin 1992:11
[45] Perez 1957
[46] Whitehead 1988:125
[47] Menezes 1978b:45; Whitehead 1988:184
[48] Whitehead 1988:125,127,128
[49] Whitehead 1988:155-6
[50] Hemming 1978b; Farage 1991; Whitehead 1988:168
[51] Farage 1991; Rivière 1995:3; Hemming 1978b
[52] Farage 1991; Whitehead 1988:155; Benjamin 1992:11
[53] Menezes 1977:5
[54] Whitehead 1988:155. Benjamin (1992) gives different but comparable figures.
[55] Benjamin 1992:15
[56] Menezes 1977:47; Whitehead 1988
[57] Cited in Benjamin 1992:15-16
[58] Benjamin 1992:18
[59] Menezes 1977:48
[60] Benjamin and Pierre 1995
[61] Whitehead 1988:127
[62] Whitehead 1988:134
[63] Cited in Whitehead 1988:141
[64] Whitehead 1988:141
[65] Menezes 1977:7,255; Benjamin and Pierre 1995
[66] Menezes 1977:99; Benjamin 1992:17
[67] Government Notices, 17 November 1949:1606; Menezes 1977:55
[68] Menezes 1977:8,51,182
[69] Menezes 1977:63,65-67
[70] Rivière 1995:6
[71] Menezes 1977:70
[72] Benjamin and Pierre 1995
[73] Menezes 1977:18,22
[74] Government Notices, 17 November 1949:1606
[75] Menezes 1977:76,86,88,89,95
[76] Menezes 1977:124,126
[77] Benjamin 1992:8
[78] Menezes 1977:134-136
[79] Menezes 1977:17
[80] Menezes 1977:172
[81] Cited in Menezes 1977:246
[82] Rivière 1995; cf Menezes 1977:166
[83] Butt Colson 1983
[84] Rivière 1995:67
[85] Menezes 1977
[86] Rivière 1995:164,169
[87] Farage 1991; Rivière 1995

CHAPTER 2
PLANTATION POLITICS

'In short, sugar has been the major formative influence in our history. It was a major factor behind the introduction of Negro slaves with all its political, economic and social implications. It encouraged the emergence of a class of wealthy planters, sometimes absentee, owning large estates and exercising important political influence; and because even they could not command the capital necessary for sugar production, the economy was increasingly controlled by creditors in Holland and England, to which such a large part of the profits were sent that very little money remained in the colony... The legacy of sugar is indeed an important one.'[1]

The gradual transformation in the status of Amerindians in the Guyanese colonies resulted from the changing emphasis of the economy. As European settlements based on Amerindian trade stabilized, they were gradually able to build up their plantations. As we have seen, by the mid-eighteenth century trade with the Amerindians had been eclipsed by exports from these estates.

Initially, the plantations were very small-scale and were established on the better drained, less fertile upland soils around the trading posts. These weaker soils favoured the cultivation of coffee and cotton, which were in fact more important than sugar until the nineteenth century. As historian Vere Daly notes, the ideal conditions for sugar cultivation were not found until towards the middle of the eighteenth century when the Demerara river was opened up and the planters of the Essequibo moved down from the lighter soils of the interior to the coastal strip.[2]

The development of the plantation economy was hampered by a number of factors. Labour was in short supply and had to be imported in the form of slaves from Africa – itself implying a major capital investment. The processing technologies were large and expensive and also had to be imported, mainly from Europe. Processing sugar, in particular, required a mill, a boiler-house and a curing house, as well as mules which were bought in from Venezuela. Economies of scale meant that profitable sugar plantations and mills had to be large, requiring considerable investment. As Daly puts it, 'sugar was a rich man's crop which could only be grown by those commanding considerable capital or credit.'[3] Although it was the Dutch who initiated the process, from the 1740s onwards much of the capital and many of the planters were English.

The exploitation of the swampy lowland soils, for the most part rich alluvial clays, increased reliance on foreign capital and imported labour, for the development of these areas implied massive expenditure on sea-defences and drainage. According to Daly, in addition to sea-defences, every square mile of land prepared for sugar cultivation required 49 miles of drainage and 16 miles of irrigation trenches. Thus, the 'original construction of sugar plantations in Guiana required the removal of approximately 10 million tons of earth.'[4] This vast feat was only made possible by the work of thousands of black slaves. Developing these sugar estates was also a long-term commitment. According to local lore, newly reclaimed lowland soils were too salty for sugar production and better suited to cotton and coffee. Only after five years did salt levels decline enough for sugar to be profitably grown.[5]

The extent of British investment in the Dutch colonies of Guiana partially explains British interest in taking over. Following the French revolution, many planters in Guiana had in fact sided with the republican Dutch government set up by French invaders in Holland. Their enthusiasm for 'Liberty, Equality and Fraternity' was quickly dampened, however, when the new French republican commissioner in the Caribbean declared freedom for African slaves. Maroon and slave uprisings in 1794 and 1795 in Suriname and Guiana had to be put down by force with the help of Amerindian allies.

Planters were anyway obliged to take the British side in the Napoleonic Wars by their commercial links. Without an export market their plantations were valueless. By 1790, the Caribbean region was supplying seventy per cent of the cotton being woven into manufactured cloth by the new cotton mills of Britain's industrial revolution. Moreover, since British ships commanded the oceans, only British ships and British merchants could be relied on to carry the export crops. A very large proportion of the crop in cotton, sugar and coffee had to be sent annually to Britain to pay off loans incurred in setting up the estates. In 1795, for example, no less than 10 million pounds of cotton, 15 million pounds of coffee and 15 million pounds of sugar had to be sent to Britain merely to pay off debts to British merchants.[6] It was commercial ties such as these which encouraged the British to accept jurisdiction over the three Dutch colonies of Essequibo, Demerara and Berbice as the Napoleonic Wars drew to their close. After various reversals, largely determined by events in far-off Europe, British sovereignty was accepted by treaty in 1803.

The freeing of African slaves in the 1830s created an acute labour shortage for the plantations, which was overcome by a variety of means. Indentured labourers were imported in large numbers; many were Chinese until the 1860s, some were Portuguese until the 1880s, some were Africans, but above all they were 'East Indians', as they are known in Guyana, from the Indian sub-continent. Between 1851 and 1917, 228,743 indentured East Indian labourers were brought in to Guyana to work the plantations.[7]

The plantocracy took many other measures to ensure a malleable workforce on the estates. Alternative employment and livelihoods for freed slaves and East Indians who had worked off their obligations as indentured labourers were discouraged. Land prices were maintained at artificially high levels; a complex web of laws made it hard for blacks and East Indians to obtain rights to land. The domination of the Combined Court by the planters limited public expenditure on the free villages – dams, village drainage and roads were all denied support – but the public purse was generously opened to pay for the irrigation and drainage deemed necessary for the estates. Unscrupulous planters even resorted to flooding lands where smallholders were trying to establish themselves.

Obedience to the colonial authorities and the needs of the plantocracy was enforced by a high degree of militarization and a plethora of legal restrictions embodied in labour ordinances. The maxim enunciated by one planter but practised by all was that the 'coolie', the derogatory term for the East Indian labourer, should either be 'at work, in hospital or in prison'. The rigour with which labour laws were applied and the level of resentment and resistance which this provoked are indicated by the fact that between 1866 and 1870, 65,084 cases were recorded involving a breach of the ordinances. This averages out to 18.5 convictions every day for the five-year period.[8]

The planters also adopted a divide-and-rule policy to keep the labour force from organizing, by fomenting antagonism between the races. As one contemporary wrote:

> The coolie despises the negro because he considers him... not so highly civilised as himself; while the negro... despises the coolie because he is so immensely inferior to himself in physical strength. There will never be much danger of seditious disturbances among the East Indian immigrants... so long as large numbers of negroes continue to be employed with them.[9]

As another planter noted in 1874:

> They do not intermix and that, of course, is one of the great safeties in the colony when there has been any rioting. If our negroes were toublesome every coolie on the estate would stand by one. If the coolie attacked me I could with confidence trust my negro friends for keeping me from injury.[10]

The society which developed was framed by these labour relations. At the top of the social order were white planters, who had the support of the colonial authorities and controlled the majority of land and capital. Chinese and Portuguese, freed from the restrictive laws and able to acquire land, emerged as a class of vigorous smallholders practising market gardening, which provided the basis for their later prominence in commerce, charcoaling and gold-mining. Free villages of miserably poor black ex-slaves eked out a living on marginal lands or worked as seasonal labour on the estates, to which East Indian indentured and ex-indentured labourers were more closely tied year round. Altogether, over ninety per cent of the population was concentrated along the narrow coastal strip, while the Amerindians, out of sight and out of mind, continued to populate the interior.

As Ralph Premdas has remarked:

> Thus a deeply divided society was formed. The foundations of inter-ethnic rivalry were forged on the anvil of the colonial policy of immigration and divide-and-rule. There is no evidence of any sort of inherent antipathy among the imported immigrants. It was, however, the manner in which colonial society was organized, stratified, and exploited that triggered and sustained inter-communal fears and rivalries.[11]

The closing years of the nineteenth century saw important changes in the economy and social order, however. A black middle class began to emerge in urban areas, achieving advancement through education, the service sector and clerical employment. At the same time, East Indians began to achieve a new economic base in rural areas by developing rice farms on land granted them in exchange for foregoing their return passages to India. This growing rural peasant and middle class expanded into cattle-farming, copra production and market gardening. Meanwhile, driven mainly by technological improvements in the sugar industry which required heavy capital investment and favoured further economies of scale, the plantations became increasingly concentrated in fewer and fewer hands. By 1904, four firms, all of which had their headquarters in the UK, controlled eighty per cent of the sugar industry.[12]

Political changes reflected this shift in economic power. The gradual eclipse of the class of white planters by the transnational sugar corporations allowed constitutional changes which gave the colonial authorities greater powers to confront the growing middle class and an increasingly articulate labour force. In 1905, riots by rebellious sugar workers spiralled out of control leading to police shootings, deaths and injuries. The event laid the ground for the emergence of a vigorous trade union movement, which developed close ties with the British Labour Party, and while initially focused on issues such as wages, conditions of work and working hours, had a clear political agenda, demanding broader emancipation for the working class and greater participation in the rule of the colony. The very first constitution of the British Guiana Labour Union, founded in 1919, called for the creation of a socialist state.[13]

The colonial rulers and sugar companies both feared and resisted the labour movement. In 1924, further bloody riots ensued when police fired on a crowd marching to demand wage increases for stevedores – twelve died and a further fifteen were wounded. Despite these provocations, the labour movement maintained its discipline and in 1939 the powerful Sugar Producers' Association finally formally recognized a trade union, following the death of four workers at the hands of the police. Legislation regarding minimum wages, workers' compensation and the right to organize gradually followed.

Towards Independence

The slow move towards independence for Britain's colonies in the Caribbean became inevitable following the Second World War. According to the Latin America Bureau, the political climate in the Caribbean did not fundamentally threaten business interests: 'neither the political nor economic systems by which the islands functioned were called into question by the major political parties. The basic grievance was that West Indians were not governing them.'[14]

Guyana was the exception to that pattern. The emergence of the People's Progressive Party (PPP) in 1951 broke consensus in the country about maintaining either the political or the economic system which had dominated the colonial period. Born out of the labour movement and a fierce opposition to the exploitative practices of the sugar transnationals, the PPP stood for independence, workers' rights and a rapid transition to socialism. Worried by this challenge to their business interests, Britain and the United States delayed independence until they felt comfortable about handing over power to a more pliable regime. Creating this situation required a decade from the mid-1950s to the mid-1960s of bloodshed, arson, murder and traumatic racial violence.

The details of this story have been well told elsewhere,[15] and only an outline need be given here. In an attempt to contain the labour movement and Guyanese aspirations for independence, the colonial government began to permit limited self-government under colonial tutelage, first through a small partially-elected Legislative Council and then through a local parliament modelled on the British system. Full adult suffrage was achieved in 1953 and the country's first elections held. In the run up to these elections, two formidable politicians, both PPP, emerged as key players. Cheddi Jagan, a doctrinaire left-winger and East Indian, with a background in the labour movement, established himself as a sugar workers' champion with a powerful following among East Indians. Forbes Burnham, a creole lawyer with a less obviously socialist agenda, built up a constituency among the urban black workers and middle class. Based on this dominant coalition, the PPP led by Cheddi Jagan swept to power on a platform of political independence, greater economic benefits for workers and fierce condemnation of the dominant sugar multinational, Booker McConnell.

The new administration immediately set about social and political reforms, first ensuring land security for rice farmers and new press freedoms. A labour relations bill was prepared to be put before parliament which, in line with international law, would have required employers to recognize trade unions. Fearing for the interests of capital, the colonial government suspended the constitution while whipping up a frenzied attack in the press on the PPP, alleging communist subversion and a plot to burn down Georgetown. Burnham and Jagan were prevented from travelling to Britain to clarify matters and after a campaign of repression and harassment, Jagan was jailed for six months hard labour for violating a restriction order and sent off to the Mazaruni Penal Settlement to prevent communications with his sympathizers. The police closed the headquarters of the PPP.

These pressures and consequent loss of confidence in the PPP, particularly among urban and middle-class members, forced a split in the party, which later took on a racial character. Cheddi Jagan managed to retain control of the PPP, which while holding true to its left-wing character became increasingly a vehicle for East Indian interests, and Forbes Burnham established an apparently more middle-ground party, the People's National Congress (PNC), which drew its support from urban and black areas. Despite the provocations, the PPP was able to retain power in the subsequent 1957 elections, but at the cost of increasing political polarization. The scene was set for a gradual descent into the racial violence which flared up in the early 1960s.

The Venezuelan Connection

The territories on either side of the disputed frontier between Venezuela and Guyana have been important political footballs for nearly two centuries. During the eighteenth century, the Dutch had claimed the whole of the Essequibo basin, including the Cuyuni and Mazaruni tributaries, as their trading territory and that of their Carib allies. However, as the Spanish missions gradually penetrated the Imataca Mountains and the Caribs were subdued, the claim to the Upper Cuyuni became harder to sustain, until the Wars of Independence overwhelmed these loyalist strongholds. Then the heavy financial debts incurred by Venezuela in these wars encouraged wild notions about what should be done with Venezuela south of the Orinoco.

In 1819, a group of British merchants in Angostura proposed creating a new state within the newly independent Federation of States, comprising all of present-day Venezuela east of the Caroni including the Delta Amacuro.

To be called Nuevo Erin with a new capital Nuevo Dublin, the state would have been opened to colonization by Irish settlers and run as a tax-free enclave by British administrators. After detailed consideration by the Missions Committee, the idea was rejected by the national congress.[16]

Venezuela broke away from its confederation with Colombia and Ecuador in 1832 but this did not curtail speculation about the borders. While the British surveyed the boundary and defined a line more or less along the present frontier, the Venezuelans as inheritors of Spanish possessions claimed the whole Guyana territory up to the Essequibo.[17] However, in 1861 a group of leading Venezuelan ranchers formally submitted proposals to Queen Victoria for the transfer of the whole of Venezuela south of the Orinoco to Britain in exchange for payment of the Venezuelan national debt.[18]

That plan came to nothing, but four years later the whole area was granted as a concession to the North American, Henry Price, giving him exclusive rights to exploit and settle it, free of all import duties and export taxes on cotton and tobacco. The agreement reached with the American entrepreneur granted all settlers the right of Venezuelan citizenship after a year of residence, freedom of the press and religion, and representation in Congress. However, owing to the complete absence of infrastructure or investment, only 38 American settlers are recorded as having taken advantage of this opportunity and within a few years the Price concession was consigned to oblivion[19].

The rubber boom and gold rush in eastern Bolívar State and British Guiana's north-west district led to growing interest in the region, however. While foreign companies were granted monopolies for the extraction of forest products from huge areas of the south of the country, the Venezuelan government began to press its claim to the whole of the territory of British Guiana up to the Essequibo river. To counter the explosion of Venezuelan mining in the Yuruari, the British opened all land east of the surveyed line to mining concessions and in 1890 proclaimed the North West District. Under pressure from the US, the dispute was referred to an international arbitration panel with four judges and, in 1899, a 'full, perfect and final settlement' was reached.

However, as Guyanese independence approached, Venezuela again voiced its claim to the territory west of the Essequibo on the basis of allegations that some of the judges in the 1899 arbitration had been pressured into finding in favour of the British Crown. Border incidents multiplied and in 1969 Venezuela was accused of supporting the Rupununi rebellion. Supported by Brazil, Guyana rejected the Venezuelan claim and embarked on a policy of frontier development – mining and agricultural schemes in the North West and hydropower in the Upper Mazaruni. The dispute remains unresolved.[20]

31

The colonial government was in a quandary. Since East Indians were in a majority, the PPP was unassailable so long as the British, first-past-the-post electoral system was retained. Even the emergence of a strong, middle-class, right-wing party, United Force (UF), which had the backing of business, the churches and through them the Amerindians, was not enough to tip the balance. Again in 1961, the PPP won the elections with twenty seats to the PNC's eleven and UF's four.

A campaign of dirty tricks and racial violence was unleashed with the colonial authorities either turning a blind eye or actually encouraging the process. The electoral system was revised to one of proportional representation. The civil service led a general strike – backed by massive funds from the CIA which allowed strike pay to be paid for eighty days – that brought the Jagan government to its knees. A new election was called in 1964. Despite numerous electoral irregularities, the PPP managed to poll more votes than in the previous elections, but the new system of proportional representation denied them an overall majority in parliament. The PPP won 24 seats, the PNC 22 and UF seven. The British Governor ignored the PPP and invited the PNC to form a government which it did in coalition with UF.

Independence
Thinking it had got what it wanted, the colonial government granted Guyana independence two years later. Forbes Burnham became the first prime minister of independent Guyana with the head of UF, businessman Peter D'Aguiar, given responsibility for finance and economic development.

The tax regime was revised to favour foreign business interests, part of a UF strategy to attract US$900 million in foreign investment with the aim of boosting industrialization along the lines of the free-enterprise model being developed in Puerto Rico. The changes favoured the sugar transnational, Booker McConnell, which by now controlled eight of the twelve huge sugar estates into which the plantations were concentrated, three more being held by the Demerara Company and one by a Guyanese planting family. Booker McConnell was also prominent in fisheries, cattle, timber, insurance, advertising and retail. At the same time, the independent rice-growing sector owned mainly by Indo-Guyanese, which had flourished under the PPP, was run down.

The government's industrialization efforts were, however, a failure and incurred heavy debts. Corruption became endemic and eventually led UF to abandon the coalition in disgust and move to the opposition. Despite this loss of support from the business sector, the PNC managed to strengthen its hold on power through fraudulent elections.

In 1970, the PNC declared Guyana a 'Cooperative Republic' and Burnham began to implement his programme of 'socialist' reforms. These aimed at both limiting the influence of foreign capital and undermining the power-base of Guyanese businessmen, big property owners and land cultivators.[21] Established in the name of the people, the new government-backed cooperatives were in fact dominated by PNC allies and cronies. The government also took control of imports and exports, with the stated aim of promoting import substitution, but again the mechanism was subverted by patronage networks. At the same time, starting with the bauxite industry, all major foreign businesses were nationalized over the following six years and bought out at an overall cost of around US$250 million. The move brought eighty per cent of the economy under state control and created the opportunity for a massive expansion of the bureaucracy, with yet more jobs being dispensed to party favourites.

Despite an immediate but continuous decline in production and efficiency, the economy was cushioned from serious problems by substantial price increases in all main commodities. Sugar prices quadrupled between 1973 and 1975, rice prices doubled in the same period and bauxite and alumina also increased substantially.

While Guyana cultivated an image abroad as a leader of the Non-Aligned Movement and champion of the third world, electoral fraud and media manipulation became entrenched back home. Over the next decade, one-party rule was established in all but name and constitutional reforms were introduced which allowed the PNC to govern without a popular base, through an Executive Presidency with near 'imperial powers'. Black political opponents, notably Walter Rodney, who had established an opposition movement, the Working People's Alliance (WPA), based on Marxist ideology and a multi-racial platform, were assassinated. Meanwhile the PPP maintained its leadership of the opposition from exile, having been ruthlessly suppressed under the terms of a new National Security Act, which led to many being held in detention for long periods without trial.

By 1980, 'Guyana had become a land of horrors. Democracy was no longer on trial here. The question was whether it would survive this [Rodney's] official crucifixion.' According to Ralph Premdas:

> State terror had become entrenched and pervasive as a mode of maintaining the PNC power... Rape, burglary and arbitary arrests by the security forces had become so prevalent that Indian villages became places of terror.[22]

While the economy declined (see Chapter 3) and corruption flourished, the situation for the poor became increasingly precarious. Food items such as milk,

33

cheese, wheat, flour, chicken, salt, butter, split peas and coffee all became virtually unavailable to the average working-class household. The steady trickle of educated Guyanese emigrating overseas became a flood. The military and paramilitaries were expanded to include nearly one in 35 of the population, though predominantly black, and various ill-conceived projects in hinterland development were attempted which were consumed by termites and lianas as soon as start-up funds were exhausted.

The situation was clearly confusing for the PPP. While it supported 'socialist' reforms in Guyana, it was openly critical of the corruption and racially structured cronyism of Burnham's brand of 'Cooperativism', yet found the PNC had the support of both Cuba and the Soviet Union. As a result, the PPP vacillated between leaving parliament, refusing to take up seats, re-entering under protest, boycotting proceedings and finally re-entering again. Outside parliament the PPP had no more success, the PNC government successfully defeating a record 135-day strike in the sugar industry, called by the PPP in 1977, by bringing in party cadres to replace the striking workers.

In the end it was the failure of the PNC's economic programme's and the death of Forbes Burnham himself, which led to its losing power. As the debt burden mounted, the Guyanese dollar collapsed, exports declined and the aid agencies grew increasingly tired of supporting the country. Repeated and undeniable electoral fraud, coupled with bankruptcy and defaults on debt repayments obliged the aid agencies to insist on both economic and political reforms. While economic reforms and structural adjustment were imposed, the country gradually restored press freedoms and parliamentary democracy. Privatization was embarked on and a new economic boom began in timber and mining, as the country was once again opened to transnationals. It was too late to save Desmond Hoyte, the new leader of the PNC, however. Signs of economic recovery had not been translated into benefits for the poor. In 1992, veteran leader Cheddi Jagan led the PPP back into power to inherit a country shattered by a twenty-year, fraudulent experiment in 'socialism'.

[1] Daly 1975:56
[2] Daly 1975:55
[3] Daly 1975:54
[4] Daly 1975:73. According to the Latin America Bureau (LAB), by 1948 the total amount of clay moved to make these trenches had increased to an estimated one hundred million tons.
[5] Daly 1975:103
[6] Daly 1975:100-101
[7] LAB 1984:16
[8] LAB 1984:18
[9] Cited in LAB 1984:17
[10] Cited in LAB 1984:17
[11] Premdas 1996:46
[12] LAB 1984:23
[13] LAB 1984:24-27. See Rodney (1981) for a detailed account of class and labour issues.
[14] LAB 1984:29
[15] Jagan 1966; Daly 1975; Lutchman 1976; LAB 1984
[16] Perera 1993:23-24
[17] Daly 1975:278
[18] Perera 1993:25
[19] Perera 1993:26-28
[20] Daly 1975; LAB 1984
[21] Premdas 1996:56
[22] Premdas 1996:61

CHAPTER 3
DEVELOPMENT DOMINATION

At independence, Guyana inherited an economy almost wholly dependent on exports of primary commodities – mainly bauxite, sugar and rice, supplemented by minerals and some specialist timbers. The industries producing these goods were largely owned by foreign, mainly British and American companies, whose influence over the colonial state had been paramount. As noted, prior to independence British and American foreign policy towards Guiana was aimed primarily at protecting these interests and resisting what were seen as dangerous left-wing or 'communist' efforts to expropriate foreign-owned businesses. This policy had successfully engineered the failure of the PPP to run the country and handed power over to a coalition government led by the PNC.

In the event, however, the economic programmes introduced by Forbes Burnham's PNC were almost as inimical to the interests of foreign capital as those the transnationals feared would have been introduced under the PPP. The new Constitution of Guyana called for a type of socialism based on 'cooperative efforts' and 'the extension of socialist ownership and the economic laws of socialism'.[1] Burnham's policies nationalized most of the country's productive industries but also forged a highly centralized bureaucratic state, which practised a 'form of elitist state capitalism... in which the ruling group continued to profit, essentially unchallenged, from the process of capital accumulation.'[2]

Foreign mining companies were taken over. The bauxite companies were bought out in their entirety and were run by the state-owned mining company, GUYMINE. The state assumed a 52 per cent share of the African Manganese Company's operations at Matthews Ridge, an arrangement the company found unfavourable and from which it withdrew in 1968. The sugar industries were also nationalized and, after foreign owners had been compensated, the concerns were merged under the management of a single parastatal, GUYSUCO. Rice production was also heavily controlled by the state, with all marketing under the control of the Guyana Rice Board. Indeed, sales of most goods were heavily regulated, the majority being channelled through the parastatal retailing company, Guyana Stores Ltd.

Economic Decline
Not surprisingly, the judgement of the international financial agencies on Burnham's 'Cooperative Socialism' has been severe. The nationalization of key sectors of the economy, they conclude, all but destroyed private-sector initiative

36

and created a very unfavourable environment for foreign investment. After the oil price hike of 1973 and the collapse of world prices for basic commodities like sugar and bauxite, the economy moved heavily into arrears. Between 1980 and 1988, real gross domestic product continually declined at nearly three per cent annually.[3]

Inefficiencies in management and a political reluctance to support sectors dominated by Indo-Guyanese meant that, even where markets were available, supply was unable to meet demand. Sugar and bauxite production declined throughout the late 1970s and 1980s and the industries ran up huge deficits while continuing to function with ill-serviced and decaying old machinery.

Public infrastructure – telecommunications, electricity services, water supply, roads, railways, canals and drainage systems – fell into disrepair. The country only remained afloat due to massive borrowing, and by 1989 the national debt had climbed to 600 per cent of GDP, whereas output had declined to 68 per cent of the 1976 figure.[4]

The macro-economic crisis led to a serious decline in the standard of living, as basic foods, fuels and spare parts became unavailable. Illicit currency exchange mechanisms were established to dodge half-hearted government efforts to foil capital flight. A black market in smuggled goods thrived, with contraband entering through Trinidad, Venezuela and Suriname, while gold and cattle were exported to Brazil to the south. The emergence of this parallel economy encouraged drug-trafficking as Andean cocaine producers sought alternative export corridors to avoid the crackdown on Colombian and Peruvian exports passing directly through Central America and the Caribbean. The breakdown of customs controls in English-speaking Guyana provided a ready entry point into the North American and European drugs markets through the eastern Caribbean.

At the same time, declining real wages and local hardship prompted a massive exodus of Guyanese citizens, especially among the more educated and well-connected. As a result, while the population plateaued off at between 700,000 and 800,000, the numbers of Guyanese living abroad increased to an estimated 200,000. For those who remained behind, life became increasingly difficult and indeed harsh.

By the early 1980s, the government began to default on debt repayments and it became clear to all but the most dogmatic that the country could not survive as an export-dependent economy without radical changes. The experiment in 'Cooperative Socialism' had failed.

Structural Adjustment

The IMF/World Bank prescription to deal with this chronic problem was, of course, structural adjustment, which means, essentially, a cut back in government spending coupled with promotion of foreign-exchange-generating exports. The preferred approach of the agencies was to re-open the country to foreign capital. However, because the promotion of foreign investment implied increasing foreign control of the economy, it was a policy that Burnham for a long time resisted. Alternative means of reviving the flagging economy were instead attempted by the aid agencies short of the full-blown reforms preferred by the development banks.

Thus, in line with national policy, the first IMF Stand-By Arrangement to bail out the economy was negotiated in 1978 and the World Bank pushed through a Programme Loan the following year. The main aim of the Bank's loan was to promote exports through *public-sector* investments. Additional funds were provided to promote exports of greenheart from the state-owned timber company, Demerara Woods Ltd. The programme was a failure, however, and exports continued to decline.

By the early 1980s, the Bank began to push more assertively for structural reforms in public-sector spending. A second Programme loan was redesigned – as the Bank later admitted with inadequate preparation and consequently little real government support – and became one of the World Bank's first 'Structural Adjustment Loans'. The sum involved was boosted from the US$10 million initially proposed to US$22 million. Emphasis was placed on devaluing the currency and laying off 'excess' public-sector employees. The problem remained, however, that cutting back expenditure did little to address the country's underlying problem of stagnant production, which resulted from eighty per cent of the economy being under state control. For that an alternative strategy had to be sought.

The IMF/World Bank formula, as elsewhere, was to link reductions in public-sector spending with a revitalization of export-oriented production by the *private* sector. This would require basic policy changes from the government, the privatization of some state assets and the creation of a fiscal climate to attract otherwise nervous foreign investors. This aspect of the Bank's hastily laid Structural Adjustment Loan was also a failure exactly because the government would not countenance such a reversal of policy. As Dominic Hogg noted in his report for Friends of the Earth, one main reason for this reluctance was the PNC government's suspicion that such reforms would 'favour, mostly, the Indo-Guyanese population, whose allegiance lay more with the WPA and PPP than with the PNC.'[5]

Hogg cites an internal IMF memorandum of 1982 which observed that:

There has apparently emerged a serious rift in the ruling party on the issue of 'privatization' of the economy and particularly on the question of the participation of foreign companies in the ownership and management of the bauxite sector. The Prime Minister... has reportedly aligned himself with the group that opposes the 'recolonization' of the economy... In recent speeches, [the President, Forbes Burnham] has repeated the theme that his Government will not 'surrender' the economy to multinationals and has even chided public officials for suggesting a return to the former dependence on foreign multinationals.[6]

As a result of this fundamental disagreement with the whole thrust of structural adjustment reform, the IMF formally terminated its support, the World Bank suspended the second tranche of its Structural Adjustment Loan and other foreign donors, notably the InterAmerican Development Bank and the Caribbean Development Bank, began to scale back their aid. Starved of balance of payments support, the economy spiralled into further decline. By 1985 the country was effectively bankrupt and was massively in arrears on its debt repayments.

The death of Forbes Burnham in August 1985, however, freed the country of its ideological straitjacket, which was an obstacle to both foreign capital and to local alternatives, and paved the way for government policies more amenable to IMF/World Bank prescriptions. Desmond Hoyte replaced Burnham as president and was secured in office by another fraudulent election. Privatization of the economy began to be discussed again, but given the continuing depressed market in bauxite and sugar, the investment banks had to look elsewhere for means to promote foreign exchange earnings.

As early as 1986, the World Bank began to argue that Guyana's future economic expansion depended on increasing natural resource exports, and that same year the government set up the Guyana Natural Resource Agency in order to promote investment in natural resource-based industries. According to the World Bank's 'Proposal for Economic Recovery':

the long term viability of the economy will depend on the Government's success in expanding and diversifying non-traditional exports (eg gold, diamonds, timber and manufacturing). It is in this context that the Government needs to streamline its policy towards the private sector and clarify the role and relationship of the public sector vis-a-vis the private sector.[7]

As the following chapters show, efforts to boost foreign investment in logging and mining soon began in earnest, but while foreign mining companies

39

began to be wooed on relatively attractive terms from the mid-1980s onwards, logging remained essentially a Guyanese and public-sector enterprise until 1989.

By 1986, Hoyte's expressed commitment to structural adjustment and liberalization laid the grounds for a *rapprochement* with the IMF, which was an essential prerequisite for any renegotiation of the country's massive debt with the other donors. Negotiations with the IMF commenced in April the same year and a joint IMF/World Bank mission visited the country in early 1987 to hammer out an agreed policy for reform. Development assistance aimed at providing balance of payments support once more became possible.

What emerged from the two years of negotiations with the IMF and World Bank was a three-year 'Economic Recovery Program' under the direct supervision of the IMF. Launched in mid-1988, the programme had three principal goals: to encourage free markets in goods and services by creating a suitable environment for private, especially foreign, investment; to reduce the size of the public sector; and to restore good relations with the main donor countries and agencies. To kick start the process, the government announced a new Investment Code in July 1988, which, as Dominic Hogg points out,[8] is regarded as one of the most liberal in South America. It also laid the basis for the privatization of state-owned enterprises.

The extent to which 'Cooperative Socialism' had been rejected in favour of development based on foreign investment – in line with World Bank and IMF prescriptions – could not be more marked. Setting out its investment policy in 1988, the government stated:

> There are in general no restrictions on the proportion of private ownership of any enterprise. Similarly, there are no restrictions on the proportion of foreign ownership... There are no restrictions specially applicable to foreign individuals or to companies incorporated in Guyana, including those owned by foreigners, in relation to the acquisition of physical assets, including land... As a matter of policy, there is no area of economic activity from which foreign or domestic investment is debarred, or to which the public sector has an exclusive right... It is no part of Government's policy to nationalize property. The objective circumstances which led to nationalizations during the 1970s no longer exist. The era of nationalizations is therefore considered to be at an end.[9]

The new policy soon bore fruit; the macro-economic balance sheet began to look healthier and foreign companies started a search for lucrative contracts. In 1989, a large part of the country's foreign debt was rescheduled and a major proportion of bilateral debts were forgiven. The same year, the government moved to reform the exchange control structure with the aim of legalizing the parallel markets that had emerged in the 1970s and 1980s. Meanwhile, the World Bank continued to push new exports. Apart from the considerable programme aid provided through its structural adjustment loans, the Bank also made available to the government new 'special drawing rights' in 1990 through its soft loan facility, the International Development Agency, explicitly linked to the 'development and expansion of non-traditional sectors (gold, forestry and manufacturing)'.[10]

The Price of Reform
But the transition from 'Cooperative Socialism' to the World Bank's vision of 'sustained growth' led by fiscal probity and foreign direct investment was not an easy one. Devaluation and the removal of price controls on all but a small number of basic commodities brought further hardship to Guyanese citizens, which were only partly offset by a hastily patched together social 'safety net' – the Social Impact Amelioration Programme (SIMAP) – which was severely hampered by a lack of institutional capacity to deliver promised services to affected groups.

Cutbacks in government spending, the decline of real earnings resulting from inflation and devaluation, and public-sector lay-offs hit the poor hard. Real wages in the public sector fell by 18 per cent compared to 1986. Government investment in infrastructure actually declined: the road system deteriorated, the sea-wall protecting coastal agriculture from flooding was breached in several places and sewerage and water supply systems collapsed. Public spending on the health sector was half what it had been in 1984 and education spending fell to a third of of pre-adjustment levels. The result was considerable disaffection. Strikes increased and were partly responsible for the fact that, in 1990, GDP actually declined by 3.2 per cent.[11]

Nevertheless, the government persevered, accompanying its economic reforms with political liberalization. By 1993, the World Bank was holding up Guyana as a shining example of courageous and far-reaching reform. 'Few countries', the Bank noted proudly 'have moved so far, so fast.' Within four years the government had eliminated almost all price controls, established a floating exchange rate for the Guyanese dollar, eliminated import licensing, reduced import tariffs, launched a major programme of privatization of state assets, introduced private-sector management of the sugar industry, reduced the government payroll and raised taxes. GDP began to increase markedly from 1991 onwards and a galloping inflation rate was gradually brought under control. Arrears on debt repayments were eliminated and bilateral debts forgiven or rescheduled, though repayments were still accounting for over fifty per cent of foreign exchange earnings.

In late 1992, elections were held, the first to be judged essentially fair by the international community since independence. The PPP, still headed by veteran party leader Cheddi Jagan, swept back into power.

President Jagan found himself, after over thirty years in political limbo, in control of a country quite different from the one he had last had charge of in the early 1960s. Since independence, his old enemies, the colonial transnational corporations, had been chased from the country. Yet since then the country had also endured a disastrous experiment in so-called 'Cooperative Socialism', which, whatever the special faults that may be laid at the door of the PNC, only mirrored the experience of socialist economies throughout the communist world. Socialism as a creed had apparently been discredited, the Berlin Wall dismantled and market-based reforms embraced even by China. More than that, Guyana itself had once again been opened up to foreign capital and new transnationals were again key players in the country's political economy.

The PPP government continued to oversee some improvement in Guyana's macro-economic situation throughout the 1990s. Real GDP growth in 1996 was 7.9 per cent, with a similar figure estimated for 1997. Inflation remained low at 4.5 per cent in 1996, while Guyana's balance of trade improved. Due to debt forgiveness and rescheduling, the national debt fell from US$2.1 billion in 1995 to US$1.5 billion in 1997.

Yet despite these achievements, the dilemmas facing the government are familiar to many developing countries. Having been yoked into the global economy by the impositions of colonial governments and companies, Guyana could not hope to reject the demands of foreign capital after independence while remaining dependent on foreign aid and trade. Burnham's state-run enterprises had failed to keep the country afloat, being run mainly to benefit the party elite, while at the same time international prices of raw materials had crashed. Consequently, the country had gone bankrupt and had now been once again prised open to foreign companies by the presence of the development agencies whose domination was so apparent.

It has been a difficult time for the PPP government, made worse by Jagan's death in March 1997. Many of the fundamental truths that the party espoused during the 1950s have had to be discarded. The government has been obliged to accept that neither Guyana's people nor its economy will tolerate a return to public ownership. Despite its suspicions of foreign interests, the PPP has also been forced to recognize that a lack of domestic capital leaves only foreign investment as the means to refloat the private sector. The PPP has had to accept the IMF and World Bank's development model as the only option available *so long as the country aims to remain dependent on exports.*

It was also clear from President Jagan's public pronouncements that he was personally deeply ambivalent about this situation. His instincts remained those of an old-style Marxist, yet circumstances obliged him to accept the capitalist road. In a speech delivered to a conference in 1994, he called for a 'New Global Humanitarian Order', funded by savings from world-wide disarmament, but his remarks on the domestic economy were altogether less radical:

> As regards the role of the public sector and the private sector in sustainable development, we do not take a dogmatic, inflexible position. However, we believe that we must exercise sovereignty over our land, resources, values and traditions. We do not share the view of those with an ideological bias for their implicit advocacy of privatisation/divestment over the state sector. We have repeatedly stated that in the context of Guyana with a wrecked economy and underdeveloped human resource base, the private sector will be the engine of growth, with the state sector playing a complementary and facilitating role and, at the same time, ensuring economic growth with social justice and ecological justice.[12]

As later chapters show, this attempt to reconcile private-sector investment with political sovereignty has led to contradictory positions, especially since domestic investment in Guyana is so weak. Distrust of North American transnationals led him to advocate certain policies, aimed at attracting 'Southern' rather than 'Northern' capital and promoting 'South-South cooperation'. Since 1992 the government has therefore courted companies and investors from South East Asia as a way of breaking dependency on the more traditional sources of investment in the US, Britain and Canada.

Jagan's death and his replacement by former Prime Minister, Sam Hinds, may not change this policy significantly. The course of economic development recommended by the World Bank and IMF and being carried through by Finance Minister Bharrat Jagdeo is set to continue. It is debatable whether such a development model has brought either social or ecological justice to Guyana. Some of the country's political class may be benefiting from liberalization, but the costs for others have been heavy. In particular, the arrival of foreign capital, whatever its origins, threatens serious consequences for Guyana's Amerindians and the environment in the country's interior.

This chapter draws heavily on the study carried out for Friends of the Earth by Dominic Hogg (1993) titled: 'The SAP in the Forest: the Environmental and Social Impacts of Structural Adjustment Programmes in the Philippines, Ghana and Guyana.' I am grateful to Friends of the Earth for their permission to cite this study.

[1] World Bank 1993b:3
[2] Hogg 1993:132
[3] World Bank 1993b:3
[4] World Bank 1993b
[5] Hogg 1993:136
[6] Hogg 1993:136
[7] Cited in Hogg 1993:144
[8] Hogg 1993:139
[9] Cited in Hogg 1993:145
[10] Hogg 1993:141
[11] World Bank 1993b
[12] Jagan 1994:33

CHAPTER 4
ROADS AND RANCHES

'The rancher is considered an intruder with no territorial rights, a person who has come with his cattle onto tribal lands and then unjustifiably sought to restrict tribal activities. The opinion is freely expressed on any occasion upon which the rancher protests against what he considers to be an infringement of his own rights by members of the tribe. The rancher as a rule seeks to interfere as little as possible with Amerindian freedom of action and movement, except for not wishing his livestock stolen, or his water holes and streams poisoned with fish-poisons. The Makushi point of view, however, is that they are his own ancestral savannahs, ponds and streams, to do as he likes with, and that cattle are a destructive nuisance, which often, by destroying his fields and breaking down the fences they make necessary, cause him severe privation. He naturally feels no compunction in recouping himself by occasionally slaughtering one of the rancher's animals.'[1]

On Guyana's southern frontier with Brazil the forests give way to an extensive, seasonally flooded savannah transected by watercourses and gallery forests. The savannah drains into open ponds and marshes and small meandering creeks, some of which, like the Pirara, wend their way down to the Takutu and Ireng rivers on the border and so south across the wide plains of northern Brazil to the Rio Branco at Boa Vista. Other creeks, separated by the slightest rise in the ground, drain eastward into the Rupununi which flows down to the mighty Essequibo. The upland thus forms a natural crossing point between the Amazon basin and the Caribbean and was used as a trading path by the Amerindians for centuries before the European invasion. Makushi and Wapishana Indians have inhabited these savannahs longer than recorded knowledge, but from the seventeenth century they were embroiled in the turmoil of slave wars and trading expeditions that linked these upland areas to the Portuguese and Dutch posts on the coast.

Leaving aside the occasional Dutch trader passing through the area in the mid-eighteenth century, the region first experienced European colonization when the Portuguese established a settlement in what is now Roraima State in 1773. A stone fort was established at São Joaquim at the confluence of the Takutu and Uraricoera rivers in 1776, with a garrison of some thirty men and their dependents. The wide savannahs were immediately seen as apt for cattle-raising, and in the

1790s the first bull and several cows were shipped upriver to provide a herd for the garrison. Shortly thereafter private ranches began to be established and by 1798 a total of 900 head of cattle were said to be grazing the coarse grasslands. Only forty years later, the German explorer and later government official, Robert Schomburgk, employed by the Royal Geographical Society, reported that the ranches had over 3,000 head of cattle and some 500 horses, with in addition a few thousand feral cattle roaming wild. By the end of the nineteenth century the herd had expanded to over 55,000 head.[2] Once ready for market, the cattle made their way south along rough trails to the edges of the forests where they were sent down the Rio Branco and Negro on rafts.[3]

The ranching economy on the Guyanese side of the border, the line of which was not agreed until 1904, developed as an independent enterprise rather more slowly. True, the Dutch governor, Storm van 'S Gravesande had, in 1750, recommended colonizing the savannah to raise much-needed cattle and horses and to secure the frontier against Portuguese and Spanish territorial claims, but these ideas came to nothing. This was not followed up until the ephemeral Pirara mission of the 1840s. Consequently, it was not until 1860, when a lone Dutch settler named DeRooy established the first small herd on the northern savannah, that coastal occupation can be said to have begun.[4]

After that date a trickle of other colonists ventured south, but little real change was experienced until the 1890s when a small number of pioneering Scottish farmers settled in the region and began to fence and manage the coarse grass savannahs. They gained rights to extensive areas by acquiring pastoral leases from the British colonial administration in Georgetown to what were then classified as Crown lands in exchange for nominal rents. Most prominent of these was H.P.C. Melville who intermarried with the local Amerindians and in the early twentieth century was vested with government authority to oversee the region.[5]

The ranchers soon found that the very poor soils of the savannahs and the tough grasses that grew on them did not allow intensive cattle-ranching. On the contrary, the cattle were allowed to roam over vast areas, with a mean population density of less than one head of cattle per hectare. However, the huge extent of the savannahs, which encompass more than one and a half million hectares on the Guyanese side of the frontier, allowed a steady expansion of the herd. Especially after the Second World War, various experiments, not all successful, were made to improve the pastures and regulate the herds in fenced enclosures. By the 1960s, the Guyanese herd on the Rupununi savannahs had grown to as many as 60,000 head, by no means all of which were grazing on officially leased lands.

Frontier Inequalities

Ranching has undoubtedly brought wealth to the region, but this wealth has not been evenly distributed, being concentrated in the hands of the 500 or so non-Amerindians in the district who have the connections and capital to secure priority to lands and invest in veterinary services and fencing. The major costs, however, have been borne by the Amerindians who have lost vast tracts of their ancestral lands to the ranchers and have suffered severe health problems due to introduced diseases.[6]

Mirroring the social order that developed in Roraima State in Brazil, the area's ranching society had, and to a great extent still has, a near feudal character. Ranchers of European descent claim control of most of the valuable land and employ poor labourers and Amerindians as cowhands, most often still referred to by the Brazilian term, *vaqueiros*. Less trained Amerindians work for the ranchers on an *ad hoc* basis as occasional labour, while the remaining Amerindians make a living as best they can on what is left of their lands.

Before the administration began to establish an independent presence in Lethem during the 1940s, the Amerindians were almost entirely dependent on the landowners and the few missionaries for their interaction with the government. Nearly all trade with the outside world was also mediated through the ranchers, although the active market in wild rubber, *balata*, from the 1900s to the 1940s, did provide seasonal employment to some 300 Amerindians every year, and an equivalent number of coastal workers who visited the region to bleed the trees for the concessionaires. Economically, balata bleeding was the most important activity of the period, with annual yields reaching nearly 500 tonnes at the industry's peak.[7]

It would be an exaggeration to say that the ranchers exercised *droit de seigneur* over Amerindian women, but mixed marriages and concubinage were commonplace and the unequal nature of these liaisons (no white women married into an Amerindian village) starkly revealed the hierarchical nature of the society: ranchers of European descent at the top, cowhands and skilled farmworkers in the middle, Amerindians at the bottom.

Inequality in the land tenure situation was equally pronounced. After 1919, minimal legal protections were provided to the Amerindians whose lands had been taken over by pastoral leases. According to the regulations, presently incorporated into the State Lands Act, ranchers are not allowed to erect corrals or cattle-pens within a three-mile radius of an Amerindian settlement and they are also obliged to 'make good' any damage done to villages and crops.[8] Formal rights in land were given not to the Amerindians but to the ranchers, yet even they were only able to obtain pastoral leases which needed renewing annually.

By the late 1940s, around half a million hectares of Amerindian land had been granted as pastoral leases to private ranchers in the northern savannah and a similar area granted to the para-statal Rupununi Development Company in the south. 'This does not leave the Indian much grazing land for developing a cattle industry', remarked a colonial survey carried out in 1948: 'there appears to be no possibility of developing a permanent industry in cattle rearing both for the Rancher and for the Amerindians under present conditions of land tenure.'[9]

The impact of ranching on Amerindian culture has also been marked. Smallpox swept through the Makushi and Wapishana in the 1840s,[10] and the Makushi in particular were severely affected by their 'traumatic' involvement in the ranching economy, 'fenced in and fenced out by rancher occupation.'[11] The system of dependence on the ranchers was especially damaging. Wrote one Administrator:

> Under the pernicious influence of this system the Indian became a dependent retainer, almost a serf, of the ranchers instead of an independent employee. It deprived him of the sense of responsibility, because his immediate requirements would be supplied by his 'patron', and also the possibility of ever becoming other than was. He neglected his fields, surrendering his self-supporting independence to a reliance on the goodwill of his master... Tribal customs and control have decreased and now these Indians are a dependent peasantry.[12]

The anthropologist, Iris Myers, who lived among the Makushi for several years, was an intimate witness of this decline, caused by repeated epidemics and the usurpation of Makushi lands by ranchers. She recounts that:

> The despair felt at overwhelming circumstances which they are powerless to control and the rapid dying out of the tribe, has led to an increase in 'paiwarri' drinking, which means that a large portion of the cassava goes into its manufacture. One frequently hears the excuse: – 'I am not going to leave my field to be enjoyed by others. I shall at least have some pleasure from it before I die'... A vicious circle is formed – sickness and despair leading to hunger and malnutrition predisposing to sickness.[13]

Although to the south, the Wapishana had evolved a more viable means of mixing old customs and new practices due to much better relations with the Rupununi Development Company, even there land disputes were common as the company sought to expand its fenced areas. The balance of power was clear. Whereas the company had leases to more than half a million hectares, only 7,280 hectares had been set aside as an Amerindian reserve.[14] Later, however, when the company's own herds declined, it was persuaded to relinquish land back to the Amerindians to allow for the development of their own herds.[15] No such transfers occurred in the northern savannahs. The 1948 report recommended that extensive areas of land be returned to the Amerindians to allow them to develop their own cattle industry.

The situation later became complicated by the fact that marked inequalities developed among the Amerindians. Amerindian herds are not shared among the community but are individually owned and mostly belong to a number of wealthier Amerindian men, many of whom are Arawaks from Moruka brought in as teachers in the late colonial period.[16]

Rancher Rebellion

Rupununi rancher society had developed as a pioneering frontier settlement, isolated from the coast, enclosed and self-sufficient. The tough frontier life created its own social norms and loyalties, feudal perhaps to the outsider, but with their own logic and system of values. A fierce sense of independence made the ranchers scornful of the soft life of coastlanders and dismissive of the legal niceties and administrative meddling of government. Consequently, the gradual extension of state control over the region from the 1950s onwards generated tensions and even resentment, which intensified in proportion to outside interference.

Discontent in the Rupununi grew during the early years of independence. Opposed to the racial politics that dominated affairs in Georgetown, the ranchers and many of their Amerindian dependents and cowhands, who had close links to the Catholic Church and its missions in the area, supported United Force. As the power of UF in the coalition government waned, the ranchers found themselves increasingly marginalized by decisions made in the capital. When, in 1968, UF pulled out of the coalition, discontent in the Rupununi grew, especially with PNC favouritism in handling land disputes and dealing out pastoral leases. The ranchers felt particularly uneasy as their land tenure was still insecure: they still only had one-year pastoral leases which they feared the government might refuse to renew any time they were out of favour. Their concerns were sharpened when the Burnham administration announced plans to establish coastlander settlers in the northern savannahs.

The fraudulent elections the same year were apparently the last straw. On 2 January 1969, a group of ranchers and Amerindians, allegedly after careful preparations, seized all government offices in Lethem, taking the administrators captive. According to official reports five policemen and a civilian were killed resisting the rebellion.

Exactly what the rebels hoped to achieve by this revolt is still not clear, and it may be that they did not know themselves. Rejecting government authority, they were allegedly planning to establish their own secessionist enclave, which, they hoped, would be supported by the Venezuelan government, which was at the time vigorously pressing its own claim to the whole of the country west of the Essequibo. According to some accounts, the Venezuelan government had foreknowledge of the affair and even supplied arms and ammunition to the rebels, giving the impression that their uprising would be strongly supported by the Venezuelan army.

If this was the case, which is doubtful, the rebels were to be cruelly disappointed. No foreign support materialized. Instead, shortly after the rebellion and without giving time for any dialogue or negotiation, the Guyana Defence Force flew in a well-armed unit to attack them. Ranches were torched to the ground and a fierce firefight ensued in Lethem in which, it was alleged, a number of ranchers and Amerindians were killed. The rebel leaders were forced to flee to Brazil and then to Venezuela, where many did find refuge.

The crushing of the rebellion led to strong criticisms in the press; the government was accused of heavy-handedness and poorly substantiated allegations were made of massacres, mass burials, the rape of Amerindian girls and pillage, while the rebels were also accused of misguided political ambitions, unprovoked violence and murder. Unable to apprehend any of the presumed ringleaders, the ranchers who had fled across the frontier, the army took 28 Amerindians captive, ten of whom were not released for fifteen months though they were never found guilty of any offence.[17]

None of these half-truths has ever been properly investigated and a full tale of the rebellion has yet to be told. Instead, the whole affair was followed by a cover-up, which partly provoked the wild speculations about what had occurred. However, the action led to serious consequences for both the ranchers and the Amerindians. Government support for the ranchers was withdrawn, subsidized flights by the Guyana Airways Corporation were cut back and the cattle herd declined by 85-90 per cent to only 12,000 head, due to the flight of the ringleaders to Venezuela and the decline of the air freight service. The revolt had raised the bogey of secession and the loyalty of the Amerindians to Guyana was openly questioned by the government.

One immediate consequence was that the report of the Amerindian Lands Commission, discussed in more detail in Chapter 7 and which was presented to government the same year, 1969, had to be particularly cautious in its recommendations. This may be one reason why the land titles recommended by the Commission in the frontier districts were much smaller than the areas claimed by the Amerindians.

The rebellion also provided the government with an excuse to delay granting lands to Amerindians. Rather than acting on the recommendations of the Lands

Commission, in 1970 the government instead extracted an agreement from certain Amerindian leaders called to Georgetown that titling should only proceed when convenient to the government. Instead of granting the titles, the government provided funds for a heightened military presence in the interior. When titles were finally granted to some communities in 1976, key frontier areas were excluded and a clause was written into the amended Amerindian Act which allowed the government to annul titles if there was evidence of disloyalty. No such condition is imposed on the property rights of other Guyanese citizens.

Land issues continue to be a problem throughout the Rupununi and the south of the country. Amerindian communities complain that their titles are too small, are encroached upon by ranchers and settlers, and are neither mapped nor demarcated. The inadequacy of the Amerindians' land titles has encouraged politically connected ranchers to annex their lands, knowing that the Amerindians lack access to means of redress. A number of communities entirely lack titles, while other villages have expanded and divided in the nearly thirty years since the Lands Commission surveyed their area and now require additional areas.

The issue of land titles has been repeatedly brought up by the Amerindians in their meetings with government. In 1994, for example, Christopher Duncan of Aishalton, a Wapishana from the South Rupununi stated:

> We are happy and most grateful to have our land titles granted but we wish to appeal on behalf of Rupunau, Katoonarib and Parikwarunau, which are young communities that have sprung up in the course of recent years. They are vibrant communities and have interim Village Councils that need to be recognised. Repeated applications for land titles and representation have been made to the past and present administrations, so far to no avail. We feel they need recognition and autonomy as they cannot continue to exist under the mother villages of Sand Creek, Sawariwau and Ambrose respectively.
>
> All our communities are crying out for extension of their grazing lands in order to accommodate the increasing cattle population. Repeated appeals have been made at different forum to seek the release of land which the Rupununi Development Company is not now beneficially occupying since their cattle population is declining. We request the assistance of Government to effect the release of lands.
>
> Due to the upsurge of activity in our area, especially in cattle rustling, illegal trading and mining by Brazilians as well as free movement of vehicles across our border, we do not feel secure and we urge that proper security measures be enforced to help curb these activities. One recent sad experience was the incident where a GDF patrol de-

51

tained some Brazilian miners at Gunn's Strip and after their release later, they threatened retaliation on the Wai Wais for reporting them.[18]

Land disputes in the area have become quite heated. Violent attacks on village councillors of the Amerindian community of Moco-Moco were reported in November 1995, when two Amerindians had to be hospitalized after being attacked by a coastal settler.[19]

The Road From Brazil

Unfortunately, the government has taken no steps to sort out the confused land situation in the south of the country, but, on the contrary, has become deeply involved in Brazilian plans to open up the interior by building a road connecting Manaus and Boa Vista to Georgetown.

In fact, the idea of connecting central Brazil to Guyana by an overland route had been proposed long before. Indeed, as early as 1837 the British official, Robert Schomburgk, had mooted the idea of building a railroad connection between the coast and Brazil.[20] With the expansion of the cattle industry in the Rupununi savannahs in the early years of the twentieth century, a rough trail was cut so that cattle could be brought down to market on the coast. The trail, which was opened up between 1917 and 1919, wound across the savannahs to the Essequibo at Kurupukari and then sliced through the forests between the Berbice and Demerara down to the Cannister Falls, areas *en route* being cleared for rough pasture to give the animals somewhere to forage while undertaking the arduous two-week trek.

However, after the Second World War this trail gradually fell into disuse. The establishment of a slaughterhouse and refrigeration plant at Lethem linked by a highly subsidized airfreight service to the coast provided an alternative means of exporting meat. The Rupununi herd expanded rapidly to fill this market. Following the Rupununi rebellion and as part of the government's policy of securing national frontiers, between 1971-1973 a rough trail was cut by the Ministry of Works and Hydraulics between Mabura Hill and Kurupukari, which allowed access to the Rupununi by four-wheel-drive vehicles during the dry season. This road soon fell into disrepair and was for years closed. Very occasionally a jeep would be hazarded along this perilous trail, more out of bravado than with any real purpose.

During the 1970s and 1980s, Brazilian private interests began to press heavily for a proper road connection. In 1971 a joint declaration was signed between Guyana and Brazil for bilateral cooperation in the construction of roads. Then, in 1982 an agreement was entered into to build a bridge across the Takutu near Lethem, though this was never completed, and the same year a 'Memorandum of Understanding on the Interconnection of Guyanese and Brazilian Highway

Networks' was signed between the two countries, identifying the need to establish a road connection between Lethem and Mabura Hill. Lack of funding for the construction delayed implementation, however.[21]

Brazilian pressure for a road connection was nevertheless sustained, supported by some Guyanese businessmen, calling themselves the 'Safari' group, who began their own efforts to upgrade the trail between Mabura Hill and Kurupukari. In 1989 the Hoyte administration eventually agreed to allow the construction of the road, the primary aim being 'to facilitate the traffic of goods and people from the State of Roraima in Brazil to Guyana's capital, Georgetown.' The primacy of Brazilian interests in the project was thus made clear.[22]

The same year, the first phase of road construction commenced along the route of the old cattle trail. To finance this initial stage of the project, the Brazilian government made a concessional loan of US$15 million through its external lending agency, CACEX, and this sum was used to pay for the construction of an all-weather road from Lethem in the Rupununi savannahs through to the Essequibo river at Kurupukari. The tied aid package secured the services of the Brazilian mining transnational, Paranapanema, which has a notorious record within Brazil for its abuse of indigenous rights, to construct the road and establish ferries on the Takutu at Lethem and on the Essequibo at Kurupukari to allow traffic across the rivers.

Human rights organizations were quick to protest. Survival International pointed out that the consequences of this project were likely to be similar to those long associated with road-building throughout the Amazonian region. 'The road link will penetrate right into the central Guyanese forests. Accelerated forest loss seems likely as are illegal cross-border penetrations by colonists and miners such as have already occurred in Venezuela, Peru, Paraguay and Bolivia. These kinds of problems are likely to be quite severe and quite beyond the capacity of the Guyanese Government institutions to control', the organization noted. 'Commercialization of ranching [expected to develop rapidly once the road is completed] in the Rupununi savannahs is likely to have very negative effects on the Indians there, in terms of land invasion, the displacement of the indigenous peoples' own herds and introduced diseases.' Both Survival International and the Guyana Human Rights Association called on the government to carry out a social and environmental impact study before continuing with the road-building. The government did not comply with these requests.[23]

A study by the University of Guyana showed that some of these concerns were well founded. As a result of the road, Brazilians were found to be moving in and out of south Guyana without regulation, while Amerindian lands had been taken over without proper consultation and without payment of compensation for damaged crops.[24]

53

The road has now been completed from Lethem to Kurupukari on the Essequibo, though it is of very variable quality and some parts are of single lane width, lack proper culverts and are rapidly being washed out. Since 1991, ex-British army Bedford 4x4 trucks, run by Georgetown-based haulage companies, have begun an irregular service between the frontier and the capital taking supplies (mainly food) down to Lethem and Brazilian exports to Georgetown at about one-third of the cost of airfreight. The very poor quality of the trail between Kurupukari and Mabura Hill, where the track has been churned into mud impassable to other less rugged vehicles, means that the trucks take up to 24 hours to accomplish the 150-kilometre stretch. The Bedfords can only achieve their mission due to their awesomely powerful winches and four-wheel drive.

Amerindian communities on the road express mixed opinions about the potential benefits of it being upgraded. Whereas some believe the road may lead to their demise as distinct peoples, others see that the road link could provide essential communications, allowing the communities to travel to the capital for trading and health reasons. On two points all are agreed; strict controls on movement across the border and up and down the road must be instituted and Amerindian lands must be secured and clearly demarcated first *before* the road building proceeds.

In 1992, the Brazilian government offered Guyana a further US$14 million, in a similar package to the first, for Paranapanema to finish the last section of uncompleted road between Kurupukari and Mabura Hill. However, the deal fell through due to objections from the IMF, whose continued financial support for structural adjustment in Guyana gives it the right to veto government acceptance of further foreign loans. In October 1993, the Brazilian State Governor of Roraima stepped up the pressure for the completion of the road which he claimed was vital to promote the development of northern Brazil. Offering to complete the road in exchange for bartered lumber, rice and sugar to the value of US$5 million, the Governor urged that the road construction be initiated immediately and be completed within six months.

The advantages of the road to the northern Brazilian states are obvious: ready access for Brazilian exporters to the small market in Georgetown and through its port to the larger Caribbean market and NAFTA region. It is estimated that trucking freight up to a container port in Georgetown could reduce the time taken to ship goods from central Brazil to North America by up to a week, avoiding the long haul to Manaus, transshipment down the Amazon and a further day's sailing north along the Atlantic coast.

The advantages to Guyana are not so clear, and there is no evidence that the government has studied the likely impact of the road on domestic businesses and haulage contractors: would they be outcompeted by the economies of scale of Brazilian companies? would a flush of cheap imports undermine local producers and upset the country's balance of payments? would new settlers and property speculation cause housing and land prices to soar beyond the reach of local residents both in the Rupununi and on the coast?

Despite repeated calls for a social and environmental impact study, the government strenuously resisted submitting its plans to any such scrutiny. Yet already, without the road even being completed, illegal cross-border penetrations from Brazil have become a serious problem in the Rupununi and Pakaraimas regions. Rustling has increased over the years and land conflicts between ranchers and indigenous communities are gradually intensifying. Border controls at Lethem are absent and, until very recently, it was possible to travel all the way from Brazil to Georgetown without once having one's papers checked. At the time, there were no customs checks on goods moving north apart from a sporadic check on the bridge across the Demerara at Linden.

According to the World Rainforest Movement, it can confidently be predicted that *if such laxness continues*, the completion of the road will lead to an increasing invasion of Guyana by landless settlers, miners, timber cutters and urban squatters. Already there are growing reports of drug-smuggling from South America through Guyana which provides a convenient transshipment point for the Caribbean and North America. The road could encourage this. There has also been an upsurge of gun-running across the border, with reports of machine guns being brought in from Brazil and Suriname.[25]

The World Rainforest Movement and the Guyana Human Rights Association have pointed out that the uncontrolled inflow of people into Guyana could have serious consequences for Amerindian communities, but towns like Georgetown could also suffer. Typically Amazonian towns that are connected by roads double in size in five years and continue growing. Population growth overwhelms town planning, leading to shanties on the outskirts, water shortages, sanitation problems and all the social pathologies associated with poverty and inadequate housing. In 1993, the World Bank, too expressed doubts about the merits of the road noting that:

> This road is controversial in that it is not economically justifiable at this time, or in the near future, in terms of costs and benefits to road users. In addition, the potential harmful impacts of the road on the environment and indigenous populations have not been adequately studied.[26]

Concern was also voiced by Janette Forte and Anne Benjamin of the Amerindian Research Unit of the University of Guyana:

To date there has been no public discussion of what consequences a road designed and built by Brazilians to meet Brazilian needs might have on our interior, our indigenous peoples, indeed on the issue of sovereignty itself... At this juncture, we simply lack the personnel, technology and financial resources, to maintain our sovereignty vis-a-vis Brazil. Why plunge headlong into this venture before conducting social and environmental impact assessments?[27]

By 1994, heightened awareness about the environmental threats to the country's interior coincided with renewed pressure by non-governmental organizations (NGOs). The Amerindian Peoples Association's lobbying of the World Bank, which was at that time funding an 'Infrastructure Rehabilitation Project' which included road-building, obliged the government to accept that an Environmental Impact Study should be carried out before the road was completed. NGOs stressed that once the study had been commissioned and carried out, with the full participation of the affected groups, the results should be published and subjected to public debate before a decision was made on whether to pursue the road.

In compliance with the first part of this demand, a study was commissioned from the British consultancy, Environmental Resources Management (ERM) in association with the Guyanese company David Klautky and Associates, and was paid for by the World Bank. The process was frustratingly flawed in a number of respects. In the first place, the study was limited by its terms of reference to look only at the impact of the road between Lethem and Linden, rather than at the wider implications of the road for the country as a whole, as had been urged by the NGOs. Secondly, the British consultants were given no hint of what sort of road the government actually proposed building – whether it was to be a rough laterite road, an all-weather, graded, gravel road or a tarmac highway – which made it hard to guess what kind of traffic would use the road and in what volumes. The government also tried to stifle public debate about the road and discouraged the consultants from holding public meetings to gather local peoples' opinions.

Despite these limitations the study, completed in April 1995, was a useful one and made some highly pertinent recommendations to the government on how the impacts of the road could be mitigated and Guyana's interests best served.

In the first place, the report stated, the road had two quite different objectives. One was to promote exports from Roraima State in Brazil and the other was to promote the development of Guyana as a unified state. Whereas Brazil's interests required the construction of an all-weather gravel road passable to international freight traffic year-round, Guyana's immediate needs would be better served by a rough 'forest road' suitable for four-wheel-drive vehicles. The report 'strongly recommended' that the cheaper and rougher track be chosen and that all other road improvements be delayed until government institutions had the capacity to regulate industries in the interior.[28]

The report pointed out that the road could offer real advantages for the communities in the interior by promoting increased employment in ranching, logging, agricultural production and allowing more ready access for goods and services, such as education and health-care. However, the costs to local communities could be high. The road threatens to increase pressure on Amerindian lands, resulting in loss of subsistence and the takeover of their traditional territories. The report also noted that the government does not have a policy for compensating indigenous communities for lands expropriated for building the road and indeed compensation has still not been paid for the land lost to the first phase of the road built between 1989 and 1991. Mining and logging operations in the interior may be accelerated by the opening up of the road, posing further problems for local communities. Interactions with migrants, molestation of women by the road-construction crews, prostitution, increased venereal diseases and drunkenness, and increasing male absenteeism, as males move off to the coast in search of work, could lead to serious social problems and a break-down of local cultures. Introduced communicable diseases, including malaria which is already rife in the interior, could also intensify if the road is completed. The report listed numerous environmental risks associated with the road. Increased small-scale mining, in particular, threatens to pollute river systems and may upset forest management regimes, while increased hunting and illegal wildlife trapping may deplete the fauna.

The report also warns that the creation of the highway will be likely to trigger the development of a whole network of feeder roads throughout the interior, giving access to mines, logging operations and agricultural programmes. The road thus implies widespread impacts throughout the southern interior and not just along the immediate course of the road itself.

To mitigate these impacts, the study recommends that the road be made as modest as possible, as already mentioned, to discourage heavy freight and passenger traffic building up on the road before government institutions can control it. The report also argues that before the road is opened up Amerindian land titles should be surveyed and secured, that the titles should be extended and that the Amerindian Act should be revised to provide stronger protections. Amerindian captains should be given stronger powers to control access to community lands, it recommends.

Unfortunately, the government seems to have paid little heed to this detailed study. In late 1995, the government decided to contract the Guyana Defence

Force to upgrade the final stretch of the road between Kurupukari and the main forest road built by the logging company Demerara Timbers southwards from Mabura Hill, at a cost of G$40 million.[29] The long-awaited all-weather road between Boa Vista and Georgetown thus looks set to become a reality in the near future. However, no measures have yet been announced to secure the interests of the Amerindians.

Nor has the government shown itself keen to share the findings of the environmental impact study with those who had first pushed for it. After the government had sat on the report for ten months, apparently without taking any action to comply with its recommendations, the environmental organizations were again obliged to write to the World Bank and demand the release of the study and the holding of a public workshop to discuss its findings. Under pressure from the World Bank, whose operational procedures require it to adopt a 'participatory' approach to development, the government finally agreed to a workshop to be held in Georgetown in April 1996. The meeting was never held.

The way the government dealt with the Amerindian component of the assessment was even more questionable. As part of the study, the ERM had been requested to produce an Indigenous Peoples Development Plan, but the government asked that this be written up as a separate, confidential document, on the grounds that it touched a sensitive issue and should have only limited distribution. Once again the Amerindians find that they are being excluded from decision-making about their own future.

During all this controversy, the 'Safari' group has been promoting a second road-building project between Linden and eastern Venezuela. The route, which in places remains little more than a foot trail, winds its way from Linden to Omai and so to Bartica from where it straggles up overland to Ianna, Matthews Ridge, Five Star and on to the border, where it will link up with the far more developed Venezuelan road network. If the road is ever built, it will inevitably lead to a major expansion of gold mining and more pressure on the already highly invaded lands of the Carib Indians. It appears that this project has been proceeding with the government's blessing and minor financial support, despite the fact that no efforts have been made to consult the local communities or carry out an impact assessment.

Illegal roads have also proliferated across the southern border from Brazil. From the air, a whole web of rough jeep trails can be observed wriggling north from the Brazilian ranching town of Normandia. The roads cross the frontier to make their way towards the mining enclaves on the Ireng and around Monkey Mountain. Here make-shift townships populated mainly by Brazilian *garimpeiros* have established themselves in the centre of the Patamona Indians' territory. Almost unconnected to Guyana, these encampments export their gold south to the markets in Boa Vista, from where they are also supplied with Brazilian goods, rum, mercury and prostitutes.

The New River Controversy with Suriname

Only when the three Dutch colonies of Berbice, Demerara and Essequibo were ceded to Britain in 1803 did a pressing need emerge for a definition of the colonial boundary between Dutch and British possessions. However, a survey carried out in 1840 appeared to lay the matter to rest, when Robert Schomburgk's expedition traced the Corentyne river up to its source at the top of the Kutari creek. It was not until 1899, when the territorial dispute with Venezuela came to a head, that the Dutch first questioned this boundary suggesting that the frontier lay along the largest and longest headwater river of the Corentyne, the 'New River' as the British called it. The Dutch thus laid claim to a 1.5-million hectare triangle of territory east

Disputed New River Area

59

of the New River. The claim was ignored and in 1936 a joint expedition between Brazil, Britain and the Netherlands fixed a tri-boundary point at the Kutari head. The matter was, it seemed, resolved.

Not so. In 1966, the Dutch revived their claim in the context of grandiose plans to turn the Lower Corentyne into a development pole, with a new city and town at Apoera – on the other side of the river from Orealla – huge bauxite mines to be opened at Bakhuis and railroads to connect the two. Vast hydro-electric dams were planned to service this centre and the Dutch engineers, nervous of Guyana's approaching independence, considered control of the headwaters of the Corentyne essential for the security of their project, which would involve large sums of Dutch development aid as well as major Dutch companies. Despite talks in London, no agreement was reached and the issue was shelved, but shortly after independence border incidents arose and the Guyana Police Force expelled a hydrographic survey in 1967. The Dutch then sent in Surinamese troops who established a camp on the New River. The following year Guyana, exercising its newly independent muscles, sent in the Guyana Defence Force, who expelled the Surinamese forces and renamed the site Camp Jaguar. An internationally brokered settlement in 1970 led to a mutual agreement to demilitarize the still disputed triangle. Since then the GDF has made only occasional forays into the region to expel illegal Brazilian miners who have established mines and airstrips in the area.

Concern about Surinamese intentions in the area were revived in 1994, when it was revealed that the Surinamese government was considering issuing a massive nine million-hectare logging concession to an shadowy Indonesian logging company, MUSA. The concession included the northern part of the New River Triangle. The concession was never granted but the boundary dispute remains unresolved.[30]

[1] Myers 1993:45
[2] Hemming 1990.
[3] Rivière 1972
[4] Baldwin 1946
[5] Baldwin 1946
[6] Peberdy 1948
[7] Baldwin 1946
[8] Benjamin and Pierre 1995
[9] Peberdy 1948:31
[10] Rivière 1995:152
[11] Peberdy 1948
[12] Baldwin 1946:55
[13] Myers 1993:24-25
[14] Peberdy 1948
[15] Benjamin and Pierre 1995
[16] Timehri Group 1967
[17] Ridgwell 1972
[18] Cited in Forte 1994:29
[19] Catholic Standard, 12 November 1995
[20] Rivière 1995:174
[21] ERM 1995
[22] ERM 1995
[23] Colchester 1991
[24] Forte 1989
[25] Guyana Review, June 1995:12
[26] Guyana Public Sector Review, May 1993:148
[27] Forte and Benjamin 1993:1
[28] ERM 1995
[29] Guyana Review, November 1995
[30] Colchester 1995; Guyana Review, September 1995:12-14

CHAPTER 5
UNDERMINING THE INTERIOR

'Mining is causing concern to residents of the communities. Water is contaminated when dredges are in operation. Residents are unable to get fish for domestic purposes and for aquarium trading. The use of mercury by miners is dangerous to all residents who depend on the river for water for all purposes, including drinking. In their greed for gold, miners pay no attention to the damages they cause. Fallen trees and the creation of new sand banks – the results of their mining activities – block the rivers causing travel in boats to be impossible. Both rivers and forests support the life of our people. Man knows that when nature dies, he too will die.'
Salome Henry, Amerindian spokesperson[1]

When Columbus first sighted the coast of South America on his third voyage in 1498, he hailed it as the 'Earthly Paradise' of biblical legend and on coming ashore his sailors eagerly exchanged trinkets for the small gold plugs and amulets that the Amerindians wore. Within half a century an enduring myth was propagated that in the interior of the Guianas lay the lost city of Manoa, by a huge lake called Parima, ruled by a gilded king, El Dorado, 'the golden one', whose streets were paved with gold and whose citizens enjoyed boundless wealth.

In pursuit of these fantasies, which were later fuelled by the lucrative conquests of the Aztec and Inca Empires, *conquistadores* and other reckless explorers scoured the interior of the continent in search of the fabled city. Many of these expeditions were brutal in their exploitation of Indian labour and spread a swathe of desolation through the region, while rewarding the gold hunters with little more than fevers, hunger and death.[2]

Dreams of these fabulous riches lasted into the twentieth century, but the more pragmatic Dutch traders who established their forts and factories on the coast in the seventeenth century soon turned to exchanging their industrial goods for dyes, timbers and other forest products. All the same, the dreams never entirely faded, not least because the rivers of the region do harbour gold, most of it long washed out from the original rock and deposited in alluvial beds and other quaternary sediments. Moreover, the Cretaceous sandstones and conglomerates of the Roraima massif, which extend west into Venezuela and east and south through the Pakaraimas and Marudi Mountains, were later found to be rich in diamonds.

61

The Gold Rush

The rush to exploit the gold of the region was triggered by lucrative finds in western Guyana in the 1840s and eastern Venezuela in the 1860s. Panners, using techniques refined in the gold rushes of North America, had found rich auriferous deposits in the Sierra Imataca and Upper Cuyuni. These consisited of alluvial gold both in river sands and gravels and in near-surface reefs, which were dug out by hand, pockmarking the area with small pits. The boom refocused Venezuela's interest in the region and fomented its territorial claims to the whole of the Cuyuni basin and all the lands west of the Essequibo. Meanwhile, a major gold rush got underway in Guyana. A first concerted attempt to mine gold was made by a local syndicate on the Mazaruni in 1863 and 1864. By the 1880s, a boom took off and production soared from 40 oz in 1882 to 11,906 oz in 1887. Partly to fend off Venezuela's territorial claim and partly to bring order to the uncontrolled frontier mining camps which mushroomed through the region, the British Guiana administration opened the North West to mining claims in 1887 and three years later the North West District, with its boundary along the Schomburgk line, was formally declared.[3]

Mining, which offered wealth and an escape from the plantations to the poor, was viewed with alarm by the colonial planters, as they feared losing their captive labour force. But despite trying to hobble small-scale miners with red tape, the plantocracy was unable to resist the gold rush. By the turn of the century an estimated 6,000 black 'pork-knockers' (so-called because of the barrels of pork they used as a staple food) were at work in the interior and gold production reached 138,000 oz in 1893. Diamond production peaked somewhat later, reaching a record 214,000 carats in 1923.[4]

Although such high levels of production could not be maintained for long and soon declined once the easiest deposits were worked out, the mining way of life established in the late nineteenth century became an integral part of the Guyana hinterland. The miners depended on the tried and tested technology of the gold pan, which when carefully wielded by skilled hands remains one of the most efficient means of extracting gold from alluvial deposits. Today miners still use the alluvium and water to brush any small air bubbles off the gold flecks so that they sink to the centre of the pan, allowing the panner to swirl water around the gold and wash off the lighter soil and alluvial material.

The method is efficient but time-consuming, and other techniques that had been refined in the California gold rush of 1849 were soon introduced by foreign adventurers from these fields. First of these was the 'long tom', a long wooden box lined with sacking or felt blankets, which empties into a further box at the end, with a riffled bed. The heavier-than-stone gold particles become rubbed clean of air and separated from the parent alluvium as they are washed along the

Location of Mines

VENEZUELA

Morawhanna

Arakaka

Imataca Mtns

Matthews Ridge

Barama

Towakaima

WAKENAAM IS.
LEGUAN IS.

GEORGETOWN

Cuyuni

Puruni

Mazaruni

Essequibo

Bartica

Demerara

Kurupung

Kamarang

Upper
Mazaruni

Kaburi

Essequibo

Demerara

Omai

Linden

Berbice

Mahdia

Potaro

Konawaruk

Berbice

Corentyne

Monkey
Mountain

Kwakwani

Siparuni

SURINAME

BRAZIL

Kanuku Mtns

Rewa

Wenamu

Barima

capital

national
boundary

regional
boundary

rivers

mines

mountains

Rupununi

Marudi Mtns

New

0   km   100

63

blanketed sluice and are further trapped in the end box in which mercury can be poured to form an amalgam. Made doubly heavy by the mercury, the amalgam is easily separated from the other materials. By simply flaming the amalgam, normally with a blow torch, the mercury can be boiled off and the pure gold recovered. A refinement of the 'long tom' is the 'dollar', which is made of a stepped series of sluices, also with a box at the end. According to David Cleary, who has made a detailed study of these techniques, both technologies require a work crew of six to ten men: digging the alluvium, sieving it, carrying it to the top of the sluice or sluices, pouring through the water, and extracting the gold with mercury. Miners in Guyana also adopted another technology developed in California and the Yukon, the 'rocker', which was also referred to by the pork-knockers as the 'shakey shakey' and which was widely used in the 1930s for areas where the gold was coarse grained or found in nuggets.

As Cleary points out, the basic advantage of such technology is that 'it is practically free. All that is needed to build one is a certain amount of knowledge, some wood and a minimum of mechanical competence... This means that people with little or no capital can construct a machine...'[5] These facts help explain why Guyanese of African descent have been so much drawn to placer mining. Historically deprived of land and any employment other than on the sugar estates, and without capital, Africans of an adventurous bent have been willing to accept the hazards of life in the bush to try their hand at prospecting. 'Pork-knocker' society has developed its own sub-culture and customary norms for operating. While outwardly chaotic, happy-go-lucky and egalitarian, each mine involves individuals in well-defined roles depending on who owns the claims, who the machinery and who works the deposit. Owners, partners and workers interact according to these norms and each receives a well-defined percentage of the take from the operations. Some mine owners in remote locations in the interior, like Wellesley Baird at Baramita, have become wealthy, self-made men running virtually autonomous villages. By concubinage and marriage with Amerindian women they have fathered large families of mixed descent who dominate the communities' economic and political lives.[6]

The North West remained the main focus for mining in Guyana until the 1930s but restless gold-seekers spread throughout the interior from the earliest years of the century. This trend was encouraged by the discovery of diamonds in the Mazaruni in 1887 and later in the Upper Cotingo just over the border in Brazil in 1912.[7] Mining spread south, up the Puruni, Barima and Barama in the 1880s, up the Cuyuni in the 1890s, up the Demerara in the 1900s and into the Middle Mazaruni by 1920. In the 1930s, the pressure on the Middle Mazaruni became so intense that the area, previously reserved to Amerindians, was opened as a mining district and the Akawaio were exposed to thousands of pork-knockers who streamed into their territory to search for the gold and diamonds in the river banks.

Amerindian Impact

Given mining's increasingly important role in the economy, the administration became keen to promote it in ways that reduced conflicts between those making claims and to ensure that revenues accrued to the exchequer. They gave little heed to the needs or rights of the original owners of the land, the Amerindians. As Anna Benjamin and Laureen Pierre of the Amerindian Research Unit (ARU) have remarked:

> Mining traditionally has been given precedence over all other eco-
> nomic activities in the interior. From the beginning, mining districts
> were declared... wherever a gold strike occurred, and usually with scant
> reference to any other consideration. The presence of indigenous com-
> munities in a given locale, therefore was no bar to the declaration of a
> mining district, once it was known to be auriferous or diamantiferous.[8]

Although colonial laws, designed to protect Amerindians, prevented mining districts from being set up within Amerindian reserves, the legislation was easily circumvented. Amerindian areas could be dereserved at the stroke of a pen and then gazetted as a mining district. The Mazaruni is a case in point. The lower and middle river were opened to mining in the 1930s by the colonial administration. In 1959, immediately after a major diamond strike was reported, one-third of the Upper Mazaruni Amerindian District around Imbaimadai was excised and gazetted as a mining district by the PPP. In 1977, the PNC passed regulations opening the rivers of the Upper Mazaruni to diamond mining, using pumps and divers. The following year the whole of the Upper Mazaruni was declared a Mining Area.[9] It was only in 1991 that the Amerindians were granted titles to a small part of the original Upper Mazaruni reserve, but mining was still permitted along the rivers and in the gaps between the community titles. Today multinational companies have secured exploration rights to search the whole area, including titled lands. When it comes to mining the Amerindians find they have no protection.

Not surprisingly, these mining invasions and *laissez-faire* policies have had a devastating impact on the Amerindians. Most to suffer have been the Caribs of the North West District who have borne the brunt of the mining industry for over a century. During the major rush into the area in the early 1900s, the government actively intervened to open it up. Here gold was found not only in alluvial deposits, but also in mineralized quartz reefs near to the surface. Small-scale miners could work such deposits with picks, crowbars and home-made ore-crushers, called 'denkies'. A regular steamship service was operated from Georgetown to Morawhanna, from where smaller boats plied the Barima up to Arakaka and the Barama up to Saint Bedes. Arakaka, in the very centre of the Caribs' ancestral lands, expanded into a thriving township around a medium-sized stamp mill set up by a foreign company, Barima Gold Mines. To encourage access to the Barama headwaters above the numerous rapids and falls, the colonial administration also drove a road through to Towakaima. In the 1930s, successful Guyanese and foreign miners developed mechanized mines at Baramita with fanciful names like 'Golden City', 'Millionaire' and 'Old World Mine'.[10]

When, after the Second World War, the administration carried out a survey of the Amerindians they discovered a shocking situation in the interior. Health conditions were so abysmal in the Matthews Ridge and Baramita area that one administrator noted the Caribs 'do not live, they merely exist'. 'The Upper Barama River Caribs' he continued 'are the most impoverished and traumatic aboriginal group that I have encountered throughout the length and breadth of British Guiana'. The colonial administration, he observed, far from curbing the invasion, had actively promoted it by constructing a base for flying boats to supply the mining zone, while making no provisions to further the welfare or protect the interests of the Amerindians. The Caribs' once elaborate material culture had vanished and they were left in a 'morbid condition' working as porters for the miners, while the women were used as concubines.[11]

The report recommended that a reserve be established to protect the Caribs against further intrusions. However, the advice was ignored, and in 1953 the administration funded the cutting of a long grass strip at Baramita, suitable for landing Dakotas. Prostitution and alcoholism became rife. While the grass strip was being completed, the float planes flew in 'machinery, fuel and girls, to keep the men contented.' Recalls Wellesley Baird, who by his own admission fathered eighteen 'known' children by various women, 'brawling sprees took place on the airstrip on Saturday nights as there were not enough girls to go round.'[12]

When the Amerindian Lands Commission visited the area fifteen years later, the situation had scarcely improved, although a small school had been established. The Amerindians still had no land base and, though mining was in decline, the Amerindians were equally degraded. Having neglected their subsistence farming for wage labour in the mines, many became destitute when the mines began to close.[13] The Commission reiterated the recommendation for a reserve, but when this was finally established in 1977 it denied the Caribs title to their lands. Today, mining, which revived in the 1980s, continues to be encouraged in the area, while health provisions remain abysmal and the government has ceased supplying teachers to the school.[14]

As in many other parts of Amazonia, the gold rush has brought a host of problems to the Amerindian communities. Most obviously, the miners have introduced new diseases to which the Amerindians have little resistance, and very high mortalities result. Anopheline mosquitoes thrive in the braided stream beds and pools left in the wake of mining, while the miners themselves rest-lessly moving about the country serve as vectors to the malaria they carry. A blood sampling study in 1992 revealed that nearly all the 40,000 people associ-ated with small-scale mining in the interior tested positive for malaria.[15] Tuber-culosis, so prevalent in mining areas where lack of hygiene, poor nutrition and ill-health provide perfect conditions for its propagation, has also become a major problem among the Amerindians of the Pakaraimas. Venereal diseases have also become a problem in many areas. Gonorrhoea is rife and is reducing fertility in Amerindian women. Recently even AIDS cases have begun to be reported.[16]

Travelling about the interior, one encounters two main responses from the Amerindians to the invasion of their areas by miners. Some groups, and this applies even to some Carib communities with the longest experience of mining, have sought to move away from the destructive cultural influences of the mines, establishing new settlements up small creeks or in interfluve areas where they can redevelop autonomous communities and subsistence economies. It is a hard choice, however, for it may mean moving out of a titled area, leaving behind the minimal services provided by the government – schools and health care – while still being exposed to the infectious diseases that enter the popu-lation through occasional trading.

More commonly, Amerindian communities have themselves been caught up in the mining fever. Amerindian labour has long been integral to the mining economy as mine-workers, porters and providers of river transport. Some Am-erindians have adopted the pork-knocker way of life and opened their own mines, and indeed some Amerindians have become quite wealthy from mining. Yet the costs to the community and culture have been severe. In the Middle Mazaruni, which was opened to mining in the 1930s, the Akawaio have been denied rights to land or any protections. As a result they are in crisis. When they demand land, the porkknockers object and tell them to move to areas where Amerindians already have title. Amerindians who have spoken out against the mining on their lands have been threatened with cutlasses after heavy drinking. In early 1994 a man was killed in Orranapai in a land dispute. As Celian Roland, elected Captain of Kurupung told the author in 1994:

67

Now they are saying we must move to the Upper Mazaruni. That makes their heart ache. They'll get no big fish up there. They are all getting this confusion but I say that we should not listen to all confusion but settle and develop our own communities... They are really aching these Indians, really aching themselves. They say they'll take up their bamboos (arrows). I think war will break out with the negroes because they cut our farms.

In a detailed and disturbing record of the impact of mining on the Akawaio and Arekuna of the Upper Mazaruni, anthropologist Audrey Butt Colson shows how the very presence of mining has seriously undermined traditional Amerindian life. Mining, she writes, has provoked a collapse of the subsistence economy. Not only has game been reduced by over-hunting to provide meat for the miners, but the involvement of the menfolk in mining leads to a steady decline in food production. New garden plots are not cut, production declines and expensive store-bought food from the coast comes to replace local food which becomes scarce and expensive. The result is the classic development paradox, where rising incomes lead to falling standards of living. Observes Butt Colson: 'Despite an apparent prosperity from the sale of diamonds, there was a fall in real income though an ever-rising cost of living, affecting in particular those unable to mine through age, sex and opportunity.' As early as 1977 malnutrition was identified as a major health problem at Kamarang, while exploitative labour relations also began to develop with poor Amerindians yoked into debt bondage to coastal miners who ran the dredges and stores. The overall results are increasing dependence on mining and permanent wealth differentiation.

Since the 1970s, with the opening of the whole area to river dredges, the government station of Kamarang has been transformed from a calm and well-ordered administrative centre, with a religious mission and active Amerindian community, into a tawdry tinsel town of grog shops, brothels and discos along one side of the airstrip. 'Red Light City', as it is known, has had a sad effect on Amerindian social life, generating what Butt Colson refers to as the typical 'pork-knocker syndrome of drink, gambling, sex, conspicuous consumption and, from time to time, violence.'[17]

Deprived of effective legal protection, village captains have been unable to expel miners from their areas and are instead obliged to negotiate the best deals they can with the miners. Corruption of community leaders is undermining village politics and fragmenting villages. Traditions of cooperation and communal living are being replaced by self-interest and mistrust.

Many young Indians have found jobs in the mines, and they are often assigned the dangerous task of diving to direct pumps and dredges along the river beds. These mine workers say that there have been numerous fatal accidents which have not been reported in the national press. They also complain that the companies do not pay compensation to injured workers or the families of workers killed in accidents.[18]

Mining has had a disproportionate impact on women and children. With the men often absent, sometimes for long periods, in the mining camps, women have had to shoulder a heavy burden of domestic duties: farming, fishing and gathering to feed and maintain their families. But with male labour absent, new gardens cannot be cleared, obliging women to seek alternative sources of income.[19] Inevitably, these long absences and separations have increased family tensions. Prostitution and promiscuity have flourished:

> Coastland miners are mostly young men, unattached, frequenting Kamarang at weekends to sell their diamonds, collect fuel and buy food. They are a source of attraction for Akawaio women, who trek to 'Red Light City' in order to 'sport with the pork-knockers'. Apart from some seductions and rapes, most deliberately embark on a prostitute's career to obtain money, as no other employment is available, and to enjoy life.[20]

The effects of these changes in lifestyle on Amerindian cultures have been marked. Old values of sharing and cooperation have been replaced by cash values and monetary exchange. Traditional beliefs and knowledge of the environment have been eroded and sophisticated arts and crafts fallen into disuse, thereby increasing dependency on mining as a mainstay of the economy. Moreover, as mining technology has become increasingly sophisticated and expensive, control of the local economies has become concentrated in fewer and fewer hands. It is often outsiders and Georgetown-based syndicates who have the capital and connections required for successful mining ventures.

New Technology

The hand-powered technologies of the early gold rushes were inherently limited and most mining was confined to the immediate banks of rivers and streams where gold- and diamond-bearing alluvium and, most important, water were readily available. As the easy deposits became worked out, the industry declined. Although mechanization of gold-mining developed in South America in the 1930s, it was capital-intensive. With world gold prices held artificially low after the war, mechanization was slow to develop and mining actually declined.[21]

However, small-scale mining boomed again in the 1970s as gold prices rose and with the introduction of mass-produced engines and new mechanized mining techniques. Dredges with suction hoses and mechanized sluices have encouraged miners to work the beds of the rivers for both gold and diamonds. The older dredges require divers who, wearing primitive diving suits, descend to the river bed to direct the nozzles into the sediments. Some more recent machines have nozzles that can be guided from the surface.

New lightweight portable engines have greatly extended the range of mining operations, with pumps providing water to mine old river terraces and water courses now far from the streams and rivers which deposited them. These so-called 'land dredges', sometimes supplied with water along hundreds of yards of plastic piping depend on powerful hoses which flush out alluvial beds. The liquified spoil is then sucked up by pumps for processing. 'Land dredging' is a relatively new trend in Guyanese mining and, according to the World Bank, is likely to favour the emergence of larger, more highly capitalized companies which can afford the costly overheads of prospecting.[22] By 1995, four relatively large Guyanese mining companies had emerged; Mazda Mining Ltd, which has a major mine on the Konawaruk,[23] Perreira Co, Correia's Holdings Ltd and Alfro Alphonso. According to the Commissioner of Geology and Mines, Brian Sucre, the top ten local companies extract about sixty per cent of the country's declared gold production.[24]

Georgetown-based companies have also developed so-called 'missile-dredges', huge remote-controlled vacuum cleaners, shaped like torpedoes, mounted on river dredges, which pump water into alluvial deposits and suck them up to process the minerals. The missile-dredges can dig deep into the river banks, sometimes as far as seventy metres, liquefying mud and gravel as they go. Missile-dredge operators appear oblivious to the damage they are causing. Fox and Danns record one case of a dredge even being used to invade an Amerindian cemetery on the river bank, 'ancestral remains from as recent as six years ago were sucked out of their graves and propelled into the Demerara river through hoses.'[25]

An estimated 40,000 to 60,000 Guyanese are now involved in small-scale mining.[26] The 14,500 small mining claims and about 800 Medium Mining Licences so far issued by the Guyana Geology and Mines Commission cover over 650 kilometres of rivers as well as one million hectares of land and are worked by approximately 1,500 licensed land and river dredges and untold illegal ones.[27] The proliferation of these machines has massively increased the amount of tailings left in the wake of mining. Wide areas are cleared of trees and top soil with chains-saws and hoses to allow access to the sub-soil deposits. Mercury use has increased exponentially as the gold-mining has expanded.

Environment Under Attack

Flying over the mining areas, the environmental impact of mining is obvious. What were once clear rivers flowing between forested banks have become wide washes of mud and debris, criss-crossed by meandering red-brown streams of water and slurry searching for a way through the tailings, with stagnant pools and a moonscape of spoil heaps and sandbanks along the banks. Navigation has been seriously impeded in some rivers and the turbid waters have caused fish stocks to crash, further affecting the Amerindian diet. The Mazaruni Christian Council complains that the Upper Mazaruni 'may soon be a mud choked gutter almost cleared of fauna and flora and the rainforest at its most magnificent.'[28] The situation on the Middle Mazaruni is worse. Says Celian Roland, elected captain of Kurupung:

> There are porkknockers all along the river with their dredges. You see the condition of the river, it is all choked with big banks of sand. The river is all choked up. You have to be a river captain to pick your way through the shallows in a boat.

Mining sites are almost never reclaimed and there is considerable concern that the abandoned pits may be producing 'acid-mine drainage' which finds its way into waters used for fishing and human consumption.[29]

Since the late 1980s there has been growing concern in Guyana about the environmental impact of mining, but the government has preferred inaction to public debate. A study carried out for the Commonwealth Secretariat in 1990 warned of the very serious consequences of mining. The report highlighted in particular that 'missile mining results in the destruction of the river banks, changes in river morphology and hydrology, greatly increases sedimentation in rivers and has profound effects on fish habitats' and recommended that the use of these dredges be prohibited. The government, however, chose not to circulate the report and missile dredges proliferated.[30]

Studies of gold-mining areas in Brazil and Venezuela have revealed that severe mercury pollution has had serious impacts on animal and human health.[31] Mercury poisoning from mining has been found to be debilitating and sometimes fatal, causing trembling, headaches, blurred vision and eventually unconsciousness and death. Most at risk are the miners themselves who rarely use protective clothing and so inhale the mercury as it is flamed off the amalgam. Mercury also enters the river system directly through spillage and in rainfall when the mercury vapour condenses and falls back to earth. In acidic waters, mercury is rapidly methylated and enters the food chain, accumulating most heavily in the tissues of predator species like larger fish. If these animals are eaten the mercury then concentrates in humans.[32] In French Guiana dangerously high levels of mercury have been found in humans living downriver of mining areas.[33] In Venezuela concentrations of mercury in fish in the Guri dam, down river of numerous mining ventures, are so high that a number of the main marketed species have been banned from human consumption.

71

These findings in neighbouring countries have not been followed up by government studies in Guyana. However, in 1994, after army Chief-of-Staff Brigadier Joe Singh expressed concern that the Konawaruk River was 'dying' as a result of uncontrolled mining, the environmental pressure group, GEMCO, carried out an independent assessment of the river and found that siltation and mercury pollution was indeed prevalent. The group urged that more detailed studies be carried out to assess the nature and extent of the contamination.[34]

The problem is that not only does the Guyana Geology and Mines Commission (GGMC) lack the biologists, toxicologists and laboratories needed to carry out a proper study of these environmental problems, but that there are no regulations to control the environmental impacts of mining anyway. Indeed, so feeble is the outreach of the Commission that even the regulations regarding filing claims, staking out concessions, declaring finds and paying royalties are regularly evaded. In 1993, the World Bank estimated that as much as three-quarters of gold production is undeclared. According to the Bank: 'Most producers under-report their production to avoid payment of royalties and taxes, and because of practical difficulties attached to selling gold legally in Georgetown.'[35] Quite simply, the GGMC lacks the staff and resources required to monitor adequately what is happening in the interior and consequently most mining is unregulated and unsupervised. To make matters worse, in the early 1990s the technical capabilities of the GGMC deteriorated. Noted the World Bank:

> There is no longer in fact any geological survey, the mines inspection and arbitration mandate is essentially not exercised, and the GGMC is unable to maintain an accurate file of locations of mining properties. Settlements of mining disputes through the GGMC are slow, costly and have been accompanied by accusations of favoritism... Administration of the mining sector suffers from a serious lack of transparency. Many documents and procedures are not available to the public.[36]

The Commissioner of Geology and Mines, Brian Sucre, admits the scale of the problem. 'Twenty to fifteen years ago there were 1,000 claims, today we have 12,000 and the Commission has not yet caught up with the industry.'[37]

The headwater mining camps, in particular, are almost completely beyond government control. According to the Amerindians, mines officers are rarely able to visit their settlements and as a result no regulations are enforced. As the Akawaio community of Jawalla pointed out to the 'Amirang' or Amerindian conference (see p.153) in 1994:

> We in the Upper Mazaruni solely live by way of fishing and hunting. We have experienced that there is no longer fishes in any great amount

as before, as a result of miners destroying the river banks and creeks on which we tremendously depend and live on. We set fish traps to catch fish but in vain... There is a serious water pollution existing in the Upper Mazaruni. The miners top-side destroy the rivers, causing the residents to suffer. The water we use for domestic purposes is no good right now. We feel the pollution is against health regulations.[38]

With the boom in gold exploration in Roraima in the 1970s and 1980s, Brazilian placer miners or *garimpeiros* also began moving across the frontier into southern Guyana. At first, the flow of these miners was a mere trickle, the prospectors trekking south into the Kanuku and Marudi Mountains. In early 1990, however, the flow turned into a flood with thousands of miners reportedly crossing into the land of the Patamona Indians at the headwaters of the Potaro river. Other groups of *garimpeiros* have moved into the south of the country along the Ireng, near Gunn's Strip and into the New River Triangle. These mining camps have a 'wild west' atmosphere. Drunkenness, prostitution and violence are common, and killings frequent. Visitors report that practically all the gold extracted leaves the country by way of Brazil, meaning that Guyana gets nothing in exchange for the plunder of resources.

Efforts by the Guyana Defence Force to control these invasions have been constrained by lack of money. Costly operations to expel miners from the Wai Wai areas and New River triangle, while praiseworthy in their intentions, have left the GDF grounded for months afterwards. Brazilian miners, however, backed by powerful syndicates in Boa Vista, have been able to rebuild and reprovision their mining camps within a few short weeks and are soon operating again with impunity. In these remote areas, the Amerindians have learned that they have little choice but to accommodate the miners as best they can, whether they wish them there or not.

Yet where communications are better, the Amerindians have increasingly spoken out against these abuses, and they raised mining as a major issue at the 1994 'Amirang'. As Wilfred Williams, of Campbelltown told the conference:

Mining which is the cause of the encroachment [on our lands] should be seriously looked into. The use of heavy duty machinery, eg missiles and land dredges, are causing environmental damage from as far as Eagle Mountain to as far as the mouth of Mahdia Creek. Though we also live by mining, we are not in favour of these machines because of the environmental damage that they cause. The mining is also encouraging the peddling of drugs, for example, cocaine and ganja, which I believe are causing our young people to be led astray and this is

73

detrimental to our society. I hope the government will also address this problem urgently.[39]

Confronted by a voracious mining industry that can neither restrain itself nor be restrained by government, many Amerindians have concluded that their only hope lies in themselves asserting rights to the sub-surface resources, so that they can regulate mining for their own benefit. The Patamona community of Kopinang, for example, stresses:

We, the Amerindians, are the original people of this country and as such we feel that we should have full rights to the ownership of our lands. Full rights where minerals (gold and diamonds) are concerned... Also to own the water rights and to claim full rights for our children.[40]

Experience in other parts of the Amazon shows that where the Amerindians are able to control what happens on their lands, they can develop means of regulating mining to their benefit.[41]

In Guyana, however, the complaints of Amerindian communities seem to have fallen on deaf ears, and the extent to which the government is prepared to challenge the might of those made rich through mining is in doubt. Recently, the US Government's Drug Enforcement Agency reported a massive increase in illegal gold imports from Guyana to the US in early 1995, which led to a major investigation of fraud by the US Department of Commerce. An estimated US$21.7 million had been illegally funnelled out of the country.[42] According to the *Guyana Review*, 'the mixture of rumour and limited fact surrounding this case suggests that several well-known and seemingly reputable businessmen have been involved in the illegal export to the United States of thousands of pounds of gold.' The journal hints at 'alleged links between the gold scam and a drug ring'.[43]

Big Mines, Big Disasters

Given the anarchy and destructiveness of the small-scale mining sector, many aid agency officials argue that the best means of getting control of the mining industry is to promote large-scale mining by big companies. Economies of scale, they believe, allow mining to be subjected to more onerous regulations and more easily monitored and supervised.

The argument is convenient in that it coincides with the same agencies' macro-economic prescriptions for structural adjustment, trade liberalization, the promotion of 'non-traditional exports', including gold and diamonds, and 'foreign direct investment'. Whereas small-scale mining is open to all – a small 'land dredge' operation costs about US$2,000 to set up and even a large river dredge costs between US$5,000 and US$10,000 – large-scale mines require investors prepared to hazard millions of dollars on costly prospecting, before mining can even begin. Few local companies in Guyana can compete in such a field. Indeed, the history of large-scale mining in Guyana amply demonstrates that this is really a field for foreigners.

Just as in neighbouring Suriname, bauxite mining became an important addition to Guyana's economy in the 1920s and as in Suriname developments implied the involvement of overseas investors as bauxite extraction requires major capital investment, heavy mining machinery and large-scale transport facilities. Globally, access to world markets is controlled by half a dozen huge corporations from North America and Europe.

Notwithstanding these similarities, the evolution and influence of bauxite mining in Guyana has not been as massive as in Suriname where it became the dominant force in the political economy.[44] In contrast with Suriname, the colonial authorities in British Guiana negotiated far better terms for the colony, thus avoiding domination by a single company and maintaining a greater degree of control of the industry.[45] Furthermore, because the majority of the bauxite mined in Guyana is high-quality calcined, non-metallurgical bauxite used for refractory, abrasive and chemical markets, it was of less strategic significance than Suriname's metallic bauxite which was considered crucial to the US war efforts in Europe and Korea.

Nevertheless, bauxite mining has been and remains an important source of employment and foreign exchange in Guyana. By independence, Guyana was supplying 75 per cent of the world market in non-metallurgical bauxite from two major bauxite mines, the first run by Demerara Bauxite, a subsidiary of Alcan Aluminium, in Linden, the second by Reynolds Metals in Kwakwani. Both sites developed substantial townships around the works. Under Burnham's policies of nationalizing key sectors of the economy, both companies were bought out by the Cooperative Republic in 1971 and 1974 respectively and were then amalgamated as a parastatal enterprise, GUYMINE.

Like other Guyanese parastatals under domestic ownership and control, GUYMINE was plagued with problems of mismanagement, poor supervision, under-investment and corruption. Production declined precipitously from 3.6 million tons in 1974 to only 895,000 tons by 1992.

The near collapse of the domestic bauxite industry under state ownership made it a prime target for reform under the World Bank and IMF's Economic Recovery Programme (ERP). While the government resisted full privatization, efforts were made to reinvigorate the industry by dividing GUYMINE into two parastatals, LINMINE and BERMINE, but this did little to improve management. Pressure from the international financial institutions to sell off the mines to private investors has so far been resisted by both the Hoyte and Jagan administrations. However, the government has allowed a kind of creeping privatization through new foreign investment in the sector. In 1991, the PNC government entered into a joint venture with Reynolds to open a new mine at Aroaima, about 115 kilometres south of Linden. The company was lured in with attractive fiscal incentives in line with ERP prescriptions. The mining agreement allows the company to operate 'free of all Guyana taxes, fees, charges, rents or royalties of any nature' for twenty years, including import taxes, consumption taxes, export duties, lease charges and permit fees. Foreign employees' incomes are also tax-free.[46]

Following this trend, from 1992 onwards the PPP government began contracting out the management of the bauxite parastatals to foreign companies, and a new deal signed in 1995 with Reynolds was meant to revive the industry. Full privatization may not be long in coming, although the world-wide glut in bauxite continues to depress the market.[47] Even the old alumina-processing plant at Linden may soon be sold off; Norsk Hydro of Norway has been taking a keen interest.[48]

Although the bauxite mines have generated important foreign exchange for Guyana and created considerable local employment, they have not been without their social and environmental costs. The World Bank has expressed disquiet over the serious impact of dust pollution on human health:

> The air quality at LINMINE is of particular concern as the prevailing wind blows the plume from the stacks directly over Linden. In Linden there is a high instance of lung diseases and asthma that is almost certainly directly related to the effluent from the stacks.[49]

The same report also stated that bauxite mines leave behind large areas of waste which are very acidic. Vegetation has been slow to reclaim these areas, while acid runoff and seepage from the spoil heaps are polluting waterways.

New technologies may also be introducing new problems. Whereas the old bauxite mines use diggers and trucks to remove overburden, the Aroaima mine adopted a new 'wet mining' technique whereby water is used to flush off overburden which is then diverted into huge ponds. After allowing sediment to settle out in these ponds, the waters are then discharged into waterways. In 1993 the World Bank expressed concern about the likely siltation of rivers, but no steps were taken in response to the warning. The following year, two serious spills from these ponds occurred, due to breaches in the dam walls, pouring filthy waste waters directly into the Berbice river. Residents down river were advised not to drink the water and alternative supplies were trucked in.[50]

The return of foreign interest in the mining sector dates from the mid-1980s when the PNC government, under pressure from the international financial institutions, began to relax conditions for foreign capital. Until that date the regulations had required any foreign company to enter into a joint agreement granting the government a majority equity share in the exploitation of any large concessions. As a result, no large ventures were initiated.[51]

Forbes Burnham, however, was keen to develop the resource-rich areas west of the Essequibo as a way of securing them from Venezuelan territorial ambitions. The collapse of his dream to construct a huge hydro-electric dam on the Upper Mazaruni, which would have flooded 4,500 Akawaio and Arekuna off their lands, led him to promote large-scale mining instead. The mid-1980s thus saw a change in policy, allowing foreign mining companies a majority stake in their operations, and a number of ventures got under way. Canada's Golden Star Resources began prospecting for gold in 1984,[52] while other multinational corporations from Australia, France, Brazil, North Korea and Yugoslavia all became active in the North West District, most on the traditional lands of the Caribs. Golden Star began to prospect for gold and diamonds at Arakaka and Baramita; Brazil's Paranapanema was reported to be mining on the Tassawini creek.[53]

While small-scale and medium-scale mining remains closed to foreign interests, large-scale mines are now open to foreign companies which can negotiate one-off 'mining agreements' with the government through the Office of the President and the Guyana Geology and Mines Commission (GGMC). These agreements are facilitated by the Guyana Natural Resources Agency, which was established with World Bank assistance in 1986 to promote private-sector investment in logging and mining. Each deal so struck defines the fiscal incentives to be offered: which taxes may be waived, for how long, the percentage on profits payable as royalties and so on.

Questions have been raised as to the wisdom of this arrangement. Instead of having a standard regime for all foreign investors in the sector, the process of negotiating separate 'mining agreements' with each company encourages a lack of transparency, favouritism, cronyism and corruption, which as the World Bank has observed, are already problems in the GGMC. Famously invisible too are the Environmental Impact Assessments required of all foreign companies, which are nowhere available to inspection by the Guyanese public.

Notwithstanding these difficulties, and notwithstanding the fickle nature of the gold market, the World Bank and many other financial advisers have heavily promoted expansion of the mining sector as a key to developing Guyana's exports. A stream of consultants have poured through Georgetown to join the chorus of siren voices urging Guyana to go for gold.

According to the Colorado School of Mines, for example, which sent an expert to Georgetown for five days in 1994 to carry out a study for the Carter

Center, 'Guyana has the potential to become one of the most attractive mining countries in five years.' To achieve this, the government should 'deregulate the mining sector' over the next 18 months, 'restructure the current legal and fiscal framework for mining, highlighting the role of foreign capital', and 'launch a world-wide campaign to draw attention to the new mining opportunities for potential investors...'. The reason for haste, says the report, is that 'Guyana is one of forty mineral-producing countries actively competing for investment dollars and has little time to delay the launching of its mineral development policy':

> The global mining investment boom is on. This will accelerate over the next three to five years and then taper off. Guyana has no time to lose if it is to take advantage of this truly global and cross-border phenomenon. To do this, the Government of Guyana must think bold and act boldly... Guyana with 750,000 people and its attractive geology can develop five to seven gold mining projects, transforming the country's economy.[54]

By this time, the first of these 'five to seven' major gold-mining ventures was already underway. After half a decade of prospecting, Golden Star Resources Ltd had negotiated a highly advantageous mining agreement to exploit a major gold find at Omai on the Middle Essequibo. A consortium, Omai Gold Mines Limited (OGML), was formed to exploit the prospect, comprising Golden Star Resources (30 per cent) Canada's Cambior Inc (65 per cent) and the Guyanese government (5 per cent) with US$163 million of political risk insurance from the World Bank's Multilateral Investment Guarantee Agency and Canada's Export Development Corporation. The operation was to be a centrepiece of the World Bank/IMF-promoted Economic Recovery Programme.

The Omai Mine

The huge, open-pit mine, which came on line in January 1993, immediately became one of South America's largest gold mines. With reserves of 2.6 million ounces to be extracted from an intrusive deposit of quartz-diorite in the greenstone parent rock, the company hoped annually to mine over 260,000 oz. of gold over eleven years. Using new technologies imported tax-free from North America, the company has installed a large crusher mill to crunch up the rock. The gold is extracted from this rock with cyanide. After the gold is chemically removed, the cyanide-laced tailings are then diluted with water and ponded in huge clay-lined dams where the ultraviolet in sunlight and oxygen in the air are supposed to gradually eliminate the cyanide through oxidation until the waters can be safely released into the environment. The company claimed that the technology was 'tried and tested', but in fact it had never before been used under tropical rainforest conditions.

78

The original deal to allow the mine to go ahead had been struck by the Hoyte administration and questions had been raised about whether Guyana was really getting a fair share of the profits. However, at the official opening of the mine in 1993, President Cheddi Jagan was full of praise for the venture; the company was 'turning a mud land into a future gold land', he told the gathered journalists.[55] Little did he know that only thirty months later he would personally announce that the mine had unleashed 'the country's worst environmental disaster', as a result of a massive tailings dam burst.

Perhaps he would not have been so enthusiastic if he had appreciated more clearly that Guyana's weak environmental standards were exactly what made investment in his country so attractive. As Golden Star Chairman David Fagin admitted a year later, his company 'had looked specifically at the Guyana Shield because of increased pressure by environmentalists and the government in the USA.'[56]

For its first two years of operation, OGML proudly touted the fact that its mine 'operated as a zero discharge gold producer',[57] something required by law of many mines in the US, but the company had all along expected that after three years of operation its tailings pond would fill to capacity and limited discharges of processed waste waters would be necessary. During the first two years of operation gold production from the mine had been very satisfactory and in late 1994 the company decided to expand production from the mill from the originally proposed 12,000 tonnes per day to 18,000 tonnes.[58]

This was despite the fact that, by then, it was already becoming all too clear to OGML that it had seriously underestimated the rate at which its tailings dams would fill up. At a mining conference in Caracas in October that year, the company's chief metallurgist puffed the company's commitment to environmental probity but noted that its tailings dam would achieve full capacity six months earlier than originally anticipated, reaching its maximum level by September 1995. Accordingly, in December 1994 OGML began negotiations with the government to secure permission to vent semi-processed leachate into the Essequibo.

The government hesitated and requested an additional environmental impact study which was hurriedly prepared and submitted in February 1995. The study revealed that the tailings pond was filling even faster than anticipated the year before: 'by July 1995 the elevation of water in the tailings pond' will be 'as high as can be tolerated'. By that date, it stated, there would be almost four million cubic metres of process water in the pond.[59] In March the company formally requested permission to commence effluent discharges into the Essequibo according to technology that it claimed was 'well-established... [and] has been implemented successfully around the world'.[60]

Non-governmental organizations in Guyana and overseas protested. They stressed that little was known of the impacts of cyanide discharges on tropical fish, though some temperate fish species like brown trout were known to be highly vulnerable to even low level concentrations of the poison. They also pointed out that OGML had skimped on measures to mitigate the environmental impact in the design of the processing facilities. Mines using cyanide leaching techniques in the US, for example, are required to construct underdrain collection grids and effluent recycling systems to ensure that no contaminated waters at all leak into ground waters or are discharged into the environment. In a report for the Amerindian Peoples Association (APA), in March 1995, British mining expert Roger Moody warned that: 'The writing is clearly on the tailings dam wall: OGML has grossly (and perhaps deliberately) over-estimated the potential of Omai as a fat earner for Guyana, while playing down the technical problems which have arisen, and the long term environmental consequences.' Based on a long observation of mines all around the world, Moody emphasized that such tailings dams 'can, of course, fail'.[61]

Under pressure, the government sent a mission to investigate the planned discharges. After carrying out a detailed study, the team concluded that the concentrations of cyanide in the effluent that OGML was planning to release would be 'unacceptably higher' than promised in the original environmental impact statement (EIS) and 'much higher' than the maximum levels allowed in many other countries. The discharges 'are considered to have potentially serious environmental and possibly health implications', observed the report. Technologies which had been promised in the EIS were not being used due to 'cost considerations'. Following the investigation, the government refused permission to OGML to discharge effluents for another six months.[62]

Countdown to Disaster
Events seemed to be slipping out of the company's control. On 15 May 1995, OGML had its first major spillage, when as a result of a power failure an automated sluice was left open and a discharge of cyanide-laced effluent gushed into the Omai river, killing several hundred fish. The 'incident' was not reported to the government by OGML for six days and it was questioned why the sluice was open anyway.[63] Guyanese environmental groups were outraged at the delay in reporting the spillage, which prevented the government's six-member inspection team from evaluating the true nature of the damage. In a press release the environment group GEMCO stated:

We believe that this is evidence of irresponsible behaviour, given the potentially hazardous nature of the entire operation, and can give rise

80

to the charge of disregard for the environment and contempt for the nation... This incident and the manner in which it was handled have vindicated opponents of cyanide use in gold recovery.[64]

President Cheddi Jagan was reported to have responded by saying that the government intended to ensure the protection of the environment even at the cost of slower economic growth.[65] But he was not running the mine; production continued regardless and in July was even further expanded to 20,000 tonnes per day.[66] The same month the company announced that it would commence construction of a second tailings dam to contain the excess effluents. By passing the waste water from one pond to another and then processing it in a treatment plant, the company hoped to reduce the levels of cyanide in its discharges to the two parts per million initially agreed to in its 1991 EIS. In response to environmentalists' concerns about the safety of the existing tailings pond and cyanide-using process, OGML General Manager, Rejean Gourde, reassured journalists, that the first tailings pond was 'impervious' to leaks.[67] Sheer hubris.

Only one month later disaster struck. At five minutes to midnight on 19 August:

> The tailings pond – a huge pit into which are piped cyanide liquids, other chemicals and mill wastes – developed cracks on two sides, two hundred metres across and six metres deep. Over the next three days, much of the contents of the dam, cascaded into the adjacent Omai river, then rushed in a massive plume down the Essequibo, the country's largest waterway. Several hundred fish died instantly.[68]

Over the next few days engineers struggled to contain the spillage and eventually managed to build a rough coffer dam with bulldozers to divert the remaining effluent into the main pit of the mine itself. Only during the fifth day was seepage into the surrounding environment finally halted. By that time three-quarters of the contents of the dam had spilled into the rivers. In all some three million cubic metres of cyanide-laced toxic waste had poured into the Essequibo, causing an international scandal and obliging President Jagan to declare the area 'an environmental disaster zone'.

In response to public outrage, the government formally closed the mine and initiated a Commission of Enquiry to look into the cause of the problem. The immediate concern, however, was with the direct impact of the cyanide-laced waters. The Omai river itself was killed off, but the sheer volume of water flowing into the Essequibo during the wet season might, it was hoped, rapidly dilute the poison. However, Amerindians, traders and miners living along the river

81

bank reported not only dead fish but also wild hogs floating belly-up and complaints about skin rashes and blistering from using river water endured for two months after the accident.[69] The government issued warnings to all residents downriver of the mine to cease using the river for washing, drinking and fishing. As well as several thousand people living in scattered communities along the banks of the Essequibo, 8,000 inhabitants of the town of Bartica were at risk.

The mining company offered to truck fresh water to all those affected and to compensate residents for losses. Scientific studies soon showed that, as expected, cyanide concentrations in the main body of the Essequibo had been diluted to safe levels shortly after the accident. However, the company's rapid reassurances that the crisis was therefore over were received with scepticism, while the manner in which it set out to settle the claims of affected residents raised a storm of controversy. A clause in the form issued by the company within days of the spill, to be filled in and signed by claimants, stated, 'This payment is accepted by me as settlement and compensation for all existing and future, direct, consequential and other damages, losses and claims of whatever nature arising out of the above incident and is paid by the Company in full settlement without admission of liability.' At this stage not even the short-term implications of the spill were clear, let alone the longer-term impacts.

WORLD RAINFOREST MOVEMENT
PRESS RELEASE   **25 August 1995**
RESPONDING TO THE OMAI DISASTER

The Guyana Government's decision to designate the Omai area 'an environmental disaster zone' and its stated commitment to hasten through environmental reforms to avoid similar problems in the future is to be welcomed. Care must be taken, however, to ensure that measures adopted by the Government are well thought through.

The World Rainforest Movement, which has been calling for greater controls on foreign companies active in the interior of Guyana for many years, advocates the following interim measures:

1. The Omai mine must be closed indefinitely. There should be no question of it reopening until a completely reformed regulatory system is seen to be in place and functioning.

2. A fully independent commission of enquiry involving all sectors of Guyanese society must be set up to examine the disaster and provided with free access to all relevant information.

3. Omai Gold Mines Limited should be obliged to release to the public its 1991 environmental impact assessment, all technical and environmental studies of the mine and the full details of its baseline geological studies,

so that the nature and extent of the contamination from the ore can be assessed.

4. Cambior Inc. and Golden Star Resources Limited must accept full responsibility for the disaster and meet the full costs of the clean up and all reparations. The companies' assets and other mines and prospects in Guyana should be frozen until these obligations are discharged.

5. The World Bank, which underwrites the Omai venture through its Multilateral Investment Guarantee Agency, must also accept responsibility for the disaster. It should institute an emergency programme to provide financial and technical assistance to the Government and to affected communities, to contain the pollution and rehabilitate the environment.

6. The draft Environmental Protection Act and form of the proposed Environmental Protection Agency should be the subject of detailed consultation with all sectors of Guyanese society, especially Amerindians who constitute the majority of the population in the interior, before they are enacted.

7. No further large-scale mining permits should be issued until these news laws, regulations and institutional reforms are in place and seen to be functioning.

NGOs including the APA, the Guyana Human Rights Association, GEMCO and international groups such as Minewatch, Friends of the Earth, Survival International and the World Rainforest Movement emphasized that apart from cyanide pollution, there was a serious long-term risk of heavy metal contamination, both from the spillage into the rivers and seepage into ground waters from the mine works and the diversion of waste into the Fennell pit. No studies were released by either the government or the company to allay these concerns.

What government surveys did later demonstrate was that communities had been severely affected by the accident. People living right by the river reported temporary skin irritations, vomiting, diarrhoea and prolonged fever. Shortage of water had caused temporary problems for many, with lack of drinking, cooking and bathing waters being widely reported. Fish supplies, a major part of their diet, were curtailed and crop failures and problems with livestock also occurred.[70] The company reported that it received 186 claims for damages.[71]

Meanwhile, the disaster was also having a wider impact on the country's economy. Besides losing revenue from the mine itself, eco-tourism operators closed some of their operations and a number of Caribbean countries banned fish and shrimp imports from Guyana. In Canada, stock markets reacted sharply to the disaster. Share prices of Golden Star and Cambior fell heavily, and nine months later Cambior was still not out of the woods. In May 1996, a group of Canadian environmental organizations, calling themselves the Guyana Legal

Defense Fund and acting on behalf of Amerindians and other affected residents in Guyana, filed claims in the Canadian courts against Cambior for C$227 million in compensation for damages.[72]

The Omai disaster also raised other serious questions. What exactly had gone wrong; was it not preventible and who shared responsibility with OGML for the dam failure? A slow-moving Commission of Enquiry was set up in Guyana to hear evidence but was widely criticized. Even the government seemed to consider it irrelevant. Long before the Commission completed its hearings and made recommendations, the government indicated that the mine should reopen in early 1996. The Enquiry revealed that the 'impervious' dam had experienced constant seepage for months and possibly years before it had collapsed, but it failed to look seriously at the question of heavy metals pollution from the mine – a matter repeatedly raised by environmental groups and the press.[73] The superficial nature of the Commission was roundly condemned by Guyanese NGOs. According to the Guyana Human Rights Association:

> Commissioned reluctantly, conducted defensively and concluded apologetically, the Enquiry process demonstrated an embarrassing degree of servility on the part of the Government of Guyana towards foreign investors. Neither of the major political parties seem to be in a position to defend the national interest when confronted by the power and influence of multinationals.[74]

However, the public did not have to wait for the Commission of Enquiry to confirm suspicions that OGML had chosen to risk overfilling its tailings dam rather than reduce production until a satisfactory solution was devised for getting rid of excess mine waste. In an extraordinary statement to the Canadian press, Knight Piesold Ltd, the engineering company contracted to design the tailings pond, washed its hands of the problem, claiming that in order to contain the excessive mine discharges OGML had increased the dam height far higher than their original engineering specifications, without their being consulted.[75] As Roger Moody summed up: 'In other words, the dam was too full, too high or too unstable – probably all three.'[76]

Nor was this the first time that greed for gold and corner-cutting on safety measures had led to an environmental disaster from cyanide processing. Indeed, the same mining financier, Robert Friedland, who underwrote Golden Star's initial operations in the Guyana Shield through his investment vehicles Ivanhoe Capital Corp and South American Goldfields,[77] was also behind the worst mining disaster in the US. In 1986, the mine of another of his companies, Galactic Resources at Summitville, Colorado, developed a massive leak of contaminated waters laced with cyanide and heavy metals. The spillage killed off 17 miles of river downstream and will cost upwards of US$60 million to clean up. The disaster was 'the Exxon Valdez of the American mining industry. Overambitious management, botched construction, reckless mining and weak state government controls combined to create one of the biggest scandals in recent mining history,' according to Thomas Hilliard of the Mineral Policy Center.[78] The head of the Guyana Natural Resources Agency, Joseph O'Lall, was warned of these precedents as early as 1993 by a US environmental group, Global Response. The information had been passed on to others in government, O'Lall said, but he had heard nothing more.[79]

The World Rainforest Movement pointed out that the World Bank also shared responsibility for the disaster. In a letter to the World Bank's Multilateral Investment Guarantee Agency (MIGA), the environmental organization stated:

> The World Bank is heavily implicated in the Omai project: since it supported the investment through MIGA; since, according to Omai Gold Mines Limited, the 1990 environmental impact assessment was reviewed by the World Bank prior to it being handed to the Government of Guyana in January 1991; and because the opening of Guyana to foreign mining companies was an explicit part of the World Bank's structural adjustment programme.[80]

Indeed in 1993, in proudly announcing its reinsurance of Cambior's investment in the Omai Gold Mine, MIGA had highlighted its environmental responsibility. In its annual report it had claimed:

> Cambior is clearly committed to acting in an environmentally responsible fashion. The Omai mining operation has implemented environmental procedures and measures that seek to harmonize economic exploitation of gold resources with protection of the environment. Cambior commissioned a comprehensive environmental impact study of the project, which was approved by independent experts selected by the Government of Guyana.[81]

Yet after the disaster, when asked if it accepted liability for the environmental impacts of tailings pollution, MIGA responded: 'even if there was an environmental disaster, it is not really our problem. It would be a little like appealing to your car insurance company after you were accused of murder.'[82] MIGA also declined to provide a copy of the contested EIA to the World Rainforest Movement, directing the organization to OGML instead.[83]

There has been extensive washing of hands all round. In February 1996, the Omai mine resumed operations, while constructing a new tailings dam with three times the capacity of the previous one.

New Prospects

The Guyanese press, if not the government, seems to have learned some clear lessons from the Omai case. As the *Guyana Review* remarked: 'The Omai incident has bared the paucity of Guyana's preparedness to cope with the possible human and ecological consequences of large-scale exploitation of its natural resources'... the imposition of 'environmental safeguards has had to compete with the powerful lobby of the mining sector'.[84] The *Catholic Standard* echoed similar sentiments:

> The world today is a highly competitive one in which we in Guyana are vying against others to attract much needed foreign investments. However, in the rush to acquire these it is vital that we do not settle for low standards and sell ourselves short. If we take the recent experience as a cue for the way in which we will transact business with companies we would like to see set up in Guyana, we only hope that the Prime Minister's dream of 'ten more Omais' will not be soon realised.[85]

Yet while efforts to push through new environmental legislation and set up more adequate government institutions to regulate the run-away mining industry have gained some impetus from the disaster, pressure from foreign mining companies has also intensified. By the end of 1994, 2,000 Medium Mining Licence applications and about fifty Large Mining Licence applications were being processed by the GGMC, totalling an additional one million hectares of mining. Warning that the Commission was too overstretched to process, let alone provide surveillance over this fast expanding industry, World Bank consultants recommend rapidly increasing staff at the GGMC.

By August 1996, mining grants and permits covered around 2.2 million hectares, over a tenth of the national territory, with in addition large areas being granted for wide-scale exploration. The pace of investment has also been increasing. According to Mines Commissioner Brian Sucre, whereas during 1995 the GGMC handed out twenty large-scale mining licences, fifty further licences were granted in the first seven months of 1996 alone.[86]

Documenting this rapidly expanding sector is no easy business. The GGMC itself lacks clear records of the permits and claims it has authorized and this information is not accessible to the public. Only some of the agreements reached with foreign investors are reported in the press. What can be gleaned by screening the papers and company reports is probably only the tip of the iceberg.

Omai is far from being the only major prospect that Golden Star has investigated. It invested over US$6.2 million in the feasibility of mining the deposits at Mahdia, which it hoped would yield around 200,000 oz. of gold over ten years.

After applying for a mining licence in 1994, the company announced that it was pulling out the following year. In January 1994 Golden Star also secured rights to survey over 1.3 million hectares in the North West, including four 'permit areas', two for gold exploration in Wenamu and Five Stars and two for diamond exploration in the Upper Mazaruni and Potaro. Golden Star also holds a 5,000-hectare prospecting licence to look for diamonds at Saganang on the Middle Mazaruni and holds another prospecting licence for Quartz Hill near the Omai mine.[87] In March 1995, OGML applied for rights to mine the area to increase ore supplies to the mill at Omai.[88] Golden Star has also acquired a 50/50 joint venture agreement with the Roraima Mining Company to investigate the possibility of mining for gold at Aranka on the Cuyuni, where the companies hold prospecting licences totalling 10,400 hectares.

Suriname: Golden Star and the Maroons

The Saramaka Maroon community of Nieuw Koffiekamp in Suriname faces forced relocation to make way for a multinational gold mine being developed by Golden Star Resources of Denver, Colorado and Cambior Inc of Montreal. The Maroon community is disputing the relocation and demanding that the companies negotiate with them as the traditional owners of the land. After years of fruitless negotiations, intimidation and violence, they are asking for international support in their struggle with the mining companies.

The Saramaka already know what it means to make way for large-scale mining. In the 1960s, many of them were forced off their original lands by a giant hydro-electric dam and reservoir, constructed to supply power to Suralco – a wholly-owned subsidiary of US-based ALCOA – for smelting bauxite into alumina and aluminium. Of the several thousand moved, some 500 were relocated to Nieuw Koffiekamp, the area now coveted by the gold-mining companies.

The Maroons are the descendants of escaped African slaves, who recreated forest-based societies in the interior of Suriname and who fought and won their freedom from the Dutch colonial administration in the eighteenth century. Treaties signed with the Dutch guaranteed their political and territorial autonomy. Since that time they have been living in the rainforests, engaged in traditional subsistence activities and small-scale mining. After the country became independent, both the Maroons and country's Amerindians repeatedly demanded recognition of their land rights in accordance with international law. These pleas have been ignored, and instead large areas of their traditional territories have been handed over to logging and mining ventures. The marginalization of the forest peoples triggered a destructive six-year civil war which was only concluded by treaty in 1992 when the government made (unkept) promises to respect the communities' land rights.

Although Surinamese law does not expressly recognize the land rights of Maroon and indigenous peoples, these rights are recognized in international human rights treaties to which Suriname is a party. However, Golden Star and Cambior refuse to treat the community as a legitimate land-owner and assert that the companies' rights under the 1994 Mineral Agreement with the government override the community's claims. Although the Nieuw Koffiekamp community lies inside the so-called Gros Rosebel concession, about eighty kilometres south of the capital, Paramaribo, the people were not consulted, informed or otherwise notified about the granting of the concession.

Trouble erupted shortly after. In March 1994, an unidentified armed force, calling itself the Surinamese Liberation Front took 26 hostages and held them at the Afobaka dam. One of their most prominent demands was the revocation of the Gros Rosebel concession. The mineral exploration went ahead, however, and a heavily guarded base camp was established one kilometre from Nieuw Koffiekamp. At the request of Golden Star, thousands of small-scale Maroon miners were forcibly evicted from the concession area, despite valid rights under Maroon customary law for many of them to remain there. Suriname's Minister of Justice even threatened to attack the miners from the 'ground and the air' if they did not vacate the concession area.

Subsequently, security measures have intensified. Golden Star has erected a number of gates and barriers, including a huge earth wall, to restrict the movements of community members on their lands, even denying them access to their agricultural plots, hunting grounds and religious sites. Both police and company security forces have established a presence and collaborate closely. Indeed, the head of Golden Star's security is the commanding officer of the police detachment at Gros Rosebel. A unit of the heavily-armed, elite, anti-terrorist Police Support Group has also been stationed at the site.

The security officers have threatened, harassed and intimidated community members. Twenty-five villagers from nearby Royal Hill were arrested and expelled from the concession at the end of September 1995 and armed police then began to patrol the area. On a number of different occasions patrols have shot live ammunition at or over the heads of Nieuw Koffiekampers, even those engaged in tending their agricultural plots and gathering forest foods.

Environmental damage has already resulted from the prospecting operations, as swathes of forest have been cut down to make way for augur pits and sampling trenches, fouling water sources. Game and wildlife habitat is depleted and animals driven away due to exploration activities, making hunting and traditional subsistence increasingly difficult. Once feasibility studies are completed, vast open-pit mines will be dug accompanied by large ponds to process crushed ore.

During 1995, the Organization of American States was invited in by the Suriname government to try to broker a tripartite agreement between the government, the community of Nieuw Koffiekamp and the mining companies. However, the negotiations were inconclusive, a sticking point being the refusal by the government and the companies to treat the Saramaka as legitimate landowners.

Golden Star and Cambior's activities around Nieuw Koffiekamp and in Guyana were recently condemned for violating fundamental human rights by the World Council of Churches' Consultation on Mining and Indigenous Peoples held in England in May 1996. The meeting concluded that the Surinamese government's failure to recognize the rights of indigenous and tribal peoples to own and control their lands and territories 'is not a valid excuse for mining companies to violate these rights'.

Other companies are also moving in. In 1994, Plaza Mining and Blue Ribbon Resources Ltd were granted a concession at Appaparu and promised to invest US$5.5 million to develop a gold mine.[89] Romanex (Guyana) Exploration Ltd, a subsidiary of Sutton Resources of Canada, is also engaged in developing what is reported as an 'Omai-like mine' on its 50-square-kilometre concession in the Marudi Mountains in southern Guyana. If feasibility studies are positive, the company will commence open pit operations to supply 3,000 tonnes of ore per day to a new mill, but none of this will be possible until the Lethem to Georgetown road is opened. Even then, the company will have to construct a feeder road due south from Lethem to supply the mine.[90]

Another Canadian company, Exall Resources, has been developing a very large gold and diamond dredging operation on the Middle Mazaruni. Canada's Cathedral Gold Corporation has been exploring for gold not far from Omai near the Akawaio community at Kaburi, in conjunction with two local companies, George Hicks Mining Company and the Kaburi Development Company.[91] Canada's Pegasus Gold and International Copper also reportedly sought prospecting licences during 1995 in the same area.[92]

Also active in the country are: Denison Mines Ltd, which is linked to a Friedland company, South American Goldfields; Gagan Gold Corp, exploring near Akaiwanna; Minorca Resources Ltd of Toronto, engaged in a joint venture with Gribaker Mining Enterprises on the Whanna creek on the Barima river above Arakaka; Adex Mining Co, also of Canada, exploiting a prospect at Pott Falls; KWG Resources Inc of Montreal which is exploring a 250-square-kilometre gold prospect at Sukabi in the Upper Potaro/Ireng area on the land of the

Patamona Indians; Idaho-based Coeur d'Alene, with its local subsidiary, Caribbean Basic Industries, which has gained exploration rights in Goete Creek in a joint venture with the Caribbean Mining Development and Investments Company Ltd.[93]

In January 1996, local miner Alfro Alphonso entered into a US$5.5 million deal with Americans Gregory Sparks and Gregory Graham to establish a new company, Bushmaster Mining Inc, to mine gold at Million Mountain on the Middle Puruni river. Supplying the mine will require breaking open a new road between Itabali Landing on the Mazaruni upstream of Bartica and the Puruni. The project will 'open up the area for other persons', noted Tony Shields of the Guyana Gold and Diamond Miners Association.[94] In March a Malaysian company, Tanahmas Gold Mining Company, owned by Solid Timbers, was granted a 12,000-acre prospecting licence on the edge of the New River Triangle. The company applied for a further 24,000 acres.[95]

Golden Star is not the only company with interests in the Upper Barama region. Canada's Canarc, which has a prospecting agreement with Echo Bay Mines Ltd, has been actively prospecting in Baramita since 1994. In May 1996 the 'big Australian', Broken Hill Proprietaries (BHP), was reported to be negotiating agreements to conduct aerial surveys in north-west Guyana and in the area between Omai and Orealla.[96] The deal was clinched in August that year and will cover 1.2 million hectares. Also in August 1996 it was revealed that Golden Star Resources had entered into an agreement with the Barama Company Ltd to explore for gold and diamonds in the whole of the logging company's 1.7 million-hectare concession,[97] and the following month a joint aerial exploration between BHP and Golden Star Resources was revealed.[98] The same month, a Brazilian company, Zamuteba Mining Co, which mines diamonds in Angola and gold in Brazil, signed an agreement to carry out gold and diamond exploration in 1.7 million acres in the Potaro-Siparuni region. A new company Vanessa (Guyana) Incorporated, a subsidiary of Vanessa Ventures of Canada, was also reported to have submitted applications for mining rights.[99]

Mining Invasion
Not surprisingly, Amerindians have been thunderstruck by this incredible expansion of mining activities. While their own claims for land lie ignored in dusty heaps in the under-resourced offices of the Minister for Amerindian Affairs and Department of Lands and Surveys, foreign companies are being allowed direct access to their ancestral territories.

Amerindians along the Venezuelan border are under especially heavy pressure, as mining companies seek to follow up on their lucrative finds across the border (see opposite). Local and foreign companies have been rushing into the

Upper Wenamu river, ancestral lands of the Akawaio and Arekuna peoples, to exploit new finds. Among the foreign-owned enterprises entering the area are Toronto-based Kretschmar International Geoscience Corporation, which has gained a fifty square-kilometre prospect, US-based Kynaston Perreira and the Texan company, HGB Ventures. Another operator, Coast Mountain, has illegally opened its own airstrip on Amerindian titled land, without any consultation. Also active in the Wenamu is another Canadian company, based in Vancouver, Guyana Goldmine, which recently took over Guyana Goldfields and which has mines at Tamberlin, Cat Fur and Military Reserve Property.[100]

Venezuela: Mining Madness

Many of the mining companies working in Guyana also have operations in neighbouring Venezuela, where a parallel mining boom has been underway in the eastern part of Bolívar State. The process intensified dramatically in the 1980s, when the government began promoting small-scale mining to help offset the national debt. Small concessions to mine diamonds and gold, subject to simplified regulations and controls, were handed out liberally by the Ministry of Energy and Mines, taking little or no account of existing indigenous communities, titles or land claims. The result was a veritable invasion of Indian lands in the eastern part of the State, especially along the road from Tumeremo to Santa Elena de Uairén. By the late 1980s at least 30,000 people were believed to be prospecting and mining in southern Venezuela, the great majority illegally. Mining also boomed along the major rivers. By 1991, for example, an estimated 12,541 non-indigenous people, twenty per cent of whom were foreigners, were engaged in mining in the Upper Caroni basin alone, substantially outnumbering the estimated 3,757 indigenous people in the same area.

Land disputes between Indians and miners proliferated, but Indian complaints to government authorities have fallen on apparently deaf ears. Since the mining laws and regulations make no mention of the need to respect indigenous rights, the authorities feel justified in ignoring their grievances. Much of the small-scale mining is informal, unregulated and illegal, but even in these circumstances complaints from indigenous communities receive little follow-up. Indeed, it is widely reported that members of the National Guard and police turn a blind eye to illegal mining in exchange for a share of the profits.

Since 1990 the government has begun to promote a more vigorous exploitation of these resources by larger-scale private companies, favouring in particular joint ventures between Venezuelan and foreign companies. In 1991 the government changed regulations and lowered taxes in order to attract foreign investment in the industry. As a result, some 367 mining concessions and leases were handed out, covering a major proportion of eastern Bolívar State and leading to bitter disputes with indigenous communities.

Thousands of small-scale miners have poured onto the lands of the Pemon, Akawaio, Carib and Arawak Indians, and over sixty foreign mining companies, most from Canada, have gained substantial concessions in the area. The social and environmental impact has been devastating and has led to a national outcry.

The situation has prompted the National Amerindian Council to call for a halt to mining in the whole Wenamu area. Amerindian spokesperson Lawrence Anselmo alleges that the numerous mining operations are causing severe damage to river banks and channels, causing water pollution and diarrhoea among children. The dredges, supplied directly by helicopters from Venezuela, which zip to and fro with impunity, are also drawing in marijuana and prostitutes from across the border, he alleges. Local villagers believe that the Guyanese security forces are themselves involved in the mining.[101] The miners, however, want to increase cross-border traffic from Venezuela, to facilitate access to their mines. In May 1996 Stanislaus Jardine, President of the Guyana Gold and Diamond Miners Association, called on the government to open up roads across the frontier.[102]

The problem for Amerindians is that under Guyanese law, all subsurface resources are considered the property of the state. While Amerindians do have privileges to carry out small-scale mining on their titled areas, it is the government which has the authority to issue mining claims to outsiders both to titled lands and other areas. Legally, the government is not obliged to consult Amerindians about mining in their areas.

It is also the case that the government has the authority to adopt a policy of not issuing mining rights to outsiders on areas owned or claimed by Amerindians. It can also choose to consult the Amerindians and involve them in decision-making. Indeed, the GGMC does profess to a policy of not giving mining permits to operate in Amerindian areas but since it has no idea where Amerindian titles are (they are not mapped) and even less idea of where their untitled land claims extend, the reality is that there are bitter disputes between miners and Amerindian communities all over the interior.

A letter to the head of the GGMC dated 17 September 1996 from the Santa Rosa Village Council of the North West District sums up these sentiments:

Dear Sir/Madam,

We respectfully wish to inform your office that based on the information we have received (see attached copy of correspondence from Golden Star Resources Ltd), We, the Captains and Councillors with the support of the Amerindian peoples we have been elected to represent in this village, do not approve of your system of granting permission to a multiInternational mining company to operate in our area.

Your office granted permission without any consultation to date. Be informed that this is the only notice from Golden Star Resources Ltd of its intention of operating in our area.

MultiInternational mining companies in general have a record of only providing temporary employment for some of our people but having long term negative impacts of undermining our culture and leaving permanent destruction and devastation of the animals and the environment on which we depend for our continued survival.

Please be informed that we do not approve of the presence of Golden Star Resources Ltd as a mining company operating in our area. We are therefore advising that your office immediately withdraw your permission to the above mining company.

We trust that you will not view it necessary to contribute to my people's genocide in exchange for monetary gains.

Thanking you in anticipation for your future cooperation.

Yours sincerely,

Mark Atkinson

Santa Rosa Village Council

The Caribs of Baramita are equally concerned by the sudden influx of mining companies:

We have lived a poor but untroubled life and Baramita is the land we know. Now we find that the entire area seems to be occupied by foreign companies. This forebodes a gloomy prospect for us... We want to live in our own way in peace.[103]

93

[1] Cited in Forte 1994:69-70
[2] Naipaul 1969; Hemming 1978
[3] Daly 1975:275-276; Menezes 1977:234
[4] Daly 1975:276; World Bank 1993a:35
[5] Cleary 1990:14
[6] Baird 1982
[7] World Bank 1993a; MacMillan 1995:24
[8] Benjamin and Pierre 1995
[9] Butt Colson 1985
[10] Gillin 1936; Baird 1982
[11] Peberdy 1948:14-20
[12] Baird 1982
[13] Baird 1982:153
[14] Colchester and MacIntyre 1994
[15] Sassoon 1993:7
[16] Amerindian Research Unit (ARU) nd
[17] Butt Colson 1983
[18] Colchester 1991
[19] Butt Colson 1983; Fox and Danns 1993; Forte 1995
[20] Butt Colson 1983
[21] Baird 1982; Cleary 1990:15
[22] World Bank 1993a:37
[23] Rescan 1994
[24] *Guyana Review*, July 1995
[25] Fox and Danns 1993:109
[26] Sanders 1995
[27] ARU nd
[28] Colchester 1991:11
[29] Moody 1994
[30] Watkins and Woolford 1990; Cremer and Warner 1990; Colchester 1991
[31] Cleary 1990
[32] MacMillan 1995
[33] Cordier and Grasmick 1994
[34] GEMCO 1994; *Stabroek News*, 9 January 1994
[35] World Bank 1993a:35
[36] World Bank 1993a:42
[37] *Stabroek Review*, 2 August 1995
[38] Cited in Forte 1994:223
[39] Cited in Forte 1994:36
[40] Forte 1994:222
[41] Gray 1986; Cleary 1990:223; MacMillan 1995:118ff
[42] *Caribbean Insight*, June 1996
[43] *Guyana Review*, October 1995; *Caribbean Insight*, July 1996

[44] Colchester 1995
[45] Lamur 1983
[46] *Stabroek News*, 30 March 1994
[47] Economist Intelligence Unit Country Profile: Guyana, Windward and Leeward Islands 1995-6:19; World Bank 1993b
[48] *Caribbean Insight*, March 1995
[49] Sassoon 1993:5
[50] Sassoon 1993:5; *Stabroek News*, 4 April 1994, 5 April 1994, 20 May 1994
[51] World Bank 1993b:44
[52] World Bank 1993a:37
[53] Colchester 1991
[54] Pang 1994
[55] Moody 1995b
[56] Moody 1995b
[57] Kozak 1994
[58] Rescan 1995
[59] Rescan 1995
[60] Moody 1995b
[61] Moody 1995a
[62] Walcott *et al* 1995; *Caribbean Insight*, June 1995; *Guyana Review*, September 1995:8
[63] *Stabroek News*, 29 May 1995
[64] *Catholic Standard*, 28 May 1995
[65] *Caribbean Insight*, June 1995
[66] *Catholic Standard*, 28 July 1996
[67] *Stabroek News*, 2 July 1995
[68] Moody 1995b
[69] *Catholic Standard*, 15 October 1995
[70] *Stabroek News*, 24 December 1995
[71] *Catholic Standard*, 24 March 1996
[72] *Toronto Globe and Mail*, 10 May 1996
[73] *Guyana Review*, October 1995; *Catholic Standard*, 21 January 1996
[74] Guyana Human Rights Association, press release, 1 February 1996
[75] *Toronto Globe and Mail*, 25 August 1995
[76] Moody 1995b
[77] Colchester 1991; *Northern Miner*, 29 May 1993
[78] Moody 1995c:23
[79] *Rocky Mountain News*, 25 August 1995
[80] Letter from Marcus Colchester, World Rainforest Movement, to Akira Iida, Vice-President of MIGA, 31 August 1995

[81] MIGA 1993:18

[82] Pratap Chatterjee, 'World Bank insures destructive mining from Peru to Indonesia', Independent Press Service, 25 August 1995

[83] Letter from Gerald T. West of MIGA to Marcus Colchester, World Rainforest Movement, 13 September 1995

[84] *Guyana Review*, September 1995

[85] *Catholic Standard*, 21 January 1996

[86] *Guyana Chronicle*, 4 August 1996, 13 August 1996

[87] GSRL 1994

[88] *Chronicle*, 8 March 1995

[89] EIU 2:1994

[90] *Stabroek News*, 13 February 1995

[91] *Chronicle*, 26 March 1995

[92] *New Nation*, 3 December 1995

[93] Moody 1995a; *Stabroek News*, 22 September 1994, 21 December 1995

[94] *Stabroek News*, 26 January 1996

[95] *Stabroek News*, 12 March 1996

[96] *Catholic Standard*, 19 May 1996

[97] *Caribbean Insight*, August 1996

[98] *Caribbean Insight*, September 1996

[99] *Barbados Advocate*, 29 August 1996

[100] *Stabroek News*, 22 September 1994; APA archives, 31 October 1995; *Catholic Standard*, 19 May 1996

[101] *Sunday Chronicle*, 11 June 1995

[102] *Sunday Chronicle*, 2 May 1996

[103] Survival International Urgent Action Bulletin, September 1996

CHAPTER 6
FORESTS FOR SALE

Guyana is one of the most forested countries in the tropics. Some three-quarters of the national territory is covered by various kinds of forests, 16,100,000 hectares in all, of which over 14 million are considered to be loggable – an area about the size of England and Wales combined. But until recently, logging in Guyana was not big business. Compared to the forests of South East Asia, Amazonian forests of the kinds found in Guyana are relatively poor in commercial timbers. So logging tends to be highly selective and up to recent times has focused on only a handful of species.

Moreover, even compared to other tropical countries, the soils are especially poor in nutrients and thus regrowth of new trees after logging is slow. On top of this, communications in the interior are particularly bad and population sparse, meaning that local labour has been in short supply. Except where mining enterprises have flourished, roads have not been developed south of the coastal belt. Even the major rivers are soon interrupted by rapids and waterfalls. Taken together, these factors long discouraged logging and, during the colonial era, logging was restricted to the more accessible forests along the coast and limited to a few timbers with special properties valued in the export market.

Ordinances were passed restricting the extraction of timber without permission as early as 1741 in Berbice, whereas in the much more extensive colony of Essequibo, the first reported laws regulating timber extraction were passed in 1803. The Dutch handed out leases for timber extraction which were considered not to affect existing Amerindian rights and the same pattern was established by early British attempts to regulate the industry. The Amerindians' traditional rights and privileges were not affected by the issuance of timber grants,[1] although in fact Amerindians complained as early as 1815 when their lands began to be taken over by woodcutters.[2]

As the timber industry gradually expanded, the Crown began to encroach on the Amerindians' rights. Under Ordinance No.12 of 1871, previous regulations regarding Amerindians were repealed and in their stead the Governor assumed the authority to define 'the privileges to be enjoyed by the Aboriginal Indians, in relation to the Rivers, Creeks, Crown Lands and Forests of the Colony and may in like manner, cancel, alter and amend any of such regulations.' From 1887 onwards, the right of Amerindians to cultivate forests granted to logging companies was restricted.[3]

The expansion of the timber industry on the lower rivers, especially on the Demerara up to the great falls some 250 kilometres inland, provided employment opportunities for Amerindians, many of whom would travel down to the wood-cutting establishments from their homelands in the highlands.[4] According to the Amerindian Research Unit (ARU), the system of employment:

> became quickly transformed into a form of debt peonage, a pattern of exploitation that still exists. Amerindians were often fleeced and de-moralised by rum. The practice of paying wages entirely in rum was not uncommon on these rivers. Selective species of wood were logged, which over time led to the disappearance of the choice wood and other commercial timbers from the more easily accessible coastal areas.[5]

Coastlanders also gained access to timbers by making use of the Amerindians' unextinguished rights to fell timber on 'Crown Land': Amerindians were bribed and paid with rum in order to dodge the forest regulations.[6]

During the 1880s, the coastal population in the interior began to increase markedly due to the gold-mining and a growing trade in *balata* – wild rubber – linked to the booming world rubber market. Whereas in the 1870s only a handful of travellers were reported in the interior, by the 1890s the numbers increased to several thousands.[7] Balata exports boomed from nothing in 1859 to 20,000 pounds in 1865, peaking at 1.6 million pounds in 1917.[8]

Right up until the 1960s, the local logging industry remained essentially seasonal, largely dependent on the wet season rains which enabled loggers to float their logs down to the small mills. Amerindians continued to comprise the chief labour force and they worked seasonally in the logging camps to earn a little cash. At the same time, several large companies emerged which were able to produce high-quality materials suitable for the export market in a very small range of species. Pride of place was given to greenheart (*Ocotea rodiae*), a durable timber favoured for marine use, in constructing piers and groynes and so on, which was exported mainly to the UK and US. Another timber, *Mora*, was exported more widely for use as railway sleepers. *Dalli*, and one or two other lesser timbers were exported to Suriname for making plywood. In all, only about 11 million cubic feet were being cut annually, controlled by a small Forest Department, which was still in its infancy.[9] The industry, constrained by a modest market and limited technology, was small and had access to only a fraction of the country's vast forest estate.

However, technical developments were to change this situation. By the 1960s, loggers in South East Asia had pioneered the use in tropical forests of powerful caterpillar tractors, wheeled skidders, chainsaws, road-building machinery and lorries and were extracting timbers from rugged terrain once considered inaccessible. From the late 1970s and 1980s, timber processing technologies were refined to deal with a far greater range of tropical timber species. New glues and mixed species were being used in the manufacture of plywood, chipboard and particle board, which vastly expanded the industry's range of products, which in turn was built up to meet an explosive increase in global demand for tropical timber. As a result, capital-intensive logging became profitable in forests once protected by their isolation and species diversity. Forests in the Philippines and on Peninsular Malaysia were rapidly depleted and the logging frontier moved on, to Borneo, Sumatra, New Guinea and the Solomon Islands.

Yet these pressures were slow to affect Guyana. Since the country's economy was protected behind the closed doors of 'Cooperative Socialism', foreign companies stayed clear. Logging continued in the coastal forests but was of low intensity and carried out with outdated machinery. The common practice was for loggers to cream the forests of the best trees of the choicest timbers and move on. It was harmful but small-scale.

Efforts by the World Bank and the IMF to promote exports during the 1970s and 1980s initiated a process of change, however. Between 1978 and 1987, as part of their policy of promoting public-sector productivity, the World Bank and European Community invested over US$35 million in a state-owned company especially established for the purpose, called Demerara Woods Ltd. Funds were privided for a US$6.5 million sawmill, imported from Italy and said to be the largest in South America, and for a huge wood gasification plant built in Germany. Neither ever functioned properly. Over US$5 million was allocated to road-building.[10]

The aim of the Demerara Woods project was to exploit what the World Bank called the 'largest stand of greenheart in the world'. However, poor financial management and lack of institutional oversight meant that the company soon ran into debt. Moreover, forestry expertise was absent and there were inadequate controls to ensure that timbers were not cut at a higher rate than they could regrow. Subsequent studies in the area showed that greenheart, which constituted 94 per cent of the timber being extracted, was regrowing at only 0.13 cubic metres per hectare per year. The company was actually harvesting timbers on the assumption it would regenerate at nearly ten times this rate.[11]

Structural Adjustment in the Forests

The policy of economic liberalization, adopted by the Hoyte government in 1986 under pressure from the World Bank and IMF and transformed into a full-blown structural adjustment programme, radically changed the context in which the timber industry could develop. A plan for the sector's growth was called for as part of a global effort by the World Bank and the United Nations Food and

Agriculture Organization (FAO) to promote tropical forestry.[12] The task was taken on by the Canadian International Development Agency (CIDA), which prepared a 'National Forestry Action Plan' within a few months. It received government endorsement in late 1989.[13]

The CIDA study found that annual timber exports were limited to only 94,000 cubic metres and that only 2.4 million hectares of the 9.1 million hectares legally classified as State Forests were under production. However, even this limited level of production was considered to be unsustainable because of poor forestry practice, while the capacity of the Guyana Forestry Commission to regulate the industry was, it found, negligible.

Nonetheless, the plan advocated a rapid increase of logging up to a maximum of 3.6 million hectares through the provision of quick-disbursing loans. Up to 62 per cent of the US$90 million budget proposed for the expansion was to be allocated to increasing production, while US$23 million was to be spent on expanding the forestry service to control the logging. To adequately monitor logging in the expanded area, the plan recommended that the number of trained forestry staff be increased from 5 to 76.

The World Rainforest Movement was quick to condemn the plan as folly.[14] Experience in other tropical forest countries had already demonstrated unequivocally that simultaneous expansion of logging and forestry institutions was a recipe for disaster. Runaway logging would constantly outpace the government's capacity to regulate the industry. As Jack Westoby, ex-director of forestry at the FAO had warned in 1987:

> Over the last two decades, massive tracts of virgin tropical forests have come under exploitation, in all three under-developed regions. That exploitation, with a few honourable exceptions, has been reckless, wasteful, even devastating. Nearly all the operations have been enclavistic, that is to say they have had no profound or durable impact on the social and economic life of the countries where they have taken place... Local needs are not being met; the employment opportunities are trifling. A significant part of the exports, as logs or as primary processed timber, is exported 'within the firm', and transfer values are fixed to facilitate the accumulation of profits outside the country,... the contribution of forestry to improving the lot of the common people has been negligible so far.[15]

Ignoring such words of caution, the Guyanese government took decisive steps to follow the agencies' prescriptions. As part of its programme of privatization, in 1989 it sold the state-owned company Guyana Timbers, which had been running at a considerable loss, to the Colonial Life Insurance Company

(CLICO) of Trinidad for a knock-down US$2.7 million. The company was incorporated locally as Caribbean Resources Ltd and gained assured access to 320,000 hectares of forests. The government, meanwhile, assumed Guyana Timbers' debts. The great forest sale had begun.

The Scourge of Tropical Forest Logging

Guyana's forestry situation is far from unique. Indeed the pattern is typical, where a runaway expansion of the timber industry streaks ahead of an inadequately staffed, under-funded and politically marginal forestry department, which fumbles along behind in a vain attempt to keep pace with developments. What is somewhat unusual about the Guyanese case is that this exponential acceleration in logging is relatively recent and, to a large extent results from deals made by a previous and largely discredited administration. Guyana thus has a chance of learning from the bad experiences of other countries and making a fresh start. This will require political courage.

The problems with an inadequately regulated and controlled industry are legion, as the well documented experiences in Papua New Guinea,[16] Malaysia,[17] Indonesia,[18] and Africa[19] testify all too well. Sustained yield objectives are soon overridden by profit motives; excessive timber is extracted and no one is there in the field to check on actual practice. Poor roading, chemical spills, and abusive labour practice damage the forests, undermine public health and bring poverty instead of wealth. Incidental damage to soils and to the residual stands caused by careless felling, poor tractor use and repeated re-entry may terminally limit the ability of a forest to regenerate. Even quite selective logging, if carelessly carried out, can cause a loss of the majority of the forest canopy, leading to erosion, laterization and a chronic decline in fauna. Scrappy regrowth, dominated by large herbs such as *Marantaceae* and secondary softwoods like *Cecropia*, impedes the regeneration of timber species.

Lack of supervision tempts loggers to underdeclare the volume of timber extracted, or misdeclare its quality, in order to avoid royalties. An almost normal practice is for companies to sell on timber to overseas parent companies or cronies at artificially low prices. The purpose is to ensure that local companies show little or no profit and thus pay no tax, while the overseas companies make all the profits. The scams are endless and it is the local communities, the national economies and the environments that they both depend on that are the real losers. Unregulated logging causes terrible waste.

The experience of other countries also shows that, unless properly supervised and made publicly accountable, the timber industry may damage the evolution of democratic institutions. The handing out of logging concessions promotes the domination of the political economy by

nepotistic, patronage politics. This undermines democratic principles and causes an increasing marginalization of rural people, who find that they can no longer rely on their political representatives to defend their interests.

The experience in South East Asia is that this political hijacking of forestry concessions leads to the demoralization and corruption of the forestry departments themselves. Frustrated forestry officials find themselves unable to control or regulate the activities of loggers whose political connections effectively protect them from criticism. Honest officials resign their posts and less scrupulous individuals prepared to overlook, or profit from, malpractice fill their positions. Damaging forest use is the inevitable consequence of abuse of office by politicians, whose vested interests in quick profits override the long term interests of the nation. Such vested interests are the most severe obstacles facing sound forest management, obstacles often coyly referred to as 'lack of political will'. Those who suffer most from all this are indigenous forest dwellers.[20]

A detailed survey of tropical forest logging carried out for the International Tropical Timber Organization showed that in 1989 less than one-eighth of one per cent of moist tropical forests were being commercially managed on an operational scale on a sustained yield basis.[21]

Privatizing the Forests

As in most other tropical forest countries, political patronage has to a large extent determined who gains large logging concessions in Guyana. Most of the large concessions given out to Guyanese nationals between 1985 and 1991 were to ministers, members of parliament and supporters of the PNC which ruled until 1992. Moreover, in the five years preceding 1989, seven companies absorbed 94 per cent of foreign assistance given to the sector, with two companies alone, Guyana Timbers and Demerara Woods getting 75 per cent.[22]

At present, some 9.1 million hectares of Guyana's forests are classified as State Forests and are under the jurisdiction of the Guyana Forestry Commission. Allocations of forest areas to concessionaires are meant to be controlled by the Commissioner for Forests and subject to the oversight of a board of directors, which includes political appointees nominated by the Office of the President. Yet the Forestry Commission is not placed within a ministry, but under the Guyana Natural Resources Agency which was itself established directly under the authority of the Office of the President, as part of the country's Structural Adjustment Programme, with the aim of speeding up 'development' in Guyana's interior.

Forests are leased out to loggers in three ways. Large tracts of forests are leased out through 'Timber Sales Agreements' which include stipulations on the annual allowable cut and the need for management plans. The terms of operation under these agreements are set out in the Forests Act and accompanying schedules, which establish which fees are payable, the royalties due on the different classes of timber and so on. 'Wood Cutting Leases' are for smaller areas of around 5,000 hectares, while 'State Forest Permissions' (SFPs) are generally for areas of under 2,000 hectares. These permits may be granted for forests outside of State Forests. The terms of extraction are set out in the State Lands Act.

With authority to hand out logging concessions vested in a small, barely accountable government office directly under presidential control, the opportunities for favouritism and malpractice abound. In practice, timber deals are rarely transparent. As the World Bank has observed:

> The [GFC] agency is clearly unable to perform its functions... The GFC is largely unable to collect the fees it is due and is unable to enforce planning requirements and environmental safeguards. Moreover, there seems to be a large amount of discretion on the treatment regarding taxes and royalties granted to different firms, and most pertinent information on how the Forestry Commission deals with individual timber operators is regarded as confidential and is not publicly available.[23]

During the early 1990s, obscurity concerning the the the Forestry Commission's operations increased. The (expatriate) Commissioner for Forests resigned and was not replaced. The Commission began to be effectively run by the Chairman of the Board, who happened to be President Jagan's brother-in-law. Beyond his brief and without even the Deputy Commissioner's knowledge, he was single-handedly negotiating logging concessions with foreign companies. The World Bank concluded that the Guyanese Forestry Commission was a perfect example of the 'capture theory of regulation', whereby the regulatory body is controlled by the industry it is supposed to regulate.[24]

The problems had already entrenched themselves under the previous government. Under the Hoyte administration's liberalization policies, foreign companies investing in forestry were accorded extraordinarily generous terms to exploit massive timber concessions. The agreements that they reached with the government have normally been kept secret, but the details of the deal done with the Malaysian/Korean consortium, the Barama Company Ltd, were leaked to the public and reveal the lengths to which the Hoyte government went to attract foreign investment.

The Barama agreement grants the company, which is eighty per cent owned by Malaysia's Samling Timbers Bhd and twenty per cent by the Korean conglomerate Sun Kyong, a 25-year licence – automatically extendable for a further 25 years – to exploit some 1.69 million hectares of forests in the North West of the country for the export of raw logs, sawn lumber, veneer and processed plywood. The company expects to export some 300,000 cubic metres of timber in the early years, rising to 1.2 million cubic metres per year after ten years. These figures may be compared to a total annual export for the entire country in 1989 of 94,000 cubic metres.[25]

The company also enjoys a ten-year tax holiday, including income tax, corporation tax, withholding tax, consumption tax, property tax and income duties on just about everything, including machinery, fuel, building materials, office equipment and medical supplies. Export taxes are only payable on greenheart, while even royalty payments have been fixed in Guyanese dollars over the first twenty-year period – a gift to the company as the currency devalues.

Yet the company is also permitted to hold external accounts, foreign currency accounts within Guyana, employ 15 per cent foreign workers (more if local labour with the right skills is unavailable) and, in the event of disputes with the government, have recourse to the arbitration of the 'International Centre for Settlement of Investment Disputes' in Washington DC, in which case the company 'shall be deemed as a national of a State other than Guyana' (Basic Agreement 1991: article 21).

The contracts setting up the Barama concession stipulate that it will attempt to extract timber according to the principle of sustained yield. Yet, whereas both the Forestry Commission and Barama admit that knowledge about how to achieve this is lacking, the company has invested in the enterprise on the basis that it will extract 25 cubic metres of timber per hectare with a cutting cycle of 25 years. This is judged to allow a sustained yield because it is assumed that the forests can naturally regenerate at a mean rate of regrowth of 1 cubic metre per hectare per year. It is very doubtful if the low canopy forests of the North West, where tree diameters are below average, can in fact regenerate merchantable timber at this rate. A survey of the concession by the Edinburgh Centre for Tropical Forests warned that excessive timber harvesting was a major risk that 'could potentially jeopardize the objective of the entire BCL programme'.[26]

The Barama agreement had been negotiated by the PNC government with the head of the Guyana Natural Resources Agency, Winston King, who after the change of government, took up a consultancy with the company. In short, the Barama concession is a classic example of the kind of enclavistic development that has led throughout much of the tropics to the over-exploitation of forests for little national gain. Even the British government was afterwards to admit that the contracts were too generous and should be revised.

Timber Pirates

Many of the foreign companies moving into Guyana have very questionable records overseas. The majority shareholder of the Barama Company Ltd, Samling Timbers Sdn Bhd comes from Sarawak, Malaysian Borneo, where its operations have brought it into repeated conflict with the indigenous Dayaks of the interior. Logging in Sarawak is being carried out at such a furious pace that the primary forests will be almost completely logged out within a decade. So unsustainable is the rate of extraction that the World Bank characterizes the Malaysian timber business as a 'sunset industry'. For over a decade, Dayak groups have been putting up barricades to prevent the logging of their ancestral lands. However, so close are the connections between the loggers and politicians that, despite an official recognition of native customary rights and a forestry policy which gives a priority to local needs over exports, the government's response has been mass arrests and harassment through the courts. Several hundred Dayaks have been arrested and laws have been changed to make their blockades of the logging company roads illegal.

As Malaysia's forests face exhaustion, many of these companies have begun operations in neighbouring Pacific countries. Berjaya Sdn Bhd has already tangled with environmentalists in Malaysia, who have fought to halt its destructive hotel complexes. In Penang, campaigners successfully foiled a Berjaya attempt to turn the forested water catchment of the island into a leisure and golfing complex, and under heavy public pressure, state officials were obliged to reject the project. However, despite protests, Berjaya is going ahead with another controversial tourism development on the island of Pulau Redang, one of the world's best marine parks, with magnificent coral reefs and mangroves. The development, which has repeatedly violated conditions imposed by Malaysia's Department of the Environment, has already destroyed large areas of mangrove, caused severe soil erosion and massively increased sedimentation in the lagoons.

The Berjaya group also has timber operations in the Solomon Islands, where rampant logging has spiralled completely out of control, jumping from 300,000 cubic metres in 1991 to over 700,000 cubic metres by 1993. This year it may top 1.3 million cubic metres, according to a World Bank study, which estimates that at this rate the Solomons will have exhausted their forests within eight years.

In July 1994 one of Berjaya's senior executives was forced to leave the Solomons for trying to bribe a senior government official in order to get a concession. The official remarked that the incident:

> only highlighted the endemic corruption which surrounds the timber industry in the Solomon Islands. Sadly, this problem has only gotten out of control in the last five or six years, a period which coincides with the big influx of foreign timber companies.

Malaysia's foremost environmental organization, Sahabat Alam Malaysia, in a letter to the Guyanese President dated 19 August 1994, urged Dr Jagan to maintain the freeze on concession hand-outs. 'We are indeed shocked to hear that many of the companies seeking concessions in Guyana are the same responsible for destructive logging and illegal business practices in several South-East Asian countries, including Malaysia, Papua New Guinea, the Solomon Islands and Vanuatu... These timber companies have recklessly over-exploited forests in several countries, creating severe social, environmental and political problems.'

Guyana also has reason to be concerned about the credentials of the Prime Group, which is alleged to have close links to Rimbunan Hijau, another Sarawakian company. Rimbanun Hijau already controls an estimated 2.5 million acres of forest in Sarawak and some 7.5 million acres in Papua New Guinea. As logging has declined in Sarawak, Rimbunan Hijau has diversified, clearing forests for large-scale oil palm plantations and further displacing indigenous communities from their traditional lands.

Rimbunan Hijau also controls between sixty and eighty per cent of timber exports from Papua New Guinea, where social and environmental problems have been the cause of repeated scandals. In 1993 Papua New Guinea community development organizers made a public declaration to the Commonwealth Forestry Conference describing the operations of Malaysian companies as 'rape and robbery'. Most of the operations are illegal and characterized by 'massive corruption in the issue of timber permits, failure to monitor exports and failure to control visas and working permits'.

PNG Government officials have also been outspoken and have accused two Malaysian timber companies of bribing 109 members of parliament to support an amendment to a new Forestry Act that would have allowed the companies to acquire more logging concessions. Like many other loggers in Papua New Guinea, Rimbunan Hijau has managed to make a shining profit from its logging operations despite recording huge accumulated losses in PNG. These creative tax avoidance measures allow RH and many of its 24 known subsidiaries registered in PNG to cream the country of its choicest timbers while Papua New Guinea gains hardly any benefits.

The official Commission of Inquiry into the timber trade in Papua New Guinea, carried out in 1990 by Judge Thomas Barnett, highlighted the destructive effect of the foreign logging companies operating there and concluded that:

It would be fair to say, of some of these companies, that they are now roaming the countryside with the self-assurance of robber barons; bribing politicians and leaders, creating social disharmony and ignoring laws in order to gain access to, rip out, and export the last remnants of the province's timber. These companies are fooling the landowners and making use of corrupt, gullible, and

> unthinking politicians. It downgrades Papua New Guinea's sovereign status that such rapacious foreign exploitation has been allowed to continue with such devastating effects to the social and physical environment, and with so few positive benefits. [27]
>
> **Another member of the Prime Group, Turama Forest Industries Pty Ltd which operates in Papua New Guinea has been found to be in serious breach of the terms of its concession licence, of failing to comply with forestry regulations and causing serious environmental degradation. In 1991, the company's operation was suspended for breach of contract and the company has been accused of transfer-pricing to avoid payment of taxes.**

A second controversial operation is Demerara Timbers, which controls about half a million hectares on the Middle Essequibo and Upper Demerara. Although full details of the contract establishing this operation have never been made public, the company has advertized the generous fiscal incentives that it was able to secure from the government (including a five-year tax holiday) in order to attract foreign investors.

Ownership of Demerara Timbers has been something of a mystery for much of its operation. The initial buyers, British financier Lord Beaverbrook with his colleague, Rupert Galliers-Pratt, paid US$16 million to acquire the original concession and the associated mill from the parastatal, Demerara Woods Ltd, by means of a shell company called Timber Holdings of the Cayman Islands, which Beaverbrook and Galliers-Pratt claimed was underwritten by their companies, Beaverbrook Investments of Switzerland and the Devanebro Foundation of Liechtenstein. After only a short time the company was passed on to the United Dutch company in a deal whereby Beaverbrook and Galliers-Pratt retained a fifty per cent share in Demerara Timbers, while United Dutch agreed to capitalize the company with an additional US$40 million. However, owing to financial problems back in Europe, United Dutch went into receivership. Bids were solicited for Demerara Timbers and among those interested was the Commonwealth Development Corporation, which looked into the possibility of buying the company with additional capital from the World Bank's private-sector arm, the International Finance Corporation. The deal was not concluded and Demerara Timbers limped through the following years, dogged by rumours of impending buyouts by Malaysian investors. Finally, in 1995, the company was bought out by the Singapore-based Prime Group, which is made up of a group of South East Asian businessmen who took over the ailing import-export firm Inchcape in the late 1980s.

Two years earlier, the Guyana Forestry Commission had opened negotiations with this same group of investors to lease some 600,000 hectares of forest in the Middle Mazaruni. Calling themselves Mazaruni Forest Industries Ltd

(MFIL), the consortium was reported to include companies such as BP Batu Ampar Wood Industries of Indonesia, Turama Forest Industries Pty Ltd of Papua New Guinea, Forest Management Services of Singapore and the SK Timber Corporation of Malaysia. At the same time, a Canadian company, Buchanan Forest Industries Ltd, was reported to be keen to open up a 1.4 million-hectare concession in the Berbice area.[28]

Malaysian interests were also thought to be behind the operations of Caribbean Resources Ltd, owned by CLICO. Newspapers reported that CLICO had closed a US$150 million deal with another Singapore-based company, Forest Marketing Services, to supply Guyanese timber to the Philippines, Korea and US. In December 1993, funded by the Barama Company, President Jagan made a special tour of the capitals of South East Asia, China and Japan to encourage further 'foreign direct investment' and 'South-South cooperation'. The results became apparent in January 1994 with news of yet another impending deal with Leeling Timbers, a company jointly owned by the Leeling Timber Group of Malaysia and the Hyundai Wood Company Ltd of South Korea, for 1.2 million hectares. Leeling announced plans to invest US$60 million in logging and veneer and furniture production in Guyana, with the aim of producing for the Caribbean, North American and European markets, taking advantage of lower tariff barriers due to the CARICOM and Lomé trade agreements. The same month, Malaysian billionaire, Vincent Tan, visited the country and indicated that his company, Berjaya Sdn Bhd, was also interested in a timber concession in the extreme south of the country.

The trend set in motion by the World Bank and IMF's structural adjustment reforms appeared to have spiralled out of control. In line with donor prescriptions on the need to offer fiscal incentives to encourage foreign investment, foreign companies were able to secure extraordinarily beneficial contracts, which include tax holidays, minimal royalty payments and the right to export unprocessed timbers. Concern at this trend was sharpened by the fact that the majority of the new investors were Asian companies which, having exhausted the forests of South East Asia, were moving west, bringing with them their capital, second-hand machinery, labour force and marketing connections.

The process is startlingly apparent to anyone visiting the Barama Company in the North West District. There, the whole operation is run by a Korean businessman, the actual timber extraction is managed by Filipino logging operators, while the tractors are driven by indigenous Iban, a Dayak people of Sarawak, thus symbolically recapitulating the global 'blitzkrieg' of the tropical logging industry, which, primarily to service the huge market in East Asia, has in turn logged out the forests of the Philippines and Borneo before moving on to the New World.

Logging Concessions

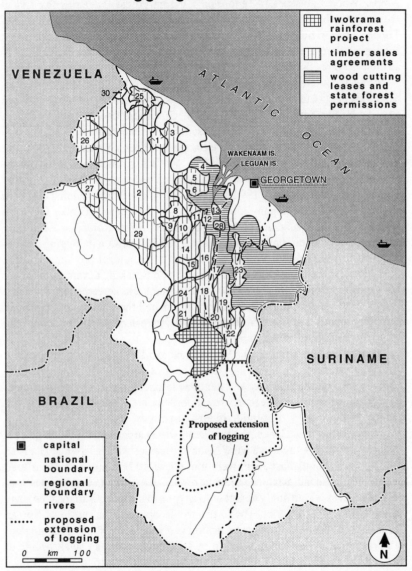

Table 1: Major Forestry Concessions in Guyana

Date	License Holder	Map
01/90	Amazon Caribbean Guyana Ltd.	1
04/91	Barama Company Ltd.	2
02/90	A. Mazaharally & Sons	3
01/88	Quan/Vergenoegen Sawmill Ltd.	4
06/85	A. Mazaharally & Sons	5
04/85	Toolsie Persaud Ltd.	6
07/85	Guyana Saw Mills (SS Rahaman)	7
01/91	Willems Timber Trading Ltd.	8
04/85	Toolsie Persaud Ltd.	9
09/85	A. Mazaharally & Sons	10
10/85	Willems Timber Trading Ltd.	11
10/85	Willems Timber Trading Ltd.	12
02/85	N. Sawh	13
04/89	Caribbean Resources Ltd(CLICO)	14
11/89	Interior Forest Industries	15
03/85	Interior Forest Industries	16
04/90	N. Sawh	17
02/91	Demerara Timbers Ltd.(Prime Group)	18
03/91	Demerara Timbers Ltd.(Prime Group)	19
03/91	Demerara Timbers Ltd.(Prime Group)	20
03/91	Demerara Timbers Ltd.(Prime Group)	21
05/91	UNAMCO (Case/Berjaya)	22
08/85	Mondeen	23
01/92	ALGLAS (Alan Glasgow Ltd.)	24
02/93	Case Timbers/Berjaya	25
02/93	Case Timbers*	26
04/93	Makapa Woods	27
03/93	Tony Parsaram	28
03/93	Mazaruni Forest Industries Ltd.**	29
06/93	Da Silva	30

*Relinquished in favour of takeover of UNAMCO concession
** Relinquished in favour of DTL concessions, now sought by Buchanan Forest Products
Note that these data are compiled from unofficial sources and are not considered to be fully accurate. Official information of this kind is not publicly available.

Foreign loggers are not the only irresponsible operators in the country. Few, if any, Guyanese loggers are investing in forest management, almost none have proper management plans based on inventories of the timber in their concessions. Most practise what is called 'high-grading', the extraction of only the choicest timbers (mainly greenheart), leaving behind depleted forests that invite re-entry and the subsequent extraction of second grades of timber.

By early 1993, unofficial data suggested that the area of State Forest leased out to concessionaires had increased to some 7.1 million hectares, about eighty per cent of the State Forests. In addition, it was estimated that there were approximately 374 SFPs, comprising a further 1.1 million hectares concentrated in the Demerara, Berbice and Corentyne areas. Most of this timber was being processed by the 72 small-scale mills that had been licensed.[29] Illegal timber cutting was also on the increase, the lumber being rapidly processed by so-called 'sprinters', small-scale portable saws which move around from one timber area to another.

Small-scale operators using chainsaws have also become a problem. Although they provide an important service in providing rough lumber to the domestic market – and help to keep down the price which can otherwise be maintained at an inflated level by the small cartel of timber operators – most of their operations are unregulated, poorly managed and often illegal. According to the Guyana Forestry Commission, the chainsaw operators, whose trade has few overheads and becomes profitable after a mere two weeks of work, commonly cut immature trees, enter the residual stands of other concessionaires and work out otherwise inaccessible areas that act as important biological reserves. In attempting to crack down on these operations, the GFC has been fining an average of ten operators per week. There have been so many chainsaw operators seeking State Forest Permissions that virtually all available areas have been handed out. It is clear that the whole forestry sector is out of control.[30] The new deals being cut with foreign companies now extend the logging into the very south of the country, outside classified State Forests.

Voices of Protest
By 1993 Guyanese and international NGOs began to speak out loudly against the situation. They insisted that Guyana stood to lose more from these irregularities than just a fair financial return. There were already indications that the kind of social and environmental impacts witnessed in South East Asia were being repeated in Guyana: alienation of indigenous peoples from their lands, unsustainable logging, destroyed or degraded habitats. Many of the companies moving into Guyana were the very same ones in conflict with indigenous peoples in Sarawak, Papua New Guinea and the Solomons. Perhaps most worrying,

Guyana's tentative steps towards a more liberal political order threatened to be derailed by the cronyism and corruption endemic in the logging industry elsewhere.

Accordingly in January 1994, Guyanese NGOs, including the Amerindian Peoples Association, the Guyana Human Rights Association, the Guyanese Council of Churches as well as trade unions, backed by many international environmental and human rights organizations, called for a freeze on the handing out of logging concessions. The message was reinforced by a short visit to Guyana by Greenpeace's flagship vessel at the invitation of the APA. The call was further echoed by Guyana's Forest Producers Association, representing the domestic timber industry, which argued that the tax breaks handed out to foreign investors placed them at an unfair disadvantage.[31] In June 1996 Toni Williams of the Forest Producers Association reiterated this position to the World Commission on Forests and Sustainable Development in Costa Rica.

Guyana is in the unique position of still having its tropical rainforests intact and should be learning from others' mistakes but it is not. The Government of Guyana is trying to solve the country's immediate fiscal, economic, social and political conflicts elsewhere in society by inviting foreign multinationals into the forest sector. Foreign investors in forestry and mining are given incentives that national producers do not enjoy and there is no way that the national producers can compete in this unbalanced situation.

The immediate monetary gain for Guyana by inviting multinationals to the country is creating havoc for the national producers. National producers are told that, if they are uneconomical they must get out of the business and make way for foreign investors. In fact the President has announced that they were lined up.

The Government, after referring to the levels of forest revenue collection in other tropical forest countries, has increased the royalties and acreage fees to punitive levels without any consideration of the present state of the industry in Guyana, the market conditions or the unique characteristics of Guyana's Forests. These increases have taken away the last possible avenues the national producers have to generate capital for upgrading the local industry which suffered severely from lack of foreign exchange in the past two decades.

Most of the national producers have put their companies on the market in the hope of settling their debts and getting out of the business before it becomes too late. Presently we are looking at 20,000 dependents in the industry, 10,000 of whom depend on the national producers for their livelihood.

111

Guyana needs to look at the quality of its forests and create its own systems that have so far been sustainable. The forest management planning process outlines a 100% inventory of all commercial species, the financial costs for which must be borne by the producers. Nationals find this economically impossible and the pressures on them from all sides will result in the demise of the local industry, perhaps this is the 'hidden agenda'. National producers look for evidence that will prove otherwise.

NGO Statement to the Caribbean Group for Cooperation in Economic Development

The CGCED needs to recognise that the donor community shares a major part of the responsibility for the critical situation of Guyana's interior forests, rivers and peoples. Guyana remains in a parlous financial situation, burdened by a massive foreign debt and subject to heavy pressure from the donor community to privatise its institutions and open up the country to foreign investment. The result is that the country is hastily liquidating its natural resource base before an adequate regulatory structure is in place to ensure both proper financial returns and socially and environmentally sound management. We are therefore calling on the CGCED and the Government of Guyana to come up with a constructive solution to this problem.

On the one hand the Government of Guyana should be required to provide undertakings to:

1. Halt the hand out of further logging concessions, while freezing all those new areas presently under negotiation.
2. Establish a Commission of Enquiry to look into the activities of the timber industry as a whole.
3. Halt the hand out of further mining concessions, while freezing all those new areas presently under negotiation.
4. Renegotiate disadvantageous logging and mining contracts entered into by the previous administration.
5. Carry out an Independent, open and participatory social and environmental assessment of the proposed Boa Vista to Georgetown road and have its findings publicly discussed and adequately acted upon before the road is completed.
6. Establish revised procedures acceptable to the Amerindians' representative institutions to examine and give recognition to Amerindian land claims.
7. Establish forthwith the promised Commission of Enquiry into the claims of the Amerindians affected by the Barama Company Limited.

On the other hand, the donor institutions that are members of the CGCED should, conditional on the above commitments, pledge themselves to:

1. Find means to permanently lessen the burden of debt on Guyana.
2. Revise their current and proposed programmes to promote structural adjustment, privatisation and to encourage 'foreign direct investment' to avoid further negative social and environmental consequences.

There should be no support for further initiatives to develop the interior through aid and FDI until an effective institutional and policy framework is in place within Guyana to control these problems...

The priority for Guyana must be to develop a coherent and responsible policy regarding development in the interior, the institutional capacity to implement it and the regulations to enforce it. It should not be diverted from this task by premature insistence on the establishment of an elaborate protected areas network which risks drawing resources and expertise away from the immediate need which is to secure the rights of local communities and regulate runaway extractive industries.

Amerindian Peoples Association
Guyana Human Rights Associaton
World Rainforest Movement
Friends of the Earth (UK)

The campaigners' concerns were echoed in the national press and struck a chord with the donor agencies, which feared a barrage of domestic criticism if they did not show concern. At the time, the Guyana Forestry Commission barely had five qualified employees and was patently unable to regulate the huge areas of forest already under concession. Led by Britain's Overseas Development Administration (ODA) and supported by World Bank officials, donors informally agreed to express concerns to the government about the hand out of logging concessions, while the ODA made its proposed aid project to strengthen the Forestry Commision conditional on a concession freeze.

Upset by the bad image it was getting abroad, the government agreed and the President's brother-in-law was removed from his position as Chairman of the Board of the Forestry Commission. Some four million hectares of Guyana's forests had, temporarily at least, been saved from the chainsaws.

Under its agreement with the ODA, the Guyanese government gave an undertaking that in order to ensure sound forest management and profitable returns to the Guyanese Exchequer no new timber permits should be issued for a minimum of three years after May 1995 or until the Forestry Commission was able to regulate the industry. Meanwhile, with the technical and financial support of the ODA, the Forestry Commission would attempt to build up the numbers and training of its staff and revise forestry regulations and royalties with the initial aim of establishing control over the nearly nine million hectares of forests already under concession, while making the industry a profitable source of national revenue.

Guyanese foresters had agreed that it would take years before this was achieved and that meanwhile concessionaires were subject to minimal supervision. A study carried out for the World Bank in late 1995 showed that loggers were getting their timber in Guyana extraordinarily cheaply; royalties, taxes and forest fees being paid by loggers in Guyana were some of the lowest in the tropics, less than a tenth of those paid in most African and Asian countries. Moreover, since 1988 fees had been falling in real terms. Royalty rates were at thirty per cent of their former value, while customs duties and acreage fees had fallen by more than ninety per cent in the past decade. On top of this, foreign companies enjoyed 'generous tax breaks and other incentives creating conditions of unfair competition (for local producers)'. With Guyana liquidating its forest assets for little national gain, the report warned: 'This kind of forest mining entails a boom-and-bust pattern of development that can be highly disruptive to employment levels, trade balances, and other factors of macroeconomic stability.'[32]

Pushing Back the Frontier

Nevertheless, pressure from overseas investors to gain access to Guyana's forests has continued and there have been signs that the government may try to find a way around its commitments to the donors. In December 1995, President Jagan announced to the local press that the multilateral development banks had given him the 'green light' to hand out more logging concessions to foreign companies. The statement was promptly denied by the World Bank, but Jagan was astutely preparing the ground to reveal a less threatening deal. After protracted negotiations, permission had been granted to Malaysia's sixth largest conglomerate, the Berjaya Group, to enter into partnership with a local company called Case Timber to take over an existing 90,000 hectares, between the Upper Berbice and the Essequibo, previously held but not exploited by the local firm, Universal Amalgamated Communal Industries Ltd (UNAMCO). Berjaya had promised to inject US$15 million into extracting and processing the timber. At the same time, the deal allowing the Singapore-based Prime Group, masterminded by Alex Ling Lee Soon of Forest Resources Management, to take over Demerara Timbers with its 800,000 hectare concession was announced. In exchange, the Prime Group had been persuaded to relinquish its rights to 600,000 hectares on the Middle Mazaruni, to which it had been granted an anomalous 'exploratory' timber permit.

International Norms Regarding Natural Forest Logging

International norms relating to forestry and sustainable forest management insist on the recognition of indigenous rights.

For example, the World Bank's new Forest Policy places great emphasis on the need to respect forest dwellers' rights and detailed norms are established by the Bank for development projects in indigenous areas. The World Bank's Operational Directive on Indigenous Peoples (OD 4.20) sets out explicit steps for the involvement of indigenous peoples in project planning and the effective recognition of their land rights.

In the same vein, the International Tropical Timber Organization has established 'guidelines for the sustainable management of natural forests'. These also set out specific conditions for involving indigenous peoples in planning and management and specify the need to respect the rights of customary rights holders in accordance with the ILO's Conventions and the standards of the World Bank.

Non-governmental organizations are likewise in the process of developing standards for the acceptable extraction of timber from tropical forests. The Forestry Stewardship Council (FSC), for example, which aims to bring together enlightened loggers, timber merchants, certification organizations, environmentalists, conservation groups and indigenous peoples' organizations, has developed 'principles and criteria' for logging in natural forests, which give a high priority on the need to respect indigenous peoples' customary rights. The aim of the FSC is to establish common criteria for the accreditation of organizations which make independent evaluations of forestry practice in all types of forests to certify whether the timber is being extracted and processed to acceptable standards.

Intergovernmental efforts to 'harmonize' the 'criteria and indicators' of 'sustainable forest management' likewise emphasise the importance of indigenous peoples' rights and 'benefit-sharing'.

The days when logging operations could take place unchallenged on the lands of indigenous peoples without their free and informed consent, as expressed through their own representative institutions, are over.

Then, on 12 March 1996, the national newspaper *Stabroek News*, revealed that the Presidential Adviser for Science, Technology and the Environment, Navin Chandarpal, had been negotiating with the Malaysian company, Solid Timbers Sendirian Bhd, to grant it a 500,000-hectare timber permit in the Upper Corentyne/New River area in the extreme south of the country. This is about half the over one million hectares the company had originally sought even further south in the New River Triangle area – a territory disputed with neighbouring Suriname. Both areas are outside the jurisdiction of the Forestry Commission and way south of the country's existing road network. According to the newspaper report, the government would first pass legislation expanding the area of State Forests and then offer the company an exploratory lease to the area, under which it would carry out a forest inventory and develop a forest management and investment plan. The same report also alleged that two other South East Asian investor groups, including Alex Ling Lee Soon and Vincent Tan's Berjaya Sdn Bhd, were still seeking further areas in the south.

It seems that in order to circumvent its commitment to the agencies not to grant new logging licences, the government has invented a new kind of permit, an 'exploratory lease'. By this means it hopes to keep foreign investors interested and then grant them licences as soon as it can get away with it. The problem with this legal trick is that the category of 'exploratory lease' does not exist in Guyanese law, but granting the loggers Timber Sales Agreements or Wood Cutting Leases would be contrary to the undertaking to the ODA.

Agency officials in Georgetown have been aware of these negotiations for some time and learned that the Canadian timber company, Buchanan Forest Products, is seeking access to the 600,000-hectare concession on the Middle Mazaruni river, the unlogged area recently relinquished by Mazaruni Forest Industries. Buchanan's proposed operations on the Middle Mazaruni would bring it into conflict with a number of villages of Akawaio Indians who have inhabited the area for centuries. Under pressure from Buchanan, which enjoys support from the Canadian High Commission in Georgetown, the government is alleged to be also considering the grant of a three-year 'exploratory permit'.

Buchanan does not have an untarnished reputation back in its home province of Ontario in Canada. A report made for the Canadian Paperworkers Union in 1992 claims that Buchanan:

> has evolved into a company riddled with contradictions. On the one hand, it has a long history of doing all it can to avoid forestry, environmental and labour legislation. On the other hand, as it has grown, the Buchanan group of companies has become more mainstream.[33]

The report details how Buchanan has successfully fought to reduce labour costs and has extravagantly logged forests to maximize profits with little regard for damage to residual timber stands and little concern for timber wastage. It also alleges that Buchanan has used strongarm tactics – threatening to close mills – to pressure politicians into granting it access to forests. Of particular relevance to Guyana, the report highlights how the company thrived on lax government controls, reaping financial benefits while passing on the social and environmental costs to others.

The report alleges that the company was able to avoid prosecution for violating environmental and forest management regulations thanks to close connections with senior politicians in the environment ministry. Tracing the company's history, it reveals how *laissez-faire* and political connections allowed Buchanan to get away with repeated violations of the Crown Timber Act, especially during the 1960s, 1970s and early 1980s. In recent years, however, due to growing public concern for the environment, supervision has tightened and compliance has been more carefully enforced, obliging Buchanan to toe the line.

Despite improved compliance with forest management practices, Buchanan has nevertheless managed to keep costs low, mainly by defying trade unions and avoiding obligations to its employees:

> Buchanan's track record in labour relations has steadily deteriorated from the late 1970s and throughout the 1980s. Buchanan's defiance of union agreements, its avoidance of mandated employee benefits and treatment of contract labour in woodlands are notorious.[34]

In August 1996, the Guyana Information Service revealed that, in fact, the government intends to hand out four of these controversial exploratory permits to foreign companies. Buchanan would get its 600,000 hectares in the Mazaruni and, in addition, three Malaysian companies, Berjaya Sdn Bhd, Solid Timbers Sendirian Bhd, and Kwitaro Investments Inc, would get exploratory permits south of the present limits of State Forests. Rumours have continued to circulate that Leeling Timber is still negotiating for a concession. The additional area would be important to Berjaya which already has control of the UNAMCO/ Case Timbers concession on the Upper Berbice. The new extension to its area will justify its costly investment in a new saw mill at Kwakwani to be linked by a new 65-kilometre road to its concession and may encourage the company to also set up a plywood mill.

To legalize this process, the government announced that it would pass new laws, one to extend the area of State Forests under the GFC's jurisdiction and the second defining the processes and conditions under which exploratory permits could be issued. Astonishingly, this whole process was being facilitated by Britain's ODA, which was not only nodding the process through but even drafted the laws.

British NGOs were outraged and questioned the British government on how it could justify handing out additional forest to foreign companies when the GFC was still incapable of controlling existing concessions, revenue from logging

117

remained minimal and considering that no progress whatsoever had been made in first securing Amerindian lands. In November 1996 the NGOs wrote to the British Government pointing out that:

...the primary mandate of the ODA is the alleviation of poverty in developing countries. Yet we here have a case where the ODA, subsequent to undertaking a study which shows clearly that Amerindians are amongst the poorest sectors of Guyanese society, with serious health and educational problems which are being aggravated by unregulated logging, is not only ignoring their interests but is instead promoting the interests of foreign logging corporations from Malaysia and Canada.

Although pressure from foreign companies to enter Guyana remains intense, there are doubts as to whether it is as profitable as the Asian companies, familiar with the rich Dipterocarp forests of South East Asia, believe. Indeed, there have been signs that the finances of the generously subsidized Barama Company are less than healthy. In 1995, the company subjected itself to a major review of its management and administration and brought in personnel from a part-owned US company of Samling's based in Arizona, Sterling Pacific Assets, a subsidiary of Sun Chance Capital, to reorganize the company's chaotic stock control and transportation systems. Barama is keen to maintain the impression that it is scarcely making a profit from its activities and has made data available to substantiate the case.[35]

The implications of these findings are far from clear. On the one hand, some hope that foreign companies will withdraw from Guyana as the promised bonanza turns out to be illusory. On the other hand, it could imply that pressure on the forests will intensify as loggers recklessly liquidate all forest stocks to ensure an immediate and adequate return on their investment. The low profitability of Guyana's forests may result in their destruction.

Perhaps one of the most disturbing aspects of the pillage of forest resources is that it is bringing very little gain to the Guyanese economy. A study carried out by the World Resources Institute found that government income from logging activities in 1995 totalled less than US$1 million and concluded that 'the promise of large future earnings from investments in logging may be little more than fantasy'.[36]

In addition to logging, Guyana has also moved to increase exploitation of non-timber forest products. In 1987, 50,000 hectares of forests in the North West District were granted in a thirty-year lease to a French-owned consortium, Amazon Caribbean (Guyana) Ltd (AMCAR) to extract hearts of the manicole palm (*Euterpe oleracea*), a multi-stemmed palm which grows abundantly in the coastal forests. Since setting up its canning factory in 1988, the company has been employing some 140 people in processing 27,000 palm hearts a day, which are exported mainly to France where they sell as a luxury food item. The company relies on a floating population of mainly Amerindian cutters who work the coastal forests in canoes extracting the palm hearts and selling them, through agents who take a ten per cent mark-up, to the company.

Two serious problems have emerged with the process. In the first place, the palm heart extraction is almost certainly not sustainable. Cutters are extracting the hearts of a much less robust species, *Euterpe precatoria*, which unlike the manicole palm does not regenerate from suckers and which is probably being gradually driven to local extinction by the trade. AMCAR is also operating on the assumption that the manicole palm itself can regenerate in five years, but as one study carried out for the World Conservation Union's species survival commission, has concluded:

> There is no scientific evidence to support this assumption. After two or three harvests of all the large stems, a particular cluster may decline in vigor and die off. Since the harvest of mature stem removes a source of seeds... it is possible that accessible areas could suffer a decline in manicole palms over a 10-15 year period and threaten the sustainability of the extraction practices. Sharp declines in the quantity of manicole seeds in the wild could also have a negative impact on bird and fish populations that depend upon the fruit for food.[37]

Over-harvesting of palm hearts has already depleted mature stems in many areas. For example, villagers around Red Hill report supplying 10,000 to 15,000 hearts every week to AMCAR and the palm has now been exhausted.[38] Cutters and their families have abandoned their villages and dispersed into distant forests to seek out unexploited stands of palms.[39]

The second controversial aspect of this trade relates to the very low wages and benefits gained by the cutters who can expect to earn as little as US$3 for a full day's work. Amerindians complain of the low pay and express concern that their children are unable to get a schooling if they accompany their parents on collecting expeditions. They also claim that since they are paid as piece-workers they get no compensation in case of injuries sustained while collecting the palm hearts.[40]

Amerindians and Logging

Serious problems have arisen when mining and logging concessions have been handed out with little regard for pre-existing Amerindian claims and even titles. For example, the Barama Company's concession not only encloses four communities with titles but also overlaps the Carib reserve established in 1977.

119

It also encloses a large number of other homesteads scattered along the main rivers – Kaituma, Barima, Barama, Cuyuni – which likewise lack land titles.

In response to the pressure of international environmental organizations which pointed out that the parent company of Barama – the Sarawak-based Samling Timbers Sdn Bhd – had a long and continuing history of conflict with indigenous peoples in the area of its logging operations in Borneo, Barama contracted the forestry consultancy, the Edinburgh Centre for Tropical Forests, both to oversee the implementation of the forestry practice and to carry out an 'independent' social and environmental impact assessment of the company's future operations.

The ECTF visited the area in early 1993 and made its report public in September. It noted that 'some Amerindians [actually the majority within the concession] live in areas not legally designated as Amerindian land'.[41] The report also identified some potentially serious negative impacts of Barama's operations: the reduction or elimination of traditional food, shelter and other forest resources of local communities; increased hunting pressure, wildlife trade and illegal timber felling; increased settlement and shifting cultivation; increased mining, the likely major impact of the road network; friction with local residents; many potential social conflicts over jobs, markets, prices and split communities; pollution of the Orenoque log pond and contamination from spills of wood preservatives, insecticides and fungicides; culture shock for communities in remote areas; disruption of traditional subsistence economies; introduction of diseases by incomers, especially miners, possibly including venereal diseases and AIDS.

On the positive side, the ECTF found that while most Amerindians interviewed lacked information about the project, they expected benefits in terms of employment, improved standards of living, better health services and improved schooling. Although the ECTF found some of the Amerindians expectations to be 'high and unrealistic' – and thereby might lead to conflict over job opportunities – they did expect most of these benefits to accrue to at least some of those affected.

To mitigate the potential negative impacts of the Barama operation, the ECTF recommended *inter alia* that the company recruit a community liaison officer, regulate the use of roads, appoint an Amerindian as an 'Amerindian Liaison Officer', establish a local committee to advise on interactions with Amerindian groups in the concession, the demarcation of the boundaries of Amerindian land titles and the inclusion of Amerindian areas on Barama maps. Improved community health care, educational facilities and the promotion of community development initiatives were also recommended.

Some of these negative consequences have already begun to show up. Amerindian residents on the Port Kaituma-Matthews Ridge road have complained to the Minister of Amerindian Affairs about the pollution of their waters downstream of the Orenoque log pond, which they claim is causing them to fall sick. They also complain that they are being prevented from practising their traditional form of rotational agriculture as this encroaches on the company's concession and that some residents have even been resettled out of the logging concession to the roadside.[42]

Ever since the Barama deal was announced, the APA has been strongly critical of the fact that the concession does not respect Amerindian land rights and that there was no consultation with Amerindians in the decision to grant a logging concession in the area. Since March 1993, the organization has repeatedly called on the Minister for Amerindian Affairs to review the contract and, faced with stonewalling tactics, threatened to call for an international boycott of Guyanese timber products unless the Minister took decisive action. It was only in September 1993, after the APA, its patience finally exhausted, did call for such a boycott that the Minister acceded to its requests and promised to institute a Commission of Enquiry to review the Amerindians' claims and the Barama contract. This Commission has never been established despite repeated further calls from the APA, other national NGOs and international supporters.

The APA appears to have a strong case. Not only are the historical records of an Amerindian presence in the area unambiguous – they have inhabited the area since first contact with the Dutch in the sixteenth century[43] – but recommendations of special measures to secure at least some of their lands have been made repeatedly in the past, notably by the Peberdy Commission of 1946 and the Amerindian Lands Commission of 1969.

Moreover the contract between the Barama Company and the Guyanese government charges the government with responsibility for maintaining good relations between the company and the Amerindians and makes a specific provision for the 'Reservation of Areas' for various purposes. Article D of the Schedule attached to the Timber Sales Agreement stipulates that the government, as the 'Grantor', 'shall have the right to propose at any time to the Grantee [Barama] to reserve for silvicultural, environmental **or any other purpose**, any or such lands within the boundaries of the [concession] area... as he [the Grantor] considers to be more suited for purposes other than timber production...' (emphasis added).

Given the lack of government action to resolve the issue, in late 1994 the APA and the Forest Peoples Programme of the World Rainforest Movement carried out a joint survey of the Amerindians in the Barama concession. It transpired that many of the hundreds of Amerindians interviewed during the course of the week had never heard of the Barama Company. Most were indignant to learn that they were now living within a forestry concession being exploited by a foreign logging company. As one Amerindian resident noted bitterly: 'so we just live on their concessions now. We're like refugees. We have no place.' Very many of the communities were explicit and vocal in demanding that their land rights be secured. Said Isolina Thomas of Baramita:

> We really want our land. We really want to live here and carry on our farming and hunting. We don't want anyone to take it away. The land belongs to us to farm and for the men to hunt. We don't want it taken away by any foreigners. Our numbers are increasing and we need our land for our youngsters to farm and to hunt in in the future.

The survey also revealed details of how the small Amerindian community of Orenoque, established as a cooperative nearby to Port Kaituma under the Burnham administration in 1966, was forcibly relocated to make way for the Barama Company's log pond and office complex. Under the Burnham government, the community had been given 100 acres of land divided into 25-acre lots. Community members planted quite extensive areas with fruit trees – mangoes, oranges, pears, golden apple etc – as well as other areas with coffee bushes. The community expanded gradually to include some nine families or about sixty or seventy people. In November 1991 they were evicted from this settlement to make way for Barama. The residents claim that they were promised that the company would rebuild their houses elsewhere but some of them refused to move out. One resident alleges that Barama threatened to flatten her wooden house with a bulldozer if she did not dismantle it.

The people were then resettled at 'One Mile' out on the edge of town. They have been settled on small lots, much smaller than their original area, and which they claim they do not have title to. These areas are patently not adequate for their present needs or future development. They claim that they were promised five acres each but that these areas have not been provided. They complain that they have received no compensation for the loss of their fruit trees. No fruit trees have been replanted in their new lots. They also allege that their graveyard was desecrated and in one part of the graveyard bodies were accidentally bulldozed up and reburied in a single grave. The graveyard area was, it is alleged, hastily fenced off just before a visit by a prospective buyer, the US company Georgia-Pacific.

The buildings that have been provided for the resettled residents are very small and of very poor quality. They are unpainted and already visibly rotting (after only three years) and the foundations are weakening. They lack guttering and only one of the houses has a water supply, those on the other side of the road being without a standpipe.

Logging Amerindian Land

Under Guyanese law, forests on private lands, including those titled to Amerindian communities, are not subject to the control of the Guyana Forestry Commission and no special laws or regulations exist to regulate felling. As a result, timber companies are free to enter into formal or informal agreements with Amerindian communities without any kind of supervision or control and with some unfortunate consequences. Among those involved in this controversial trade is the Barama Company, which has found that to produce high-grade plywood it requires certain quality timbers not readily available on its concession. For the past few years, therefore, Barama has been buying an average of 2,400 cubic metres of timber every month from outside its concession, constituting 12-15 per cent of the company's supplies. Up to 1,000 cubic metres of this timber has been coming from the Amerindian community of Orealla, a mixed Amerindian village of Warau and Arawak on the Corentyne.[44]

Studies carried out by the Amerindian Research Unit show that this trade has had serious impacts. In the first place, the timber has been extracted at a far higher rate than it is regenerating, resulting in the virtual elimination of marketable timbers within a few years. Profits have been much smaller than anticipated by the villagers, as they have not taken into account the high costs of transporting logs to the point of sale or the delays in making sales and paying off loans. Like mining, community logging has taken men away from subsistence activities and as a result the family diet has worsened and women and children have suffered. The deals with the logging companies have also divided the community, as individual profit-seeking has been at odds with the community's long-term interests of maintaining the forests intact.[45]

In view of this and similar experiences, both the APA and the Guyana Organization of Indigenous Peoples have concurred that regulation should be developed to control commercial timber harvesting on Amerindian lands.[46]

The survey also heard complaints about the low wages paid by Barama. They get their labour 'as cheap as they can get it' one resident said in Port Kaituma. Another resident of Matthews Ridge concluded: 'Where they come from they just treat people as cheap labour. So that's how they treat us, we are just cheap labour to them.'[47]

Many of the other major concessions are also plagued by similar land conflicts with Amerindian communities. Akawaio on the Demerara are in conflict

123

with the Mondeen and Demerara Timbers concessions. As Salome Henry, an Akawaio Indian from Malali, reported to the national 'Amirang' in 1994:

> Both communities lack legal rights to the land occupied for thousands of years. Representations were made to the former government as well as to the present Administration but so far responses have been mere promises. Residents want to resolve the land issue as early as possible. Malali requests land on both banks of the Demerara River to a depth of 2 1/2 miles on each bank, from Wallaba to Comaparoo. Great Falls wants 2 1/2 miles depth on both banks of the Demerara River from Comaparoo to Cannister Falls.[48]

The legal situation of Amerindians in granted forest concessions is weak. According to a strict reading of the law, Amerindians are not allowed to cultivate in granted forests and may also be prohibited from hunting and fishing by the concessionaires if the latter so wish. Both Barama and Demerara Timbers restrict hunting within their concession. As Anna Benjamin and Laureen Pierre of the ARU point out:

> Some communities, of course, have no option but to pursue their livelihood on granted State Land or forest because this is where they were living when the Timber Sales Agreement or Wood Cutting Lease was signed. Such is the position with some of the Caribs in the Barama concession, who have no legal rights, other than possibly hunting and fishing, and who are therefore dependent on the good graces of the Company to be allowed to pursue their traditional life-style.[49]

In sum, in the past two decades foreign timber companies have gained control over as much as six million hectares of Guyana's forests and are actively negotiating for between two and four million hectares more. The domestic industry, which still controls about three million hectares, is under heavy pressure to sell out to overseas interests. At the same time, the Amerindians who make up the majority population in the interior, have title to only 800,000 hectares. A very large proportion of these people are landless and extremely poor, yet find the areas they live in taken over for logging. Such is the logic of the development process being promoted by the government in Georgetown and by the international financial institutions that their cries for justice and land are derided as the special pleading of an unworthy minority.

[1] Menezes 1977:16; Benjamin and Pierre 1995
[2] Menezes 1979:xxii
[3] Benjamin and Pierre 1995
[4] Butt Colson 1983; ARU nd
[5] ARU nd:8
[6] Menezes 1979:xxi
[7] Butt Colson 1983
[8] ARU nd
[9] Forbes 1959
[10] Colchester and Lohmann 1990; Hogg 1993:146
[11] Sunderland 1993
[12] Colchester and Lohmann 1990
[13] NFAP 1989
[14] Colchester and Lohmann 1990
[15] Westoby 1987:264-265
[16] Marshall 1990
[17] Colchester 1989
[18] DTE 1992
[19] Reitbergen 1989; Rice and Counsell 1993; Colchester 1993
[20] Westoby 1987; 1989; Colchester 1989; WRM/SAM 1990; Colchester and Lohmann 1990; Marshall 1990; DTE 1992; Rice and Counsell 1993; Johnson and Cabarle 1993; Colchester 1993
[21] Poore 1989
[22] NFAP 1989:21
[23] World Bank 1993a:45
[24] Stabroek News, 29 October 1993
[25] NFAP 1989:ii
[26] ECTF 1993:37
[27] Barnett 1990:5
[28] Catholic Standard, 17 October 1993; Stabroek News, 22 October 1993; Sunday Chronicle, 24 October 1993
[29] NFAP 1989
[30] Marshall 1994:83
[31] NGO statement to the Caribbean Group for Cooperation in Economic Development, Washington DC, 6-10 June 1994
[32] Flaming 1995
[33] Frood and Sanders 1992
[34] Frood and Sanders 1992
[35] Sizer 1996:42
[36] Sizer 1996:3
[37] Johnson 1994:6
[38] Forte 1995:50
[39] Forte 1995:50
[40] Forte 1995
[41] ECTF 1993:iv
[42] Interview with Emelda Jones, 17 October 1993; Stabroek News, 21 October 1993
[43] Gravesande 1992
[44] Sizer 1996:39,51
[45] Henfrey 1995; Sizer 1996
[46] Catholic Standard, 9 April 1995
[47] Colchester and MacIntyre 1994
[48] Cited in Forte 1994:69
[49] Benjamin and Pierre 1995

CHAPTER 7
AMERINDIAN SURVIVAL

'We were told that this was not Amerindian land but Crown land, but by what right our ancestral lands were removed from our ancient homeland we do not know. We are an unconquered people and have never heard that our forefathers signed away their rights by any treaty with the colonial rulers. Today the miners dominate and despoil a large area as if it were their own, and at Imbaimadai we are often treated as if we are strangers, in the place that was, not long ago, a strong and revered village with its central church and extensive farmlands. By what right? What is our offence?' Akawaio community of Chinowieng, 1994[1]

As outlined in Chapter 1, the colonial state, which had at first relied on its Amerindian allies to survive, gradually dispensed with their support, replacing Amerindian labour with African slaves, the trade in Amerindian forest products with plantation produce, and the support of the Amerindian 'bush police' with its own militias. By the 1840s, the colonial state no longer needed the Amerindians, except as a labour force for the growing gold, *balata* and timber industries.

With the economy and decision-making dominated by the concerns of the coastal plantocracy, the colonial authorities had little time and interest, and even less money, to spend on Amerindian welfare. In line with Victorian policies towards the poor in Britain, the Amerindians were thus entrusted to the care of charitable enterprises and religious missions, which from the 1830s began to expand their operations throughout the interior. As historian Sister Mary Noel Menezes puts it, the Amerindian communities were seen as 'fields ripe for harvest'.[2] Desrey Fox and George Danns, who carried out a study of the heavily missionized Akawaio of the Demerara, describe the disruptive cultural impacts that the missions had, imposing western values and prohibiting traditional marriage practices and rituals. The new religious leaders asserted their authority and undermined traditional leadership systems. Some studies have suggested that the formalized, closed marriages imposed by the missions led to an increase in extra-marital affairs, family conflicts and wife-beating. Chistianization was seen by many colonials as compensation to the Amerindians for the takeover of their land. In Menezes' words, the 'Amerindians were offered heaven for their earth'.[3]

Even the Wai Wai in the extreme south of the country were not spared. Once air transport made access to the interior more feasible in the 1950s, evangelical missionaries came south to rescue the Amerindians' souls and introduce them to Christian mores, decent clothes, modern dwellings and western knowledge. Such missionaries had scant respect for traditional healers and belief systems, judging them to be 'savage sorcerers' practising 'witchcraft' with 'superstitions' based on 'fear'.[4]

Reduced to powerlessness and dependency on the missions, the Amerindians were not well placed to object to their status as subjects of colonial jurisdiction.

Indigenous Rights in International Law

Current international law towards indigenous peoples rejects policies of integration and stresses the need to respect 'the aspiration of these peoples to exercise control over their own institutions, ways of life and economic development and to maintain and develop their identities, languages, religions, within the framework of the States in which they live' (International Labour Organization, Convention 169).

What most indigenous people themselves demand is the right to self-determination in accordance with the International Covenants on Civil and Political Rights and on Social, Cultural and Economic Rights. Whereas the ILO's Convention specifically avoids deciding whether or not indigenous peoples have such rights (ILO Convention 169, Article 1.3), the latest draft of the Universal Declaration on the Rights of Indigenous Peoples, being developed by the UN's Human Rights Commission, notes in Article 3:

Indigenous Peoples have the right to self-determination. By virtue of that right, they freely determine their political status and freely pursue their economic, social and cultural development.

International law does clearly accept the right of indigenous peoples to the use and ownership of their traditional lands. Article 11 of ILO Convention 107 of 1957 states:

The right of ownership, collective or individual, of the members of the populations concerned over the lands which these populations traditionally occupy shall be recognised.

The law established the principle that 'aboriginal title' is to be derived from immemorial possession and does not depend on any act of the state. Moreover, as Gordon Bennett's study shows,[5] the Convention considers land to be generic and to include the woods and waters upon it.

Convention 107 also established firm principles regarding the forced relocation of indigenous and tribal peoples. Under article 12 of the Convention, indigenous people cannot be relocated except according to national law for reasons of national security, economic development and their own health. If they are relocated 'as an exceptional measure', they shall be 'provided with lands of quality equal to that of the lands previously occupied by them, suitable to provide for their present needs and future

---

development... Persons thus removed shall be fully compensated for any resulting loss or injury.'

The revised convention, adopted by the ILO in 1989, further elaborates on indigenous rights to land and territories and natural resources. In addition to recognising indigenous peoples' rights to land ownership, Article 14 states that 'measures shall be taken in appropriate cases to safeguard the right of the peoples concerned to use lands not exclusively occupied by them, but to which they have traditionally had access for their subsistence and traditional activities. Particular attention shall be paid to the situation of nomadic peoples and shifting cultivators in this respect.' Article 15 of the Convention also notes:

> The rights of these peoples concerned to the natural resources pertaining to their lands shall be specifically safeguarded. These rights include the right of these people to participate in the use, management and conservation of these resources.

International law also goes some way towards defining how states and outside institutions should go about interactions with indigenous peoples. ILO Convention 169 records in Article 2 and 4 the need to respect and safeguard indigenous peoples' customs and institutions, while Article 6 obliges states to:

> a) consult the peoples concerned, through appropriate procedures and in particular through their representative institutions, whenever consideration is being given to legislative or administrative measures which may affect them directly... [and] c) establish means for the full development of the peoples' own institutions and initiatives, and in appropriate cases provide the necessary resources for this purpose.

International law regarding indigenous people is unique in a number of respects, perhaps the most important being that it recognizes *collective* rights. It thus asserts the authority of the indigenous *group* to own land and other resources, enter into negotiations and regulate the affairs of its members in line with customary laws which may be quite different to national laws. Indigenous peoples are, thus, to some extent recognized as autonomous seats of power within the state. Outsiders dealing with indigenous peoples need to recognize the political nature of their interaction with them.

Furthermore, the colonial state never chose to ask itself whether it did indeed have the right to assert sovereignty over the interior and assume ownership of the Amerindians' customary lands. Yet the British had not made such assumptions in all their other colonies. In New Zealand, the representative of the British Crown signed a treaty with the Maori which was interpreted as an act of cession but which explicitly recognized Maori rights to continue owning their lands and other resources. In Canada, the state continues to justify its control of land and assertion of sovereignty based on rights of conquest and the signing of treaties with Indian 'bands'. In Australia, the British asserted the rights of settlers to take over land, on the basis of a legal fiction, the concept of *terra nullius* (unclaimed lands), which was underpinned by the racist idea that Aborigines were not really people and could not own land because they did not cultivate it. However, the notion of *terra nullius* has been invalidated in the Australian courts and the law now recognises that Aboriginal rights to Crown lands are unextinguished where the claimants can demonstrate immemorial possession.

No such clarity exists for Guyana, by contrast. The colonial regime could not claim rights either of sovereignty or land ownership, based on conquest, cession by treaty or papal bull, yet it asserted sovereignty nonetheless. Nor has the Amerindians' status ever been tested in the Guyanese courts since, either with respect to their land rights or to self-determination. Instead, the colonial state had stealthily assimilated the Amerindians as its subjects and then claimed frontiers against other colonial states, on the basis of extending the protections of British law and order over them.

British law, as it was developed in the colony, assumed – not necessarily correctly – that all lands not already allocated to settlers could be treated as Crown Lands, owned and administered by the colonial power. However, the emerging laws at first conceded a special status to the 'Aboriginal Indians of the colony' by recognizing their 'traditional rights and privileges' to hunt, fish, gather and cultivate wherever they wished on Crown Lands, without need for a special permit.[6] However, as competing interests began to move into the interior these rights were progressively curtailed and, reflecting similar legal changes taking place in India,[7] Amerindians were instead accorded privileges, defined by regulations, to continue their subsistence activities. From 1887, Amerindians were expressly prohibited from cultivating Crown Lands granted to other parties for logging, mining, balata collection or ranching.[8]

Janette Forte, the leading anthropologist of the University of Guyana's Amerindian Research Unit (ARU), shows how low the Amerindians had been brought by that time:

> By the decade of the 1890 census, it was being predicted that the Amerindian race was on its way to extinction. By this date, Amerindians had dropped from a rank on the social hierarchy next to Europeans to one beneath Africans and East Indians, and were effectively excluded from coastal society and its economic structure.[9]

As one colonist wrote at the time:

129

I simply look upon the obliteration of the Indian as inevitable, in short, the realization of DARWIN's theory of the survival of the fittest. At the same time I think it would be well to preserve a few Indians by reservations, &c, as is done in America, just as a curiosity for future generations.[10]

Remarked another:

This race is of little or no social value and their early extinction must be looked upon as inevitable in spite of the sentimental regret of the Missionaries. At the same time it is unnecessary to hasten the process in any way, for in this matter, nature, as ever, is much more gentle than man.[11]

The Amerindians were treated as historical curiosities, and groups of them with 'articles typical for their way of life' were displayed at world exhibitions and fairs.[12]

The terrible effects of interior development on the Amerindians could not be disguised and, under pressure from the church and British humane societies such as the Aborigines Protection Society, a new paternalistic policy was adopted at the turn of the century to provide the Amerindians some protection. Laws passed in 1902 and 1910 allowed the Governor to proclaim any 'unoccupied land' an 'Indian Reservation'. As Anna Benjamin and Laureen Pierre of the ARU remark, 'effectively the autochthonous population became a ward of the Governor-in-Council who had authority to make decisions affecting its welfare.'[13]

Racist stereotyping underlay these laws. 'Half-castes' could be removed from Reservations. As a critical government official wrote half a century later: 'The establishment by the State of coastland Reserves was primarily intended to secure and to protect land holdings in Trust for aborigines of comparatively pure blood.'[14]

By the 1940s, the century-long policy of nominal 'protection' of the Amerindians, based on a notion of the need to maintain their racial distinctiveness, was thoroughly discredited. A national survey carried out for the administration by Peberdy in 1948 revealed that the 15,000 surviving Amerindians were existing in conditions of extreme squalor, ill health, poverty and cultural degeneration. Unpoliced reservations, deprived of services and development assistance, had done next to nothing to protect the Amerindians against the worst effects of exploitation by mining, logging, ranching and wage-labouring in agriculture and balata bleeding.

The report showed that the colonial government was failing dismally to enforce its own laws. No Superintendents of Reservations had been appointed, access to Reservations went unchallenged, young women were being illegally 'inveigled' to Georgetown 'as often as not to end up as streetwalkers', and protections designed to ensure fair employment conditions were largely unenforced. Peberdy accused the administration of a 'laissez-faire' attitude and questioned the priorities of the coastal government which allocated its revenues to meet the claims of coastland colonists, while denying adequate assistance to the colony's autochthonous inhabitants. The shocking report prompted a re-think of the administration's policy.[15]

Integration Policies

World-wide, government policies towards indigenous peoples have varied widely. On the one hand, some state policies, like those pursued until then in Guyana, seek to isolate indigenous people and keep them apart from the national majority, treating them as legal minors and wards of the state to be protected from outsiders by a paternalist administration. On the other hand, in a pattern that became prevalent in the 1930s and 1940s, states developed policies which seek to eradicate indigenous peoples' lifestyles and cultures and integrate them into the national mainstream. In both cases the underlying prejudice is that indigenous peoples are inferior and must either be elevated to a more modern cultural level or kept apart from their superiors. Policies of integration received the sanction of international law in 1957, with the promulgation of the ILO's Convention 107 on Tribal and Indigenous Populations. The conventional wisdom behind this approach was that indigenous peoples were doomed to extinction if they clung to their outmoded ways. They needed to be encouraged to change their ways so that they could join the national mainstream and, in the meantime, remain protected from exploitation.[16]

Oxford anthropologist, Audrey Butt Colson, who has made a careful study of policy towards the Amerindians argues that integration became the keynote of British Guiana government policy in the post-war years. The recommendation of a determining government report circulated in 1948 was that:

> a long range Amerindian Policy be adopted based on the assumption that it is necessary and desirable for these people to gradually *achieve Western Civilization*, and that accordingly all planning should be directed with this object in view.[17]

The policy recognized that it would take time to prepare the 'widely dispersed' groups with 'semi-nomadic tendencies' for civilization and in the meantime certain areas should be set aside for their use, while development schemes were promoted to hasten their integration into the market. The reservations were there to buffer the Amerindians against the rougher side of development. The colonial policy stressed:

> There must be no question of the permanent segregation of these people, and reservations should be looked upon as temporary sanctuaries and Tribal Amerindians should be left alone only until such time as it is considered that they *have reached a standard of civilization* which will enable them to take their place in the general life of the colony.[1]

The policy formally adopted by the colony emphasized that the idea was:

> to cease mollycoddling the Amerindians as though they were Museum Pieces and to give those who so desire the full privileges and responsibilities of citzenship so that they may take their proper place as an equal partner with the other communities in the economic and cultural life of the colony.[19]

The colonial government also had other plans for the interior, however. As we have seen, mining, logging and cattle-ranching were expanding and the government was also considering developing intensive agriculture in the interior. Fruit plantations and agricultural settlements were proposed for the lowlands, while the Pakaraima highlands were considered very suitable for temperate vegetable crops, in high demand in Georgetown and the Caribbean. To fit into this scheme of accelerated interior development, the Amerindians would need to be encouraged to abandon their dispersed residence patterns and concentrate about the new administrative centres, so that they could be easily reached by agricultural extension officers and more easily offered health and educational services. The concentration of the Amerindians around the new centres would also free up land for other interests like logging and mining, and even as hill resorts where coastal residents could travel for holidays.

The colonial administrators felt that the interior was underpopulated and proposed encouraging migration, particularly into the highlands. At various times, areas like the Upper Mazaruni were proposed as locations for settling migrants from St Lucia, Jews from Europe and even 'Assyrians'.

To achieve these ends, a new emphasis was placed on building up an administrative structure in the Amerindian areas. Under revised legislation passed in 1951, reservations were renamed 'Amerindian Districts', to be run by the Department of the Interior, with the Commissioner in Georgetown supported by District Commissioners and District Officers who would live and work in the Amerindian districts.[20] At the same time, in line with Britain's preferred policy of administering native people by indirect rule, the authorities sought to impose a more democratic system of governance on the Amerindian villages. The new centralized settlements were encouraged to elect their Captains who were to be supported in their work by District Councils of elected members. The Captains were to receive a small stipend, a uniform, staff of office and were vested with the powers and immunities of a rural constable. According to the Amerindian Ordinance of 1951, it was 'the duty of every captain to carry out such instructions as may be issued to him by the Commissioner or District Commissioner' and to maintain law and order in his area. The net effect of all these interventions was that the 'Amerindians were to become part of an administrative unformity in which, it transpired, national development was to be paramount.'[21]

The result was the 'administrative annexation' of the Amerindian peoples and their territories,[22] with the express aim of 'merging the remaining Amerindians with the other inhabitants of the country.'[23]

The consequences of these policies were soon to be felt. The entire Upper Mazaruni basin, for example, was designated as an 'Amerindian district' in 1945 and six years later a District Officer was posted to the region to implement the new policy. During the 1950s and 1960s the administration pursued a vigorous policy of 'voluntary' resettlement, encouraging the then highly dispersed Akawaio and Arekuna, who were spread out all over the region up to the very headwaters in small mobile homesteads, to descend to the lower reaches of their creeks and rivers to the new centres, where they could be effectively administered and provided with government services. Administration was shifted from Imbaimadai to Kamarang as a more central and convenient marketing and communications point, with a river stretch suitable for landing amphibious Grumman aircraft and soils considered more suitable for intensive farming and cash-cropping.

In the Imbaimadai area of the Upper Mazaruni, where villages and homesteads were widely scattered through the savannah, the Akawaio were persuaded that as the poor soils of the area would not allow for the intensive agriculture and peanut-farming advocated by the District Officer, they should remove themselves from the region down to a new centralized village. The move was agreed to, after the headman of one of the Imbaimadai villages died, and the community selected a new site at Jawalla. As the District Officer remarked, this consolidation of population 'would be a great help to the administration'.[24] The removal was also convenient as the British colonial administration was at the time considering settling the area upstream of Imbaimadai with refugees and opening the Imbaimadai area itself as a holiday resort. Shortly afterwards in 1959, the very same area that the Amerindians had been encouraged to abandon was dereserved on the grounds of being unused and unoccupied and was gazetted as a mining district.

Many Akawaio feel today that they were unfairly tricked into abandoning their ancestral lands in order to allow others access to the minerals. Some also feel that their old dispersed residence pattern was more ecologically sound than the present concentrated pattern which places heavy pressure on local resources.

Limits of Independence

A remarkable aspect of Guyana's gaining of independence in 1966 was the extent to which the colonial state's integrationist policies went unquestioned and were even reinforced. Indeed, the Independence Agreement itself stated that: 'It is the policy of the Government to assist the Amerindians to the stage where they can, without disadvantage to themselves, be integrated with the rest of the community.' The Forbes Burnham government duly went further than the British in pushing an assimilationist policy. In 1969 the new government did away with the Amerindian Development Committee and replaced it with an Interior Development Committee, which aimed at creating a sense of national unity and national integration in the interior. It was time for the Amerindians to stop feeling Amerindian and start identifying themselves as Guyanese.

The exception to this general rule of continuity with colonial policy was with respect to land. Under the provisions of the Independence Agreement, by which sovereignty was transferred from Britain to the newly independent government of Guyana, it was stipulated that the Amerindians should be granted legal ownership to the lands where they were 'ordinarily resident or settled':

> The Government of British Guiana has decided that the Amerindian should be granted legal ownership or rights of occupancy over areas or reservations or parts there of where any tribe or community of Amerindians is now ordinarily resident or settled and other legal rights, such as rights of passage, in respect of other lands they now by tradition or custom de facto enjoy freedoms and permissions corresponding to rights of that nature. In this context, it is intended that legal ownership shall comprise all rights normally attaching to such ownership. (Annex C, Section L of 1965 Guyana Independence Agreement)

The issue had been forced into the independence negotiations by the Amerindian, Stephen Campbell a Catholic Arawak from Santa Rosa, who had created an 'Amerindian Association' to promote indigenous interests. Campbell was a member of United Force, the right-wing party that had formed an alliance with Forbes Burnham's PNC to unseat Cheddi Jagan, and had been elected to the national legislature in 1957. UF, which enjoyed the support of big business, the Catholic Church and was the strongest vehicle for the Amerindian vote,

134

held the balance of power between the PNC and PPP. To secure Amerindian and UF support, the British and the PNC acceded to Campbell's demands to include provisions for the Amerindians to get their land into the Independence Agreement.[25]

In fulfillment of this legal obligation, an Amerindian Lands Commission was established in 1966 and made a comprehensive, but not exhaustive, review of the Amerindians' land situation and documented indigenous land claims. Behind the scenes, and out of the view of the Amerindians, there were subtle battles over the interpretation of the Independence Agreement. How much land should the Amerindians get? As one British member of the Commission admitted privately:

> In drawing up the terms of reference of the Commission, the PNC legal types pulled a fast one, which the pro-Amerindian UF did not spot in time to have it changed. Boiled down to bare facts, we are to recommend to Government the form of tenure or title to land of those areas *occupied by Amerindians at the time of independence*. This limits areas to house lots, farms and grazing land. With that out of the way, the PNC can go ahead and sell the remaining 70,000 odd square miles of the country or settle the interior with the Youth Corps and pioneer groups Burnham is forming to take over the remaining Amerindian lands which they all are convinced are the most valuable in minerals and agricultural lands in the country. There is also the question of national security. All the borders are peopled with Amerindians and their loyalty to a black government is not all it might be with Venezuela dangling millions of dollars before their eyes so it is necessary to have some of their own people in the touchy border areas.[26]

For their part, the British members of the Commission shared the view that the Amerindians' traditional territories were overlarge and that, in line with pre-independence policy, they should be encouraged to intensify their agriculture around the centralized settlements.

These considerations had a powerful effect on the Commission's final recommendations, which it made in its report in 1969. Moreover, the political moment was highly charged as the report was finalized in the immediate aftermath of the Rupununi revolt, a time when border issues were highly sensitive. Thus, although the report recommended the provision of community titles to the majority of Amerindian communities in the country, there were some notable exceptions: land titling was not recommended for a scattering of communities on the lower rivers (Mazaruni, Cuyuni and Demerara) and in the mining districts like the Middle Mazaruni and the Barama-Kaituma areas. Moreover, in a number of cases – notably in the North West District (Arawak and Warao), the Upper

Mazaruni (Akawaio and Arekuna), the South Rupununi (Wapishana) and the North Rupununi (Makushi) – the Commission recommended community titling of areas substantially smaller than the territorial claims made by the Amerindians to the Commission. Exactly these areas have now become the subjects of land disputes: between Amerindians and logging companies (North West District); miners (Upper Mazaruni); ranchers (South Rupununi) and conservationists (North Rupununi-Iwokrama project).[27]

Having received the report, the government prevaricated in applying its recommendations. It was not until international controversy about a proposed hydro-power project on the Upper Mazaruni focused attention on the government's failure to abide by its commitment at independence to secure Amerindian land rights that the it passed the Amerindian (Amendment) Act No. 6 of 1976, providing Amerindians with community title and the right to administer their areas through their Captains and Councils.[28]

The Act was not comprehensive and there were some notable exceptions where the government chose not to follow the Commission's recommendations. A number of communities in the lowlands, like the Akawaio of the Demerara, did not get the titles that the Commission had recommended,[29] probably because logging was given priority. The Amerindians of the Upper Mazaruni, where the government still planned a big dam which would displace some 3,000 Akawaio, were also left without land title. The Caribs of the Upper Barama, where the government was encouraging mining, were similarly excluded. In the extreme south the Wai Wai were ignored.[30]

Since 1976, the government has issued two further schedules. The first, in 1977, did establish the Carib and Wai Wai Amerindian districts but, in violation of the Independence Agreement, denied the Amerindians ownership rights to their lands. The second, issued in 1991, finally provided land titles to some of the other excluded communities – notably, now that it had abandoned its plans for the Upper Mazaruni dam, to the Akawaio and Arekuna of the Upper Mazaruni. Yet, even after this, the Amerindians had regained less than one-fifth of the land area that the Amerindian Lands Commission had recommended be granted to them.[31]

The community titles have also been inadequately followed up on. Although documentary proof of ownership was provided to most of the communities with textual descriptions of the boundaries, no accompanying maps showing the actual extent of community titles were provided. With only one or two exceptions, the government has not surveyed and demarcated the community titles. As a result, many communities are unclear of the actual extent of their titles and this has exacerbated disputes with non-Amerindian neighbours. Many communities report overlapping claims with settlers and ranchers.

It is now thirty years since the Amerindian Lands Commission carried out its surveys. Much has changed in the intervening period. Communities have moved, grown, divided and expanded their economic activities. At the same time, pressure on the interior has intensified but despite a rising groundswell of complaints and demands for territorial recognition, successive governments have done next to nothing to address these concerns.

The Amerindians Today

Forty years of state-directed meddling in the Amerindians' lives, in the name of 'interior development', 'integration' and 'nation-building' have not greatly benefited Guyana's indigenous communities. On the contrary, ambitious and unrooted interventions have had very damaging effects on the Amerindians' economies. British efforts to promote a rapid integration into the market through trade in vegetables, balata, basketry and other produce proved unsustainable. Once the administration ceased subsidizing the costs of air transport, the trades often became uneconomic, leaving the communities with increasingly sophisticated demands for western goods but with no obvious means of paying for them. During the PNC years, efforts to build up the communities continued but as the economy stagnated, community welfare declined dramatically.

Moreover, the newly centralized communities that were stabilized around airstrips, schools, dispensaries and clinics now place an increasingly heavy burden on their local environment. The result in many areas is the degradation of forests owing to an intensification of shifting agriculture in the immediate vicinity of the new villages. Fish and game have declined from local overhunting. The need for money also means that what surpluses there are, instead of being shared with all in the village, are sold for cash. Inequalities have grown.

As a consequence, Amerindian health is in a critical state. Malnutrition among Amerindians, especially children, is widely recorded, while anaemia is very common among women. Amerindians have the country's highest rates of respiratory tract infection and tuberculosis. The ARU considers that the malaria situation is so bad in Amerindian areas that it requires 'a national emergency response'. Although precise data are lacking, it is estimated that about a third of Amerindians carry malaria.[32] The ARU reports that venereal diseases including AIDS are also growing at disproportionate speed among Amerindians.[33]

Amerindians also have the country's lowest levels of formal education, with the smallest proportion going on to secondary and higher level grades.[34] The lack of secondary schools in the interior means that the few children who do pursue further schooling are often obliged to travel down to the coast. There they suffer discrimination and cultural pressure to conform to coastlander standards. As Captain Leonard Fredericks of the Akawaio community of Great Falls explains:

> Children are removed from here to urban areas and placed with guardians who are only interested in acquiring money that the government pays and they pay little attention to the students. They even set difficult tasks for them in the morning: cleaning up toilets and what's not and what's next, and the child is not accustomed to such life at home... Next because you are coming from a rural area I think people feel that you are of an inferior quality being the 'buckman'. You are accustomed to this and you are accustomed to that, you do not know this and you do not know that. That tends to cast some discouragement into the pupils.[35]

Moreover, because of the governments' integrationist policy and unlike many other South American countries, no effort has been made to establish educational programmes in the Amerindian peoples' own languages. Increasingly, Amerindians are calling for a change in this approach. As Wapishana leader, Christopher Duncan of Aishalton, pointed out to the 'Amirang' conference in 1994:

> We also want to see the writing of our native tongues introduced in the school curriculum since we are losing our heritage and identity with the declining use of our language especially by our younger generations. We recommend that suitable people be identified and encouraged to study linguistics and phonetics to effect proper work in writing our languages since foreigners brutalise our languages in their efforts to write same.[36]

The 'Amirang' made clear that above all else the Amerindians were concerned to resolve their land rights problems. As Mrs Gloria Lowe, an Arawak from Kabakaburi, stated at the meeting:

> We have come here to discuss many issues affecting Amerindians but we, the Arawaks, would like all of us, all the Amerindians to put our heads together as one and ask the Government to review the land titles. We would also like all our communities to be demarcated and give us our resources, both on land and under the land, to use and control. No other race must enter into our community to work our resources without our permission.[37]

Amerindians in Guyana now number some 60,000 individuals and make up some seven per cent of the national population. Numerically and in terms of social organization, they predominate throughout the interior. No longer does anyone talk of them becoming extinct and on the coast there is an acceptance, sometimes grudging, that they have a right to maintain their identities as Amerindians: that it is possible to be both Guyanese and Amerindian. This is certainly a sentiment widespread among the Amerindians themselves. As one Akawaio put it to the author in 1994:

> We were not brought in to this country as slaves. We are the original peoples and we should be respected. We may need education, but we have our own civilization and our own language and we want to build on this.

[1] Cited in Forte 1994:221
[2] Menezes 1979:215 cited in Fox and Danns 1993:29; cf Myers 1993
[3] Menezes 1982:67 cited in Fox and Danns 1993:29
[4] Dowdy 1963
[5] Bennett 1978
[6] Benjamin and Pierre 1995
[7] Gadgil and Guha 1992
[8] Benjamin and Pierre 1995
[9] ARU nd
[10] John Dalgliesh-Patterson, cited in Williams 1936:426
[11] Cited in Williams 1936:426
[12] Forte 1993:5
[13] Benjamin and Pierre 1995
[14] Peberdy 1948:17
[15] Peberdy 1948
[16] Bodley 1982
[17] Gregory-Smith 1948:3 cited in Butt Colson 1983
[18] Gregory-Smith 1948: 10 cited in Butt Colson 1983
[19] Legislative Council debate 1944, cited in Butt Colson 1983
[20] Butt Colson 1983
[21] Butt Colson 1983
[22] cf Ferguson 1992
[23] Gregory-Smith 1949:11 cited in Butt Colson 1983
[24] Seggar 1954
[25] Sanders 1995:3-4; Seggar 1968
[26] Seggar 1968
[27] Amerindian Lands Commission 1969
[28] Survival International 1976
[29] Fox and Danns 1993
[30] Colchester 1991
[31] Forte 1993:4
[32] Forte 1993:7
[33] ARU nd (a)
[34] ARU nd
[35] Fox and Danns 1993
[36] Cited in Forte 1994:30
[37] Cited in Forte 1994:14

CHAPTER 8
FUTURE OPTIONS

'The question of your land titles and areas of land which you should have. These matters, I hope, will be addressed very quickly, and clearly – not addressed from above but with your involvement. We do not see the government from above only. We want to see government come from the bottom, from the grassroots. In this regard, we have said that we want not just representative democracy but participatory democracy. The people must not only have governments which they elect periodically but be in a situation where they participate every day, every hour, every minute of their lives, to fashion their own affairs.'
President Cheddi Jagan[1]

This book has attempted to reveal the present situation of Guyana's Amerindians, summarizing how they were rendered nearly powerless by the colonial state and how since independence they have been further marginalized and exploited. Despite being the majority population in the interior, the Amerindians have little say in the development of their ancestral lands. On the contrary, decisions about their future are shaped by the priorities of coastal residents and politicians, and are dominated by the pressures and policies of international financial institutions.

This *realpolitik* has led to nearly half the country's territory of 21 million hectares being handed over to domestic and foreign logging companies and over a tenth of the area to mining concerns. Meanwhile, despite endless promises from the government, no concrete steps have been taken to secure the Amerindians' lands. The original owners of the country now hold title to only 800,000 hectares divided into 75 community lots.

The marginalization of the Amerindians is not wholly driven by economic interests. It is made more acute by the fact that the coastal Guyanese who make up ninety per cent of the population know little about the interior and rarely travel there. Culturally the coastlanders feel more strongly tied to the Caribbean and to the countries from which their ancestors came, while socially they are now more closely linked to the 200,000 Guyanese who live overseas, especially in Canada, the US and UK. Guyana looks north and not south, treating the hinterland as a savage wilderness, inhabited by 'bucks' and promising wealth to the adventurous, an empty frontier for pioneering exploitation not a landscape inhabited by equal Guyanese citizens with natural rights to their ancestral lands.

For all that, the Amerindians are far from being crushed by this continuing invasion of their lands. On the contrary, they have grown increasingly organized and outspoken and have linked up with indigenous peoples' organizations throughout the continent and the rest of the world. Those travelling in the interior of the country are also immediately struck by this contradiction: that despite centuries of exploitation and abuse, many Amerindian communities remain vigorous and viable. Indeed, in some respects, their very isolation and political marginalization has helped to protect them from coastal impositions.

Trekking through the forests of the Upper Barama and Barima, an area which has endured over a hundred years of gold fever, it is still possible to come upon small Carib villages that seem virtually unchanged since the last century. Linked to the rest of Guyana only by narrow foot-trails through the forest, almost invisible to the inexperienced, such communities appear to consist of little more than a cluster of rough thatched huts on the muddy banks of a small stream, and their material wealth is apparently limited to some cheap aluminium pans, broken knives and cutlasses, some fishhooks and nylon and a clutch of other oddments stashed in smoke-blackened cloth bags or suitcases under the eaves of the open-sided houses. The children run naked to bathe in the stream and their parents, who may keep a change of clothes for visits to the stores in Matthews Ridge, are for the most part content to dress in the traditional 'lap', or loin cloth.

Yet behind these simple appearances still lies the millenial wisdom of forest existence which allows them to live well from their surroundings, supplied with staple foods from their small plots of cassava and other crops, cut from the surrounding forests, and with game brought down by the hunters' shotguns and bows and arrows. Villages such as these have made the conscious choice to retain their traditional ways of living and avoid the disruptions of mining and logging. The villages move frequently to avoid exhausting the local forests and they have also evaded the imposed decision-making structures of the coastal administration, preferring to maintain their customary decentralized leadership pattern. As one Amerindian told the author: 'everyone is a captain around here'.[2]

Not all the communities choose to live such mobile and spartan lives. Large, long-established Amerindian communities near the coast, like those at Moruca, include well-constructed buildings, quays, shops and resthouses, with substantial schools and clinics. Even in the headwaters, some Amerindian villages have invested a great deal of time and effort, as well as money from hard-won village funds, to provide basic modern services to all village members. In the Upper Mazaruni, many villagers have made themselves handsome clinker-built houses on raised platforms, roofed with shingles cut from wallaba trees, and

141

have called on communal labour to construct impressive cottage hospitals and churches. The Upper Mazaruni has also seen the emergence of a notable religious tradition, the so-called Hallelujah Church, a fusion of traditional dances and beliefs with Christianity, producing its own catechism, hymn books and prophets, which has been accepted into the Guyana Council of Churches.

Problems of health, poorly supplied government medical and educational services, land insecurity and invasion may abound, but the Amerindians are far from passive victims. Given the right circumstances, the welfare and viability of these villages is secure in the Amerindians' own hands.

The present government came to power with promises of making just such self-development possible. In its election manifesto of 1992 the PPP stated:

> The PNC is now using the distribution of land titles to Amerindians as a political gimmick. In fact, Amerindians are complaining that they are not receiving titles to all the lands they occupy. The PPP-Civic will ensure that titles are given to Amerindians to all the lands they occupy. Communal titles will be given to all Amerindian villages/settlements through their genuine elected councils. The boundaries of villages and settlements will be clearly defined and demarcated. Amerindians will be consulted on development projects which are likely to affect their rights and interests. The new government will work towards the allocation of part of the proceeds from the extraction of minerals and precious stones within the boundaries of any settlement, which is carried out with the consent of the Amerindian council, to be given to the settlement as development revenue.[3]

As we have seen, none of these promises has been adhered to. No single title has been granted to an Amerindian community since the government assumed office. Far from making efforts to map and demarcate titled lands, it has refused permits to technicians invited into Amerindian areas to help them map their own lands. At the same time, the government has handed out logging and mining permits to foreign companies as if there was no tomorrow. Not a cent has been extracted from the companies' profits for paying into village funds. Consultation with the local communities has been minimal, making a mockery of the PPP's implication that they would seek Amerindian consent before mining took place on their lands.

Faced by those they have misled with such promises, government officials have been apologetic. In February 1996, the Senior Minister for Local Government, Moses Nagamootoo, admitted that these pledges had not been kept since 'once in office the government has had so much to do to address all the country's problems',[4] suggesting that the pressing concerns of Amerindians were not a priority.

These shortcomings may be understandable, if not excusable, in a country dominated by a coastlander vision and the very real problems of poverty along the coast. What is much harder to understand is why the government has put up so little resistance to the reinvasion of the country by foreign companies, even when they promise little financial returns to the exchequer.

Part of the answer to this puzzle perhaps lay in President Jagan's heartfelt distrust of the 'North'. He apparently saw transnational corporations from the 'South' as allies in a global game of domination between the old 'Western' powers and the resurgent nations of the 'South' and the Non-Aligned Movement. For example, at the opening of the Barama Company's plywood factory, at Land of Canaan south of Georgetown, Jagan announced:

> It is good that [investors from Malaysia and Korea] have now decided to come here... because they are coming here, not only with capital, but with knowledge of Third World backward countries, kept backward because of colonialism and neo-colonialism. They have been able to forge ahead, applying science and technology, a disciplined workforce, and setting the pace, so to speak, in the world today of growth and development.[5]

However, it is far from clear why companies from the 'South' should be any more respectful of the needs of people in more 'backward' countries than 'Northern' companies. Was the President right to assume that 'my enemies' enemies are my friends', especially considering that many of these 'Southern' companies have already tarnished reputations elsewhere in the developing world and are increasingly part-owned by shareholders from 'Northern' countries snapping up attractive investments on the Kuala Lumpur stock exchange?[6] Moreover, such reasonings hardly explain why the President should have been equally welcoming to North American mining and logging companies. If 'neo-colonialism' is seen as a threat to Guyana's political autonomy and economic development, why did the President go out of his way to smooth the way for foreign investors?

The press in Guyana has been quick to ask just these questions and has also implied that there are less healthy connections between the current administration and foreign capital. When it was revealed that President Jagan's tour of South East Asia in late 1993 to drum up further investment in forestry had been subsidized by the Barama Company, a question of conflict of interests was raised; the same question arose again when it transpired that the railings around the presidential building were a gift from the same company.[7] But trips to en-

143

courage overseas investment have not been made just to Asia. In June 1996, President Jagan travelled to Canada and came back with reports that Placer Dome, one of the original investors in the Omai goldmine later replaced by Cambior, was considering returning to Guyana.[8]

Overall, the reasons for the current administration's welcome to foreign companies (whether they are from the 'North' or the 'South' is increasingly irrelevant) can be reduced to the old dependency arguments. Without an alternative proposal for wealth generation, the government has gone along with the development formula of the international financial institutions and been obliged to pay many of the same social and environmental costs.[9] The question that is not being adequately asked, however, is: if the underlying problem for Guyana is its political and economic dependency on foreign markets and capital, will opening up the country yet further to foreign companies break this dependency or only reinforce it?

This book has also highlighted another fundamental problem with the international financial institutions' development approach. This is that the promotion of 'foreign direct investment' in the absence of effective government institutions to regulate or control such companies can be environmentally and socially devastating – a problem that has not been confined to Guyana. As the World Bank has been forced to admit during a general debate with developing country governments concerned about the impacts of structural adjustment:

> It is true that a more attractive incentive environment for private investors without adequate regulatory tools attracts private investment into potentially destructive logging, mining, agriculture and energy ventures... It is therefore important to improve the regulatory framework for the environment. The Bank is supporting such efforts. But this is a long term process and meanwhile harm can be done and is being done.[10]

In fact, when non-governmental organizations first started raising questions about the social and environmental impacts of World Bank promoted road-building, logging and mining in the 1980s and early 1990s, there was no sign that the World Bank was supporting efforts in Guyana to regulate these extractive industries. It was only after international campaigns were launched to pressure the development agencies into curbing these excesses that belated first steps were taken in this direction.

Since 1993, the development agencies have suddenly woken up to their wider responsibilties and begun to send down teams of environmental consultants to try to patch things up. The agencies have belatedly recognized that there is an almost complete lack of environmental legislation and regulations in Guyana and that the main decisions about the country's natural resources are being taken by a small coterie of advisers in the Office of the President, with little reference to other ministries, let alone the general public. Putting matters right will, in their judgement, require new laws, new institutions and 'capacity building' – new staff, new management techniques, more money and fresh training for government officials.

A start in this direction has been made by the Inter-American Development Bank (IDB), which has made further assistance to coastal zone management conditional on the government adopting an Environment Protection Act (EPA). So slow was progress in drafting and enacting this legislation that the IDB ended up having to do most of the work itself and then develop an Environmental Management Project to try to put the law into effect. The World Bank has followed this up, first by rushing through a notionally participatory environmental planning exercise, referred to as a 'National Environmental Action Plan', and then by recommending that the government carry out an ambitious Natural Resource Management Project. The Bank's proposals proved unacceptable to the Office of the President, however, as it was afraid of relinquishing powers to a new tier of bureaucracy. In the event, the World Bank has had to back down, instead spinning off one component, to develop a 'National Protected Areas System', as a grant-funded project of the Global Environment Facility, while pooling US$5 million of its technical assistance with the IDB to help set up the new Environment Protection Agency, to be established under the new Act.

Meanwhile, the German technical assistance agency, GTZ, has commenced providing funds and staff to the Guyana Natural Resources Agency to adopt computerized mapping techniques – known as 'Geographical Information Systems' in computer-speak – in order to establish an information base for land use planning and natural resource management decisions. Backing up these changes, the Atlanta-based Carter Center, has carried out a series of 'Multi-Stakeholder Consultations' in the various regions to try to establish a national consensus on land-use planning.

Direct assistance totalling some £5 million is now being provided to the Guyana Forestry Commission by Britain's Overseas Development Administration (ODA), while the Commonwealth Secretariat is providing a more modest technical assistance package to the Guyana Geology and Mines Commission. The ODA is also about to embark on another large project to modernize the Department of Lands and Surveys, with the aim of revising land tenure systems on the coast and facilitating the transfer of coastal lands, presently mostly state-owned and leased to tenant farmers, into private ownership. The Canadian International Development Agency (CIDA) is also looking to provide support to the forestry and mines commissions.

145

Whether this alphabet soup of aid agencies and projects will help bring the runaway logging and mining industries under control is still an open question. In the long term, certainly, all these institutional changes will be necessary if Guyana is to regain control of developments in the interior. However, in the short term, there are serious obstacles to be overcome.

The first is the problem that development specialists refer to as a 'lack of absorptive capacity'. With so many projects being set up at once, the government is hard-pressed to cope with the demands on its time, especially as decision-making is highly centralized and there is a chronic shortage of trained Guyanese to act as counterparts to the expatriate aid agency personnel. As a result, the aid agencies are competing for the time and attention of the few trained Guyanese in government positions. This problem is compounded by the great reluctance of the Presidential Adviser for Science, Technology and the Environment, Navin Chandarpal, to delegate any power outside the Office of the President. The result is a bottleneck on decision-making that drives impatient development agency personnel, keen to advance their pet projects, to distraction.

Currently, Guyana is awash with environmental consultants jetting in to the country to study particular aspects of the country's situation. After lightning field trips, ambitious consensus-building seminars and brain-busting perusals of the available literature, they pound away on their laptop computers and jet home again, leaving behind their worthy reports to gather dust in government offices.

It is not only the government which is to blame for this state of affairs. Not surprisingly, it has been confused by the conflicting demands of the development specialists. The development agencies seem almost schizophrenic, on the one hand demanding economic liberalization and the promotion of logging and mining by foreign companies, while on the other hand insisting on strict controls on these same industries. In the case of the World Bank, this schizophrenia has become institutionalized, with environmental staff and economists being housed in quite separate departments of the Bank's 7,000-strong bureaucracy in Washington DC. As a result, while the Bank's environmental specialists urge a revision of the over-generous contracts awarded to Omai Gold Mines, Demerara Timbers and Barama, insisting that 'sustainable development' can only be achieved if Guyana secures greater benefits from existing concessions, the Bank's macro-economists, whose goal is to promote 'sustained growth', reject the proposition out of hand as it would 'send the wrong signals' to potential foreign investors.

Many Guyanese citizens and NGOs believe Guyana's long-term interests would be better served by slowing down the inflow of foreign investors while securing greater debt relief and foreign assistance grants directed at short-term poverty alleviation programmes and the provision of basic health and education services. If logging and mining could be slowed down, there would be more time to build up the regulatory institutions needed to control them.

The development agencies, always in a hurry to see economic growth, do not share this vision, however. They would rather pursue a fast-track approach to development while simultaneously trying to patch up the damage as they go along. This kind of make-and-break mentality even undelies their conservation efforts, which are, in effect, part of an exercise of national triage – with some areas to be set aside for global biodiversity conservation, others slated for agricultural development, while the remainder of the country is treated as a sacrificial zone open to the extractive industries. Amerindians and other local communities have been granted a minimal role in these zoning decisions.

Protected Areas

So far Guyana has had little experience of the horse-trading between development specialists and environmentalists that goes on behind the facade of conservation. Guyana's one and only national park is the tiny – 11,600 hectares – protected area surrounding the Kaieteur Falls, established largely for its scenic value. It is not in a good state. 'There has been little management of the Park. The boundaries have not been demarcated and no management plan has been formulated...' Miners, who are illegally working the Potaro river for gold and diamonds above and below the falls, even occupy the Park's buildings.[11] Attempts to increase the size of the Park so that it encompasses an area large enough to conserve viable populations of fauna and flora have been fiercely resisted by the mining lobby, and it appears that the present administration is unwilling to force the issue.

More interest has been expressed by the government in the ambitious 'Iwokrama Rainforest Programme', which encompasses a 360,000 hectare area of forest between the Rupununi savannahs and the Essequibo. The project was initially criticized by international and local NGOs for failing to take account of the needs and rights of the Amerindians who live in and make use of the resources of the area. The World Rainforest Movement (WRM) also expressed concern over whether the project could be said to respond to the country's environmental priorities. In response to questions in a letter from President Jagan in 1993, the organization expressed concern that the project might absorb the country's limited institutional capacity to deal with the environment, thereby diverting attention away from the more crucial problems facing the country such as: effectively regulating logging and mining; carrying out a social and environmental impact study of the proposed Boa Vista-Georgetown road;

securing Amerindian lands; and combatting the epidemics of malaria and cholera. The WRM also expressed concern that the project, which envisaged a vigorous 'biotechnologies and biofutures' programme, based on detailed documentation of Amerindian plant lore, made no provisions to secure Amerindian intellectual property rights.

To their credit, the project's international sponsors gave very serious consideration to these concerns and the revised project now proposes some measures to deal with all of them – though how adequately is another matter.[12]

One final concern raised by the WRM has not yet been dealt with convincingly. The project proposes using half the area for experimental logging operations and creates the serious risk (so near the Brazilian border and directly on the Boa Vista-Georgetown road) that the necessary road network will facilitate the illegal penetration of the area by poachers, miners, settlers and loggers.

The forest set aside for the Iwokrama project is relatively sparsely populated even by Guyana's standards, with only one small settlement, Fairview, on the banks of the Essequibo actually falling within the reserve, but the whole area falls within the territory claimed by the Makushi people in 1966.[13] Although this claim was not upheld by the Lands Commission on the grounds that the area was too large for the Amerindians to develop and administer and instead smaller areas were recognized in 1976, some Makushi and other Amerindians do continue to make use of the wider area for farming, hunting, fishing, small-scale mining and community logging.

Since the Commonwealth Secretariat and other project sponsors were alerted by NGO protests to the social implications, there have been a number of missions to the area to consult with the local people. However, whereas the local communities now feel that their concerns have been understood and that the project will be modified accordingly, the official position seems to be that the project 'will need to pay particular attention to the participation of local people in future development' and 'local suggestions... will need to be evaluated'.[14]

The Amerindians of the area expect the project, on balance, to bring them some real benefits. In the short term, they anticipate that it will provide them with jobs as tree spotters, and as informants in herbal lore. The project should also stimulate the trade in handicrafts. In the longer term, they expect their younger community members to benefit from direct training from the visiting scientists, which should allow them, once trained, to take over the management of the area. This, they believe, will help them to become a fully recognized part of Guyanese society, while at the same time attention to traditional forest use and herbal lore will help ensure cultural continuity and respect for the traditional knowledge of the elders among the younger generation.

The Amerindians also believe that certain conditions would need to be met for the project to work well. It would first of all have to help clarify the boundaries of indigenous areas and demarcate them effectively. In addition, the Amerindians would need clear rights to be able to continue non-commercial hunting within the reserve area. Effective guard posts, coordinated by radios, would need to be established at the entrances to the reserve at Kurupukari and Annai to control access. An adequate area of forest within the reserve should be set aside to provide timber on a long-term basis to the community sawmill at Surama. A proportion of any profits made on drugs and medicines developed from the ethnobotanical research would need to be put into a development fund for the benefit of the communities. These and other matters should be established in the form of a written contract to ensure that Amerindian interests are properly protected.[15] After years in legal limbo, the Iwokrama Rainforest Programme was finally granted official recognition in early 1996 and has begun effective field work.[16]

The Kanuku Mountains have long attracted the interests of conservationists. They are believed to be home to some eighty per cent of the country's harpy eagles and contain a wide diversity of forest types including montane vegetation. The area is among the 24 priority conservation zones proposed for protected area status by biologists of the University of Guyana.[17] Two recent studies of the region, by Conservation International and the European Commission, have also recommended the establishment of a protected area in the region. The latter, set out in a comprehensive draft report,[18] proposes the creation of a 'Kanuku Amerindian National Park' of some 290,000 hectares as part of an integrated parks development programme that would directly involve the local people. As the EC study points out, there are seven Amerindian reservations, including sixteen villages and 4,600 Amerindians within the area of influence of the proposed park. EC staffers say the project will not go ahead without the explicit support of the local communities.

As with the other protected area proposals, the EC envisages the main obstacle to the Kanuku project as a lack of an effective governmental institutional counterpart. Not only is suitable National Parks legislation lacking, but there is no government agency with the capacity or interest to handle such a project. The GAHEF has now been closed and the proposed Environmental Protection Agency is still on the drawing board. Thus although some US$800,000 is presently available for the project, it is unlikely to be implemented for some time.

The Global Environment Facility's project to establish a 'National Protected Areas System' for Guyana, through the provision of a grant of US$7.5 million, is aimed at overcoming these institutional obstacles. The project envisages setting up a new Protected Areas agency, staffed with specialists from who knows where, who will oversee the establishment and management of a network of parks and reserves that include substantial examples of all the country's main ecosystems. The project has run into a number of familiar obstacles, including the queues for access to the Office of the President. The government has also made expressly clear that it is reluctant to consider any region for protected area status until exhaustive mineral surveys have been carried out. There is now some doubt whether the GEF project will go ahead. Whereas a team of Guyanese advisers recommended that an accountable and transparent public authority be established to handle the project and manage the country's protected areas, the government has sought to keep the project within the Office of the President, putting the GEF in a quandary.

Positively, the team from the GEF, recognizing that the Amerindians are the majority population in the Guyanese interior, has made an effort to promote dialogue between the communities and the government.[19] But the government has been unable to provide convincing reassurances that Amerindian land claims will be dealt with before lands are taken over for conservation.

The Amerindians are acutely aware that plans to create protected areas throughout the interior are not their own priority. Asks Benson Thomas of the Upper Mazaruni:

> My question is are the proposals for protected areas coming from indigenous peoples' initiatives or is this coming from the World Bank and the government? Do we need these protected areas? Are we destroying our nature and our animals? Or where does this all come from?... Finally, we have been given land titles. These are very precious to us and we need to manage them carefully. But we may also have to ask for more lands as our peoples grow. So, if these programmes go ahead before we have secured these areas this may be a problem for us.[20]

Harold Brown of the community of Jawalla is equally sceptical of proposals to create an 'Anthropological Reserve' around the Wai Wai in the south of the country:

> Creating these reserves for the Wai Wai – it is like caging them. All their aspirations will be directed by the government. The government will have full control over them. We have a long history of being kept apart. If we are going to treat the Wai Wai as a caged people, why not do the same for the other tribes of Guyana? No, all this is very shortsighted. The government must allow the people to develop: it must allow the people to aspire to develop themselves.[21]

The underlying problem of the development and conservation programmes in the interior is that neither have yet developed effective mechanisms for building on local initiatives rather than imposing outsiders' visions. Achieving this will be a slow process. The legacy of the Burnham years when Amerindian communities grew accustomed to being told what to do by central government without any opportunity to think or act for themselves still weighs heavily. Fortunately this is beginning to change.

From Integration to Self-Determination

Probably the most encouraging aspect of the Amerindians' situation today is their increasingly vocal and self-assured presence in the national arena. The political liberalization of Guyana with the ending of one-party rule in the 1980s has seen an indigenous resurgence, as Amerindians have taken advantage of the new political space to assert their own views. The first to emerge on the national scene was the Amerindian Peoples Association (APA), which was set up in 1991 to push for Amerindian land rights and to ensure that the Amerindians' voice was heard in policy-making at the national level. Its structure is designed to ensure that the Amerindians of the interior control the organization's advocacy while being directly represented in Georgetown.

Accordingly, the APA draws its authority from its General Assembly, which is meant to meet annually, and which elects an Executive Committee with one member representing each region, including a Chairperson, Treasurer, and Secretary. The Assembly also elects a Coordinator and a Programmes Administrator who are authorized by the Committee to pursue the goals of the Association between Assemblies in coordination with the Committee. The Coordinator and Programmes Administrator maintain a small office in Georgetown. None of the Committee members is normally resident in Georgetown, all being from interior communities.

The Assembly is comprised of representatives of Units established in some 46 Amerindian communities throughout the country. Each Unit has its own committee and office holders, elected by its membership in its respective areas. Each Unit sends two representatives to the General Assemblies. The APA has carried out vigorous campaigns against logging, mining and road-building in the interior and has energetically condemned what it sees as government attempts to sell-off Amerindian lands.

The APA is firmly in support of self-determination for its peoples, by which it means that Amerindian territorial rights should be recognized and legally secured and they should be empowered to take charge of their own affairs in their own areas. The APA argues that development in Amerindian territories should be under community control and subject to their free and informed

consent. It has urged the government to revise the presently out-dated Amerindian act and adopt the International Labour Organization's Convention 169.[22]

The APA thus rejects the government's current policy of integration and, in
line with indigenous peoples' aspirations at the international level, insists that
Amerindians should be in charge of their own destinies in the future. As the
APA's previous Coordinator told the author:

> We are not ready for 'integration' yet. If you haven't got education or
> land title, you're done. You're politically weak. You're nothing. Inte-
> gration just means your women become call girls, waitresses and bar
> girls. Your men are just labourers. And you get taken over all around –
> they take your forests and your mines. They take everything off you
> and you're nothing. The time is past when they told us what is good
> for us and what is bad for us. It is time we decided for ourselves.[23]

The Curious Case of the 'Amerindia Nation'

Ever since independence, the loyalty of Amerindians to Guyana has been
questioned by coastal Guyanese. Accordingly and quite unusually,
Amerindian land titles in Guyana can be extinguished by the government
if it suspects them of intending to secede.

In fact, the vast majority of Amerindians in Guyana are quite clear about
their nationality and are keenly aware that indigenous peoples enjoy even
fewer rights in neighbouring Venezuela.[24] However, some of those who
have taken refuge in Venezuela as economic migrants have voiced
extravagant claims to autonomy. In 1993, for instance, self-styled Arawak
'Chief' Susana Atkinson, then resident in New York, bogusly claimed that
she was unanimously elected by the country's nine Amerindian tribes
and issued a press release announcing the Declaration of Independence
of the 'Amerindia Nation' in the 'Reclamation Zone', the area claimed by
Venezuela, west of the Essequibo.[25]

The Amerindian Peoples Association was quick to denounce Ms
Atkinson as a 'trouble-maker who can only undermine the best interests
of Amerindians by pretending her mad schemes have the support of the
nine tribes of Guyana.'[26]

Amerindians in Guyana are claiming the right to self-determination, but
by this claim they are seeking to define their destinies within the
framework of the nation state and not outside it.

About the same time that the APA began to establish itself, the Guyana
Organization of Indigenous Peoples also emerged and included some members
of Stephen Campbell's 'Amerindian Association'. The organization has close

links with the present government and counts the present Minister for Amerindian Affairs among its members.

In addition to the Amerindians' own initiatives to organize and define their futures, a variety of attempts have been made to promote the indigenous voice, mainly with the aim of helping the international development agencies to interact with the Amerindians. In 1994, with funds from the Canadian government-backed 'Futures Fund', the Amerindian Research Unit of the University of Guyana organized a national gathering of Amerindians, an 'Amirang', which resulted in a well-documented summary of Amerindian perspectives about the various problems facing them.[27] The following year, a second 'Amirang' was held, also supported by the Futures Fund, resulting in the establishment of a National Amerindian Council, which initially focused on the need to review the Amerindian Act.

The process by which coastal Guyanese and foreign aid agencies have taken on themselves the task of indigenous organizing has, however, come under fire from Amerindians themselves. The APA distanced itself from the National Amerindian Council when it was created, on the grounds that the members had not consulted their communities before involving themselves and calling it the brain-child of the Futures Fund. Clarifying its concerns, the APA stated that 'it is not opposed to the formation of a coordinating structure which brings together genuinely representative organizations. However such a structure must be genuinely democratic and independent of political party activists. The new body lacks both these criteria.'[28]

These concerns have been echoed by Amerindians in the interior. As one Amerindian from the North West asks:

> With respect... to the newly formed National Amerindian Council... I would like to know where these people originated from and what tribe? Were they appointed or elected and by whom? I would also like to know the names of all the different villages that were consulted before this committee was formed?... We feel that it is high time that our intelligence is respected and this should have been done by the process of consultation with Amerindian communities and their respective representative organizations. We do not want a clique of self-appointed and politically affiliated or appointed people to continue making recommendations and proposals to Government and donor agencies using Amerindian identities. We would like to know by what criteria this body operates and by what merit the government was awarded a permanent seat on this body...[29]

In exactly the same way, controversy has now arisen about World Bank and Global Environment Facility plans to involve Amerindians in community development and protected area projects. In September 1995, a World Bank consultant who visited the country for two weeks, advised against working through the Amerindians' existing national organizations, instead arguing for the 'development of an integrated structure of representation linking disparate Amerindian villages into a national structure of communication'.[30] Accordingly, the following year, the World Bank arranged a consultation with Amerindian Captains in the Pakaraimas, which purposefully excluded the national Amerindian organizations. Indeed, during the meeting the organizations were pointedly referred to as 'Amerindian interest groups'.[31] The Amerindian organizations roundly attacked their exclusion from the meeting,[32] and a number of Amerindian Captains also expressed concern that they would be expected to assess the desirability or otherwise of protected area planning without having time to study and understand the implications of the proposals and seek alternative views.[33]

The risk is that the development agencies, in the name of participatory development and consultation, using the time-honoured trick of divide-and-rule, are seeking to create their own private patronage networks in the interior. At the same time, they are acceding to the government's reluctance to deal with the national Amerindian organizations, which with greater self-assurance, are insisting that all land use decisions in the interior, be they for logging, mining, road-building or conservation, should be preceded by the resolution of outstanding Amerindian land claims.

Looking Ahead

It is not my place to end this book with another set of outsider's proposals. Guyana has had enough of colonialisms of all kinds. On the contrary, the only workable proposals for the future of the interior will come from the Amerindians themselves. The main changes that are needed, therefore, are only that their voice is heeded and that the government keeps its word when it makes them promises.

In response to Amerindian pressure, the government has again offered reassurances that their demands for land will be respected. In February 1996, President Jagan told assembled Amerindian leaders:

> As long as Amerindian people are prepared to work hard to till the soil, to work the land, I can assure you that enough land will always be made available to you as a people of this country, the indigenous people of Guyana who inherited this soil before any of us arrived.

154

Having title to your land is important. Governments come and go, sometimes they are brutal and authoritarian, and they cancel agreements made previously. This is happening in many parts of the world. But we do not intend to dishonour any agreements we made. We want to assure that not only can you depend on the titles which you currently have, but also that we will make additional areas of land available for your use now and in future to accommodate the projected growth of your population. But the Amerindians must also understand that other Guyanese want land, and we all have to sit around the table to make an amicable settlement to serve the interests of all the people of Guyana.[34]

To back up this promise the government has also given a clear undertaking to re-establish the Amerindian Lands Commission.[35]

The government has also made a positive response to demands for a revision of the Amerindian Act. In December 1993, the National Assembly approved the appointment of a Special Select Committee to review the Act and collect alternative suggestions, although this committee seems to have been starved of funds and initiative since then.[36] And while the government does not yet seem comfortable with the language of self-determination, its expressed commitment to 'participatory democracy' in which, in the words of President Jagan, people 'participate every day, every hour, every minute of their lives, to fashion their own affairs' comes pretty close.[37] The administration, like the Amerindians, professes to aspire to a mode of governance which allows, as Minister Moses Nagamootoo puts it, 'the Amerindians to make decisions for themselves'.[38]

Even with respect to logging and mining President Jagan offered some reassurance:

I want to assure you that you must be part and parcel of the policing apparatus. We don't have enough money or resources in the Geology and Mines Commission or personnel in the Guyana Forestry Commission. We don't have enough vehicles, we don't have enough boats to police the vast interior. I say today, organize yourselves in villages and work closely not only with the police and the army and the security forces but also with the Geology and Mines Commission, with the Guyana Forestry Commission, and become part of protecting your own rights.[39]

Perhaps, then, this book should end on a positive note. The Amerindians' vision of future development in the interior is clear. They have made their

155

demands of the government and been heard. The government has agreed to these demands and has even promised concrete measures to meet them. All that is needed is for the government to keep its word. Action is now needed on the ground to secure the Amerindians' lands and help them build up their capacities to manage them.

Unlike the hasty and destructive development model being imposed by the international financial institutions and acceded to by coastal politicians and technocrats, the Amerindians have a more prudent and longer-term view of what is best for them. As the Secretary of the APA Lawrence Anselmo stressed to a District Council meeting in the Upper Mazaruni in January 1996:

> We can't make decisions in haste, as these will have consequences for five or six generations... We need to carefully weigh up what kind of development we really want. Already we are seeing the negative effects of development on our people – you all know what I mean. Our culture has been affected. Our way of life will be confused by development. We welcome it because we do not know what it means, what it leads to. We need to be careful to ensure that we get the kind of development that we really want. Our future generations, our little ones who are coming up, they will get better education in the future and they will look back at the decisions we make now. They will be sorry if they realize we have not made the right decisions for the futures of our peoples... We must not think only in terms of ourselves or our immediate grandchildren but in terms of seven generations. We want them to enjoy the same privileges that we do.

[1] Cited in Forte 1994:21
[2] Colchester and MacIntyre 1994
[3] *Time for Change, Time to Rebuild*, PPP/ Civic Manifesto, 1992
[4] GEF 1996:4
[5] *Catholic Standard*, 28 November 1993
[6] Colchester 1994
[7] *Stabroek News*, 8 January 1994
[8] *Chronicle*, 20 June 1996; *Stabroek News*, 25 June 1995
[9] Broad 1993; Reid 1996
[10] World Bank 1995:4
[11] Ramdass and Hanif 1990:22
[12] Commonwealth Secretariat 1993; NRI 1993
[13] Amerindian Lands Commission 1969; Myers 1993
[14] NRI 1993:7
[15] Interviews 19-20 October 1993
[16] Forte 1996a, 1996b
[17] Ramdass and Hanif 1990
[18] Agriconsult July 1993, not publicly available
[19] GEF 1996

[20] Field notes, 21 January 1996
[21] Field notes, 21 January 1996
[22] APA 1994
[23] Gerald McIntyre, personal communication to the author, 1 November 1994
[24] See Colchester 1995
[25] Amerindia Nation, press release, New York, 13 September 1993
[26] APA press release, 27 January 1994
[27] Forte 1994
[28] *Catholic Standard*, 30 April 1995; Jean La Rose, *Guyana Review*, August 1995
[29] Mark Atkinson, letter to the editor, *Catholic Standard*, 30 July 1995
[30] Brana-Shute 1995:8
[31] GEF 1996:72
[32] *Stabroek News*, 2 February 1996
[33] *Catholic Standard*, 14 January 1994
[34] GEF 1996:11
[35] GEF 1996:1,72
[36] *Guyana Review*, August 1995
[37] Cited in Forte 1994:21
[38] GEF 1996:5
[39] Cited in Forte 1994:21

USEFUL ADDRESSES

Amerindian Peoples Association
71 Quamina Street
Georgetown, Guyana
Tel:+ 59 22 70275
Fax:+ 59 22 74948

Guyana Human Rights Association
71 Quamina Street
Georgetown, Guyana
Tel: + 59 22 61789
Fax: + 59 22 63463

Forest Peoples Programme and
World Rainforest Movement UK
Unit 1c, Fosseway Business Centre
Stratford Road
Moreton-in-Marsh
GL56 9NQ, England
Tel: + 44 1608 652893
Fax: + 44 1608 652878
Email: wrm@gn.apc.org

Forests Monitor
114 Broad Street
Ely, CB7 4BE, England
Tel: + 44 1353 669989
Fax: + 44 1353 665092
Email: fmonitor@gn.apc.org

Survival International
11-15 Emerald Street
London WC1N 3QL, England
Tel: + 44 171 242 1441
Fax: + 44 171 242 1771

Latin America Bureau
1 Amwell Street
London EC1R 1Ul, England
Tel: + 44 171 278 2829
Fax:+44 171 278 0165
Email: lab@gn.apc.org

Rainforest Action Network
450 Sansome Street, Suite 700
San Francisco CA 94111, USA
Tel: + 1 415 398 4404
Fax: + 1 415 398 2732

IUCN-Netherlands
Plantage Middelaan 2b
1018 DD Amsterdam, Netherlands
Tel: + 31 20 626 1732
Fax: + 31 20 627 9349

WorldWide Fund for Nature
Forests for Life
CH-1196 Gland, Switzerland
Tel: + 41 223 649111
Fax: + 41 223 643239

REFERENCES AND BIBLIOGRAPHY

Amerindian Lands Commission
1969 *Report*. Georgetown.
APA
1994 Presentation to the '94 NGO Islands Forum to Complement the UN Global Conference on Sustainable Development of Small Island Developing States. Amerindian Peoples Association, Georgetown.
ARU
nd(a) *Background Paper on Amerindian Population and Health*. UNDP Consultation on Indigenous Peoples. Georgetown.
ARU
nd(b) ' *Background Paper on Mining and Amerindians*. UNDP Consultation on Indigenous Peoples. Georgetown.
ARU
nd(c) *Background Paper on Forestry and Amerindians*. UNDP Consultation on Indigenous Peoples. Georgetown.
ARU
nd(d) *Background Paper on Amerindian Land Issues*. UNDP Consultation on Indigenous Peoples. Georgetown.
Baird, Wellesley A.
1982 *Guyana Gold: The Story of Wellesley A. Baird, Guyana's Greatest Miner*. Three Continents Press, Washington.
Baldwin, Richard
1946 *The Rupununi Record*. The Barbados Advocate Company, Barbados.
Barnett, Thomas
1990 *The Barnett Report: a summary of the Report of the Commission of Inquiry into Aspects of the Timber Industry in Papua New Guinea*. Asia-Pacific Action Group, Hobart.
Benjamin, Anna
1992 'A Preliminary look at the Free

Amerindians and the Dutch Plantation System in Guyana during the Seventeenth and Eighteenth Centuries.' *Guyana Historical Journal* IV & V:1-21.
Benjamin, Anna and Laureen Pierre
1995 Review of Legislation in Relation to Land, Forestry and Mining. In *Forte* 1995: Annex 1.
Bennett, Gordon
1978 *Aboriginal Rights in International Law*. Royal Anthropological Institute and Survival International, London
Bodley, John
1982 *Victims of Progress*. Mayfield Press, Mountain View, California.
Brana-Shute, Gary
1995 *Indigenous Peoples of Guyana: Action Report*. The World Bank, Washington.
Brett, Rev.W.H.
1868 *Indian Tribes of Guiana; Their Condition and Habits*. Hill and Daldy, London
Broad, Robin
1988 *Unequal Alliance: The World Bank, the International Monetary Fund and the Philippines*. University of California Press, Berkeley.
Buve, Raymond Th.J.
1975 'Governor John Hensius: the Role of Van Assen's Predecessor in the Suriname Indian War 1678-1680.' In Peter Kloos and Henri J.M. Classen (eds) *Current Anthropology in the Netherlands*. Rotterdam Branch of the Netherlands Sociological and Anthropological Society, Rotterdam: 39-47.
Butt Colson, Audrey
1973 'Inter-tribal Trade in the Guiana Highlands.' *Antropologica* 34:1-70.
1983 National Development and the Upper Mazaruni Akawaio and Pemon. ms.

1983 'El Desarrollo nacional y los Akawaio y Pemon del Alto Mazaruni.' *América Indígena.* XLIII, no.3

Butt Colson, Audrey and Morton, John
1965 'Early Missionary Work among the Taruma and Waiwai of Southern Guiana – The Visits of Fr. Cuthbert Cary-Elwes, S.J. in 1919, 1922 and 1923.' *Folk,* Vol.24. Copenhagen

Carneiro, Robert L.
1961 'Slash-and-Burn Cultivation among the Kuikuru and its Implications for Cultural Development in the Amazon Basin.' In *The Evolution of Horticultural Systems in Native South America: Causes and Consequences, a Symposium,* ed Johannes Wilbert, pp. 47-67. *Antropológica,* Supplement Publication no.2. Caracas: Sociedad de Ciencias Naturales La Salle.
1995 'The History of Ecological Interpretations of Amazonia: Does Roosevelt Have It Right?' In *Indigenous Peoples and the Future of Amazonia. An Ecological Anthropology of an Endangered World,* edited by Leslie E. Sponsel, pp. 45-70.

Carberry, Lance
1993 'Iwokrama: Pioneer's Progress.' *Guyana Review,* August 1993.

Caulin, Fray Antonio
1778 (1966) *Historia de la Nueva Andalucia.* Tomo I & II. Biblioteca de la Academia Nacional de la Historia, Caracas.

Chambers, Frances
1989 *Guyana.* World Bibliographical Series, Volume 96. Clio Press, Oxford.

Cleary, David
1990 *Anatomy of the Amazon Gold Rush.* Macmillan, London.

Colchester, Marcus
1989 *Pirates, Squatters and Poachers: the Political Ecology of Dispossession of the Native Peoples of Sarawak.* Survival International and INSAN, Petaling Jaya, Malaysia.

1991 'Sacking Guyana.' *Multinational Monitor,* September 1991:8-14.
1992 'Forests for Sale: Guyana's Natural Resources, Going, Going, Gone....?' World Rainforest Movement, UK.
1993 *Slave and Enclave: the Political Ecology of Equatorial Africa.* World Rainforest Movement, Penang, Malaysia.
1994 Malaysian Loggers Come Out of the Woodwork. World Rainforest Movement. ms.
1995 *Forest Politics in Suriname.* International Books, Utrecht.

Colchester, Marcus and Larry Lohmann
1990 *The Tropical Forestry Action Plan: What Progress?* World Rainforest Movement, Penang, Malaysia.

Colchester, Marcus and Larry Lohmann (eds)
1993 *The Struggle for Land and the Fate of the Forests.* Zed Books, London, and World Rainforest Movement, Penang.

Colchester, M. and MacIntyre, G.
1994 Joint Survey of Barama Company Limited Concession Area. Amerindian Peoples Association/ World Rainforest Movement. ms.

Commonwealth Secretariat
1993 *Iwokrama: The Commonwealth Rainforest Programme in Guyana.* Promotional Brochure.

Coppens, Walter
1971 'Las Relaciones Comerciales de los Yekuana del Caura, Paragua.' *Antropologica* 30:28-59.

Cordier, S. and Grasmick, D.
1994 *Etude de l'impregnation par le mercure dans la population Guyanaise.* Réseau National de Santé Publique, Saint-Maurice.

Cremer and Warner
1990 *Gold Mining in Guyana: A Review of Environmental Aspects of Dredge and Small Pit Mining Operations.* Commonwealth Secretariat for the Government of Guyana.

Daly, Vere T.
1975   *A Short History of the Guyanese People*. Macmillan, London.
de Groot, Silvia W.
1977   *From Isolation Towards Integration: the Suriname Maroons and their Colonial Rulers*. Martinus Nijhoff, The Hague.
Dieter Heinen, H.
1992   'The Early Colonization of the Lower Orinoco and its Impact on Present Day Indigenous Peoples.' *Antropologica* 78:51-86.
Dowdy, Homer E.
1963   *Christ's Witchdoctor: from Savage Sorcerer to Jungle Missionary*. Hodder and Stoughton, London.
DTE
1991   *Pulping the Rainforests: the rise of Indonesia's Paper and Pulp Industry*. Down to Earth, London.
ECTF
1993   Barama Company Limited: North West Guyana Sustainable Forest Management Programme. Environmental and Social Impact Assessment by Edinburgh Centre for Tropical Forests, June 1993.
ERM
1995   *Environmental and Social Impact Assessment: Linden-Lethem Road, Guyana*. Environmental Resources Management, London.
Farage, Nadia
1991   *As Muralha dos Sertões: os povos indigenas no rio Branco e a colonização*. Paz E Terra, São Paulo.
Ferguson, James
1994   *The Anti-Politics Machine. "Development," Depoliticization, and Bureaucratic Power in Lesotho*. University of Minnesota Press, Minneapolis.
Flaming, Lorene
1995   *An Economic Analysis of the Timber Industry in Guyana. Prospects for Strengthening State Capacity and Private Incentives for Sustainable Forest Management*. The World Bank, Washington.

Fock, Niels
1963   *Waiwai: religion and society of an Amazonian Tribe*. National Museum, Copenhagen.
Forbes, G.P.A.
1959   'The Forests of British Guiana and Their Future Development.' *Timehri*: 38:57-61
Forte, Janette
1989   *The Road from Brazil*. University of Guyana, Georgetown.
1990   *The Populations of Guyanese Amerindian Settlements in the 1980s*. Amerindian Research Unit, University of Guyana.
1993   Amerindian and Poverty. Paper prepared for IDS Seminar on Poverty, March 19, 1993.
1995c   *A Selective Reading List on Guyanese Amerindians*. Occasional Publications of the Amerindian Research Unit, University of Guyana.
1996a   *Makushi Lifestyles and Biodiversity Use*. Iwokrama Rainforest Programme, Georgetown.
1996b   *Makushi Women's Ethnobotany and Ethnomedicine*. Iwokrama Rainforest Programme, Georgetown.
Forte, Janette (ed)
1994   *Proceedings of the Amirang*. National Conference of Amerindian Representatives 'Amerindians in Tomorrow's Guyana' April 11-14, 1994. Amerindian Research Unit, University of Guyana.
1995a   *Situation Analysis Indigenous Use of the Forest with Emphasis on Region 1*. University of Guyana Amerindian Research Unit.
1995b   Report of the UNDP Consultation on Indigenous Peoples and National Development held at Beterverwagting Guyana on February 14-15, 1995. Amerindian Research Unit, Georgetown.
Forte, Janette and Anna Benjamin
1993   *The Road from Roraima State*. University of Guyana, Georgetown.

161

Fox, Desrey and George K. Danns
1993   *The Indigenous Condition in
Guyana: a Situation Analysis of the
Mabura Great Falls Community.* University of Guyana, Georgetown.
Frood, David W. and Sanders, Larry
1992   *Lean and Mean. The Forest
Labyrinth of Ken Buchanan.* Canadian
Paperworks Union.
**Gadgil, Madhav and Guha,
Ramachandra**
1992   *This Fissured Land. An Ecological History of India.* Oxford University
Press.
GEMCO
1994   *Report on Results of Tests
Conducted in Konawruk.* Guyana
Environmental Monitoring and Conservation Organization Ltd, Georgetown.
Gilij, Felipe Salvador
1782 (1965)   *Ensayo de historia
Americana.* Tomo I,II & III. Biblioteca de
la Academia Nacional de la Historia,
Caracas.
Gillin, John
1936   *The Barama River Caribs of
British Guiana.* Peabody Museum,
Cambridge, Mass.
Gray, Andrew
1986   *And After the Gold Rush? Human
Rights and Self Development Among the
Amarakaeri of Southeastern Peru.*
International Work Group on Indigenous
Affairs, Document 55, Copenhagen.
**Government of Guyana Upper
Mazaruni Development Authority**
1983   *Upper Mazaruni Additional Field
Investigations. Final Report. Resettlement
of Amerindians in the Upper Mazaruni
Basin.* SWECO.
Gravesande, Caesar N.
1992   'Amerindian Jurisdiction in the
Guiana Territory in the Seventeenth and
Eighteenth Centuries.' *History Gazette* 44
(May), University of Guyana.
GSRL
1994   *Golden Star Resources Ltd
Annual Report 1993.* Denver, Colorado.

Guppy, Nicholas
1958   *Wai Wai.* E.P. Dutton, London.
Hancock, John
1835   *Observations on the Climate, Soil
and Productions of British Guiana and on
the Advantages of Emigration to, and
Colonizing the Interior of, that Country:
Together with incidental remarks on the
diseases their treatment and prevention;
founded on a long experience within the
tropics.* James Fraser, John Hatchard and
Son and George Mann, London.
Harris, C.A. and de Villiers, J.A.J.
1911   *Storm van 'S Gravesande. The
Rise of British Guiana. Compiled from His
Despatches.* Hakluyt Society, London.
Hemming, John
1978a   *Red Gold. The Conquest of the
Brazilian Indians.* Macmillan, London.
1978b   *The Search for El Dorado.*
Michael Jospeh, London.
1990   *Roraima: Brazil's Northernmost
Frontier.* Institute of Latin American
Studies, Research Paper No. 20, University of London.
Henfrey, Colin
1995   'Democracy and the Sustainability
of Livelihoods and Natural Resources: the
Issues Currently Underlying Amerindian
Development Options.' In *Forte 1995:*
72-75.
Hogg, Dominic
1993   *The SAP in the Forest: The
Environmental and Social Impacts of
Structural Adjustment Programmes in the
Philippines, Ghana and Guyana.* Friends
of the Earth, London.
Hutt, Srikant
1984   *India and the Third World.
Altruism or Hegemony?* Zed Books,
London.
Imbaimadai
1949   Proposals for Development,
Upper Mazaruni Reservation. District
Officer to Commissioner of the Interior.
Jagan, Cheddi
1966   *The West on Trial.* Michael Joseph,
London.

1994 'The Caribbean Community: Crossroads to the Future.' *Caribbean Affairs*, vol 7, no 3, 1994.

Jennings, Francis
1975 *The Invasion of America: Indians, Colonialism and the Cant of Conquest.* University of North Carolina Press, Chapel Hill.
1984 *The Ambiguous Iroquois Empire.* Norton, New York.

Johnson, Nels and Bruce Cabarle
1993 *Surviving the Cut.* World Resources Institute, Washington DC.

Johnson, Dennis V.
1994 Report on the Palm Cabbage Industry in Northwest Guyana. IUCN, Silver Spring, USA.

Kaplan, Joanna
1975 *The Piaroa.* Clarenden Press, Oxford.

Klitgaard, Robert
1988 *Controlling Corruption.* University of California Press, Berkeley.

Knapp, S.C.
1965 Report on the Amerindians of British Guiana and suggested Development Programmes. ms.

Kotkin, Joel
1993 *Tribes: how Race, Religion and Identity Determine Success in the New Global Economy.* Random House, New York.

Kozak, Alexandra
1994 Environmental Management Perspectives at Omai Gold Mines Limited. III International Gold Symposium in Venezuela, October 2-4, 1994, Caracas.

LAB
1984 *Guyana: Fraudulent Revolution.* Latin America Bureau, London.

Lacarda, L.D. and Salomons, W.
1991 Mercury in the Amazon; A Chemical Time Bomb? Report sponsored by Dutch Ministry of Housing, Physical Planning and Environment, Chemical Time Bomb Project, Den Haag.

Lamur, Carlo
1985 *The American Takeover: Industrial Emergence and ALCOA's Expansion in Guyana and Suriname 1914-1921.* Foris, Dordrecht.

Lathrap, Donald W.
1970 *The Upper Amazon.* Thames and Hudson, London.

Lutchman, Harold A.
1976 *From Colony to Cooperative Republic.* Institute of Caribbean Studies, University of Puerto Rico.
1992 'Patronage in Colonial Society: A Study of British Guiana, 1891-1928.' *History Gazette.* No.41. University of Guyana.

MacMillan, Gordon
1995 *At the End of the Rainbow? Gold, Land and People in the Brazilian Amazon.* Earthscan, London.

Marshall, George
1990 'The Political Economy of Logging: the Barnett Enquiry into Corruption in the Papua New Guinea Timber Industry.' *The Ecologist* 20(5): 174-181.

Marshall, Godfrey
1994 'The Development of the Forestry Sector (1987 to the Present).' In Forte (ed.) 1994:82-93.

Menezes, M.N.
1977 *British Policy Towards the Amerindian in British Guiana 1803-1873.* Clarendon Press, Oxford.
1982 *The Amerindians and the Europeans.* London.

Menezes, M.N. (Ed.)
1979 *The Amerindians in Guyana 1803-1873: a Documentary History.* Frank Cass, London.

MIGA
1993 *MIGA Annual Report 1993.* MIGA, Washington, DC.

Ministry of Information and Culture
1970 A Brief Outline of the Progress of Integration in Guyana. Ministry of Information and Culture, Georgetown.

Moody, Roger
1994 'The Ugly Canadian: Robert Friedland and the Poisoning of the Americas.' *Multinational Monitor.* November 1994:21-23.
1995a Swords in the Shield: Canada's Invasion of the Guyanas. Part One of Report for the Amerindian Peoples Association.
1995b Commentary on New Developments at Omai Gold Mine, Guyana.
1995c Five Minutes to Midnight: an Account of the Origins and Consequences of South America's Worst Mine Disaster. Report for the Amerindian Peoples Association. ms.
Myers, Iris
1993 'The Makushi of the Guiana – Brazilian Frontier in 1944: A Study of Culture Contact.' *Antropologica* 80: 3-99.
Myers, Norman
1989 *Deforestation Rates in Tropical Forests and their Climatic Implications.* Friends of the Earth, London
Naipaul, V.S.
1969 *The Loss of El Dorado. A History.* Penguin Books.
NFAP
1989 *National Forestry Action Plan 1990 - 2000.* Guyana Forestry Commission and Canadian International Development Agency, Georgetown, Guyana.
NRI
1993 *The Commonwealth and Government of Guyana Iwokrama Rainforest Programme: Executive Summary.* Phase 1 Site Resource Survey. National Resources Institute, Chatham, England.
Pang, Eul-Soo
1994 *Guyana Mineral Development Strategy. Mineral Policy Assessment and Recommendations.* The Government of Guyana and Global Development Initiative, The Carter Center, Atlanta.
Peberdy, A.
1948 British Guiana. Report of a Survey on Amerindian Affairs in the Remote Interior: With Additional Notes on Coastland Population Groups of Amerindian Origin. Colonial Development and Welfare Scheme No.D.246. Georgetown.
Perera, Miguel Angel
1993 *El Amazonas Venezolano: impacto y ecodesarrollo.* Fundación Centro Español de Estudios de América Latina, Madrid.
Perez, D
1946 El tratado de límites de 1750 y la expedición de Iturriaga al Orinoco. Consejo Superior de Investigaciones Científicas, Madrid.
Poore, Duncan (ed.)
1989 *No Timber Without Trees: Sustainability in the Tropical Forests.* Earthscan, London.
Premdas, Ralph
1996 'Race and Ethnic Relations in Burnhamite Guyana.' In Dabydeen, D. and Samaroo, B. (eds) *Across the Dark Waters: Ethnicity and Indian Identity in the Caribbean.* Warwick University Caribbean Studies. Macmillan Caribbean. 39-64.
Raleigh, Sir Walter
1596 *The Discoverie of the Large, Rich and Bewtiful Empire of Guiana, with a Relation of the Great and Golden city of Manoa, (which the Spaniards call El Dorado) And the provinces of Emeria, Arromaia, Amapaia and other Countries, with their rivers, adjoyning.* Performed in the year 1595 by Sir W. Ralegh, Knight, Captaine of her Majesties Guard, Lo. Warden of the Stanneries, and her Highnesse Lieutenant Generall of the Countie of Cornewall. Imprinted at London by Robert Robinson.
Ramdass, I and M. Hanif
1990 A Definition of Priority Conservation Areas in Amazonia: Guyana Country Paper. Background Paper produced for 'Workshop 1990 – a Meeting to Define Areas of Biological Significance in the Greater Amazon', Manaus, Brazil, January 1990.

REFERENCES AND BIBLIOGRAPHY

Reed, David
1996 *Structural Adjustment, the Environment, and Sustainable Development.* Earthscan Publications with WWF, London.
Reitbergen, Simon
1989 'Africa.' In Poore 1989:40-73.
Repetto, Robert and Malcolm Gillis (eds.)
1988 *Public policies and the misuse of forest resources.* Cambridge University Press, Cambridge.
RESCAN Consultants Inc.
1991 *Omai Gold Project Environmental Impact Statement.* Rescan Inc., Vancouver, Canada.
1994 *Environmental Assessment of Konawaruk River Operations.* Mazda Limited, Georgetown.
1995 Omai Gold Project Environmental Impact Statement Addendum. Tailings Effluent Management. Omai Gold Mines Ltd.
Rice, Tim and Simon Counsell
1993 *Forests Foregone: the European Community and Tropical Forests.* Friends of the Earth, London.
Ridgwell, W.M.
1972 *The Forgotten Tribes of Guyana.* Tom Stacey, London.
Rivière, Peter
1969 *Marriage among the Trio.* Clarendon Press, Oxford.
1972 *The Forgotten Frontier: Ranchers of North Brazil.* Holt-Rhinehart and Winston, New York.
1984 *Individual and Society in Guiana: A Comparative Study of Amerindian Social Organization.* Cambridge University Press, Cambridge.
1995 *Absent-Minded Imperialism. Britain and the Expansion of Empire in Nineteenth-century Brazil.* Tauris Academic Studies, I.B. Tauris Publishers, London, New York.

Rodney, Walter
1981 *A History of the Guyanese Working People, 1881-1905.* Heinemann Educational Books, London.
Roosevelt, Anna C.
1980 *Parmana: Prehistoric Maize and Manioc Subsistence Along the Amazon and Orinoco.* New York: Academic Press.
1991 *Moundbuilders of the Amazon: Geophysical Archaeology on Marajó Island, Brazil.* San Diego: Academic Press.
Sanders, Douglas
1995 *Amerindian Peoples in Guyana.* University of British Columbia.
Sassoon, Meredith
1993 'Guyana: Minerals and the Environment: Working Paper for the National Environment Action Plan.' ms.
Seggar, W.H.
1954 Some Aspects of Development of a Remote Interior District. *Timehri* 33:30-40.
1959 Amerindian Local Authority Elections. Upper Mazaruni Amerindian District. *Timehri* 38.
1959 Community Development Amongst Amerindians. *Timehri* 38:21-26.
1968 Letter from Bill Seggar to Audrey Butt Colson, 4 February 1968.
Sizer, Nigel
1996 *Profit Without Plunder: Reaping Revenue from Guyana's Tropical Forests Without Destroying Them.* World Resources Institute, Washington.
ter Steege, Hans et al.
1996 *Ecology and Logging in a Tropical Rain Forest in Guyana. With recommendations for forest management.* The Tropenbos Foundation, Wageningen, The Netherlands.
Sunderland, T.C.H.
1993 A Critical Review of the Ecology and Forestry of the Mabura Hill Concession, Guyana, with an Assessment of the Demerera Timbers Ltd Forest Management Plan 1992-1996. MSc Thesis, University of Oxford.

165

Survival International
1976   *The Damned.* Occasional Document, London.

Thomas, David John
1972   The Indigenous Trade System of Southeast Estado Bolivar, Venezuela. *Antropologica* 33:3-38.
1982   *Order Without Government, the Society of the Pemon Indians of Venezuela.* University of Illinois Press, Urbana.

Timehri Group
1967   Land and the Amerindian. ms.

Upper Mazaruni Development Authority, Guyana
1975   *Environmental Appraisal. Upper Mazaruni Hydroelectric Project.* Harza Engineering Company, Aubrey Barker Associates.

Walcott, George et al.
1995   *Report of a Special Committee Set up to Review the Environmental Impact Statement.* Omai Gold Mines Ltd.

Watkin, E.M. and Woolford, G.W.
1992   Alluvial Gold Mining in Guyana: Environmental Considerations. Mining, Metals and the Environment Conference, Manchester, UK.

Westoby, Jack
1987 *The Purpose of Forests.* Basil Blackwell, Oxford.
1989   *Introduction to World Forestry.* Basil Blackwell, Oxford.

Whitehead, Neil L.
1988   *Lords of the Tiger Spirit: A History of the Caribs in Colonial*

Venezuela and Guyana 1498-1820. Foris Publications, Dordrecht, Netherlands.

Wilbert, Johannes
1972   *Survivors of Eldorado: Four Indian Cultures of South America.* Praeger Publishers, New York, London.
1993   'Carpenters of Canoes.' In *Mystic Endowment, Religious Ethnography of the Warao Indians.* Howard University Press.

Williams, Brackette F.
1991   *Stains on My Name, War in my Veins: Guyana and the Politics of Cultural Struggle.* Duke University Press, Durham and London.

Williams, Rev.James
1936   'The Aborigines of British Guiana and Their Land.' *Anthropos* XXXI:417-432.

World Bank
1993a   *Guyana. Private Sector Development.* Washington.
1993b   *Guyana. From Economic Recovery to Sustained Growth.* Washington.
1995   SPA Donors' Meeting June 5-9, 1995. Washington.

WRM/SAM
1990   *The Battle for Sarawak's Forests.* World Rainforest Movement and Sahabat Alam Malaysia, Penang, Malaysia.

Yde, Jens
1965   *Material Culture of the Waiwái.* Nationalmuseets Skrifter Etnografisk Raekke, X. The National Museum of Copenhagen.

166

INDEX

Aborigines Protection Society, 130
acid-mine drainage, 71
Act of Capitulation, 19
African Manganese Company, 36
Aguiar, Peter D', 32
aid agencies, 2
AIDS, 67, 120, 137
Akawaio people, 7, 9, 14, 16-17, 64, 67-
9, 72, 77, 89, 91-2,
116, 123-4, 126, 133-4, 136, 138-9
Akurio people, 14
Alcan Aluminium, 75
ALCOA, 87
alcoholism, 66, 73
Amazon river, 1,7, 9, 15, 16, 22, 5, 53,
54, 55, 67, 74, 96, 109, 118
Amerindian Act, 51, 57, 154
Amerindian Lands Commission, 50, 66;
re-establishment, 154
Amerindian Peoples Association (APA),
1, 56, 80, 83, 111, 113, 121, 123,
151-2
Amerindian Research Unit (ARU), 55,
83, 97, 121, 123, 129, 152
Amerindians, 3, 131; British rule, 23,
133-4; health, 137; land claims,
47-57, 65-7, 96-7, 129-42;
political organization, 141, 151-2,
156; protected area project, 153;
reservations, 131-2, 149
'Amirang' conference, 73, 138, 152
annatto trade, 13, 17
Anselmo, Lawrence, 5, 92, 156
'Anthropolgical Reserve', proposed, 150
Arawak people, 7, 12-14, 16-17, 49, 92,
123, 134, 136, 138, 152
Arekuna people, 9, 68, 77, 91, 133, 136
Aroiama mine, 76
assimilationist policy, 134
Atkinson, Mark, 93
Atkinson, Susana, 152
Atorai people, 9
Australia, Aboriginal land, 129

Baird, Wellesley, 66
Barama mining concession, 103, 120-1,
146

Barama Company Ltd, 90, 102, 104,
107, 112, 118-19, 122-3, 143
Barima Gold Mines, 66
Barnett, Thomas, 105
bauxite, 33, 36-7, 39, 75, 87; environ-
mental impact, 76-7
Beaverbrook, Lord, 106
Benjamin, Anna, 14-15, 55, 124, 130
Berbice, 10; Slave Rebellion, 17
Berjaya sdn Bhd, 104, 107, 114-17
BERMINE, parastatal, 75
Boa Vista, road project, 1, 58-9, 73, 112,
147-8
Booker McConnell company, 30, 32
Borneo, 98, 104, 107, 120
Brazil, 1, 5, 7, 10, 15, 16, 21, 22, 31, 45,
47, 51-60, 64, 71, 73, 77, 90, 148
Britain, Labour Party, 28
British Guiana, 18-21, 131-4
British Guinea, Labour Union, 29
Broken Hill Proprietaries (BHP), 90
Brown, Harold, 150
Buchanan Forest Products, 116-17
Burnham, Forbes, 29-30, 32, 34, 36, 39,
42, 49, 75, 77, 122, 134-5, 151

CACEX, Brazilian external lending
agency, 53
Cambior Inc, 78, 83-9, 144
Campbell, Stephen, 134, 152
Canada: Export Development Corpora-
tion, 78; 'Futures Fair',
152; Indian land, 128; International
Development Agency
(CIDA), 99, 145; logging companies,
116-18 mining
companies, 92, 144
Canadian Paperworkers Union, 116
'capture' theory of regulation, 102
Capuchin missionaries, 15-16, 18, 21
Carib people, 9, 12-19, 21, 30, 58, 65-7,
92-3, 119, 124, 136, 141
Caribbean Development Bank, 39
Caribbean Group for Cooperation in
Economic Development, 112
Caribbean Resources Ltd, 100
CARICOM trade agreement, 107

Caroni people, 18
Carter Center, USA, 78, 145
cassava, 7, 12, 141
Catholic Church, 49, 134
cattle ranching, 45-8, 51; 1969 rebellion, 49-50
Central Intelligence Agency (CIA), 32
Chandarpal, Navin, 115, 146
Cleary, David, 64
'co-operative socialism', 2
cocaine, 37, 73
Colombia, 31
colonialism, sugar, 25
Colorado School of Mines, 77
Colson, Audrey Butt, 22, 68, 131
Columbus, 61
Commonwealth Development Corporation, 106
Commonwealth Forestry Commission, 105
Commonwealth Secretariat, 71, 145, 147-8
community titles, land, 136
Conan Doyle, Arthur, 5
Conservation International, 149
cotton, political economy, 26, 31
Cuba, 34
cyanide pollution, 78, 80-83

dalli trees, 97
Daly, Vere, 25, 26
Danns, George, 70, 126
David Klautky and Associates, consultancy, 56
Dayak people, Sarawak, 104, 107
debt burden, 4, 34, 37, 40-2, 112, 147; peonage, 97
Demerara, 14; river, 25
Demerara Bauxite, 75
Demerara Timbers company, 58, 106, 124, 146
Demerara Woods Ltd, 38, 98, 101
devaluation, 41
development agencies, 144, 146, 147
diamonds, 74, 77, 147; discovery, 64-5; dredging, 89;
exploration, 87; mining, 1, 61-2, 91; sale, 68
Drug Enforcement Agency, USA, 74
drug trafficking, cocaine, 37
Duncan, Christopher, 51, 138
Dutch, the: presence, 10, 12-18; alliances, 10; republican government, 26; sugar plantations, 25

Dutch West India company, 10
'East Indians', 26-8, 32
economy, 2, 3, 9, 10, 14, 15, 17, 19, 20, 22, 25, 28, 33, 36-43, 46, 48, 65, 67, 68, 69, 75, 78, 83, 98, 100, 118, 126, 137
economic liberalization, 4
eco-tourism, 83
Ecuador, 31
Edinburgh Centre for Tropical Forests, 103
education, 28, 41, 57, 118, 120, 132, 137, 138, 139, 142, 147, 152, 156
Environment Protection Act, 145
environment: legislation lack, 144; logging damage, 100-5
Environmental Protection Agency, 149
Environmental Resources Management consultancy, 56
European Commission, 149

Fagin, David, 79
fish, 7, 9, 12, 45, 137; poisoning, 80-1, 83
forest privatization, 101-3, 106-7, 110-18, 124
Forestry Stewardship Council (FSC), 115
Forte, Janette, 55
Fox, Desrey, 70, 126
Fredericks, Leonard, 138
French Guiana, 71
French Revolution, 26
Friedland, Robert, 84, 89
Friends of the Earth, 38, 83, 113

Galliers-Pratt, Rupert, 106
garimpeiros, 58, 73
GEMCO, parastatal, 80, 83
George, Randolph, 1
Georgetown, 1, 46, 54, 58, 131-2
Global Environment Facility, 149-50, 153
globalization, 4
gold mining, 1, 2, 28, 31, 37, 58, 61, 64-6, 68, 75, 91, 126, 141, 147; concessions, 77; deregulation, 78; discovery, 21; environmental damage, 71-3, 79-88; expansion, 90; fatalities, 69; illegal export, 74; technique, 70
Golden Star Resources Limited, 77-79, 83-4, 86-90, 93
Gourde, Rejean, 81
Gravesande, Storm van 'S, 15, 17, 46

greenheart trees (*ocotra rodiae*), 97-8, 103
Greenpeace, 111
gun-running, 55
Guyana: Airways Corporation, 50; 'Co-operative Republic'; Council of Churches, 111, 142; Defence Force, 50-1, 57, 60, 63; Department of Land and Surveys, 90; Forest Producers Association, 111; Forestry Commission, 99, 101-2, 106, 110, 113-14, 117, 123, 145, 155; Geology and Mines Commission(GCMC), 70, 72, 77, 92, 155; Gold and Diamond Miners Association, 90, 92; Human Rights Association, 53, 55, 83-4, 111, 113; Legal Defence Fund, 83; independence, 32; Natural Resources Agency, 39, 77, 103; Organization of Indigenous Peoples, 123, 152; soils, 96; Guyana Timbers, privatization, 99, 101
GUYMINE, parastatal, 36, 75
GUYSUC, parastatal, 36

Hallelujah Church, 142
health, 40, 41, 47, 54, 57, 67, 68, 71, 73, 76, 80, 100, 118, 120, 127, 130, 132, 137, 142, 143, 147, 148
Henry, Salome, 61, 124
Hilliard, Thomas, 85
Hinds, Sam, 43
Hogg, Dominic, 38, 40
Hoyte, Desmond, 34, 39-40, 53, 76, 79, 98, 102

Inchcape plc, 106
indentured labour, 27-8
Indigenous Peoples Development Plan, 58
Indigenous Rights, International Law, 127
intellectual property rights, Amerindian, 148
InterAmerican Development Bank (IDB), 39, 145
internal colonialism, 3
International Centre for Settlement of Investment Disputes, 103
International Development Agency, SDRs, 41
International Labour Organization, 127-8, 131, 152
International Monetary Fund (IMF), 2, 38-40, 43, 54, 75, 78, 98, 107
International Tropical Timber Organiza-

tion, 101, 115
Investment Code, 1988, 40
Iwokrama project, 147-9

Jagan, Cheddi, 1, 29-30, 32, 34, 42-3, 76, 79, 81, 102, 107, 114, 134, 140, 143-4, 147, 153-4
Jagdeo, Bharrat, 43
Jardine, Stanislaus, 92

Kaieteur Falls, national park, 147
Kamarang, 133; transformation, 68-9
Kanuku National Park, proposed, 149
King, Winston, 103
Knight Piesold Ltd, 84
Konawaruk River, 72
Korea, 2, 75, 77, 102, 107, 143

labour laws, colonial, 27
land rights, 1, 27-28, 47-8, 51, 54, 57, 65-7, 87, 90, 92, 96-7, 115, 121, 122, 126, 129-137, 138, 140, 142, 151
Latin America Bureau, 29
law, British, 129
legality, 13, 27, 47, 49, 68, 78, 116, 124, 129, 131, 134, 135, 149
Lethem, 49, 89
Linden, 76
LINMINE, parastatal, 75
logging, 1-2, 39-40, 96-7, 99; encroachment on Amerindians, 120-3; environmental damage, 101; greed, 100, 104-5, 110, 116; ownership, 107; revenues, 114; transformation, 98
Lomé trade agreement, 107
Lowe, Gloria, 138

Makushi people, 9, 45, 136; land usurpation, 48
malaria, 57, 67, 137, 148
Malaysia, 2, 90, 98, 100, 102, 104-106, 115-18, 143
Manao people, 16-17
manicole palm, 118, 119
mapping: computerized, 145; lack, 142
'Maroons', 14, 16, 19; Saramaka community, 87-9; uprisings, 26
Mazaruni area, 4, 65; Christian Council, 71; Penal Settlement, 30
Melville, H.P.C., 46
Menezes, Mary Noel, 19, 126
mercury, pollution, 70-1

Mineral Policy Center, 85
Minewatch, 83
missile dredges, 70-1, 73
missionaries, 127, 130; Jesuit, 14-15;
    Moravian, 21; Spanish, 16
Moody, Roger, 80, 84
mora trees, 97
Moruca, Amerindian communities, 141
Myers, Iris, 48

Nagamootoo, Moses, 142, 155
Napoleonic Wars, 26
National Amerindian Council, 92, 152
nationalization, 33, 36, 40, 75
New Zealand, Maori land, 128
Non-Aligned Movement, 33, 143
Non-Governmental Organizations
    (NGOs), 2, 56, 83, 84, 111-113, 117,
    118, 121, 125, 146, 147, 148
Norsk Hydro company, 76
North America, see also United States, 23,
    31, 37, 43, 54, 55, 62, 75, 78, 107,
    143

O'Lall, Joseph, 85
oil price hike, 1973, 37
Omai gold mine, 79, 81-2, 84-6, 144,
    146; Omai Gold Mines Ltd (OGML),
    78, 80-1, 87
Organization of American States (OAS),
    89
Orinoco river, 9-10, 14-15
Overseas Development Administration,
    UK, 113-14, 116-18, 145

Papua New Guinea, 100, 104-107, 110
Paranapanema, Brazilian mining com-
    pany, 53-4, 77, 90
Patamona people, 7, 58, 73-4
People's National Congress (PNC), 30,
    32-4, 36, 38, 42, 65, 76, 101, 134-5,
    137, 142
People's Progressive Party (PPP), 29-30,
    32, 34, 36, 38, 65, 76, 135, 142
Philippines, the, 44, 98, 107
Pierre, Laureen, 124, 130
Pinzón, Vincente, Yañéz, 7
Placer Dome company, 144
plantation economy, 14, 18, 25
poitos ('red slaves'), 13
pollution, 71-73, 76, 83-85, 92, 120, 121
Portugal, slavers, 15-17
poverty, 55, 100, 118, 130, 143, 147

Premdas, Ralph, 28, 33
Price, Henry, 31
Prime Group, 106, 114
privateers, English, 15
privatization, 34, 39-41, 76, 99
prostitution, 66, 69, 73

racial violence, 1960s, 30, 32
racism, 27-8, 49, 129, 130,
Raleigh, Walter, 10
Reynolds Metals, 75-6
rice, 36
Rimbunana Hijau, 105
riots, 1905, 28; 1924, 29
Riviere, Peter
roads, 1, 27, 37, 52, 55, 57, 58, 92, 96,
    104, 120
Rodney, Walter, 33
Roland, Celian, 67, 71
Roraima Mining Company, 87
Roth, Vincent, 20
Royal Geographical Society, 46
rubber, balata, 47, 97, 126, 130; boom, 31
Rupununi Development Company, 48
Rupununi revolt, 135

'safari' group, 58
Sahabat Alam, Malaysia, 105
Samling Timbers Sdn Bhd, 102, 104, 118,
    120
Sarawak, logging experience, 105
savannah, 7, 15-16
Schomburgk, Richard, 21
Schomburgk, Robert, 21, 46, 52, 59, 62
sea defences, 26
Shields, Tony, 90
slavery: African, 12, 13, 18, 25-6; British
    abolition, 19; uprisings, 26; wars, 9
Social Impact Amelioration Programme
    (SIMAP), 41
Soon, Alex Ling Lee, 114, 116
South American Goldfields, 89
South East Asia, 2, 43, 96, 97, 101, 106,
    107, 110, 116, 118, 143
South-South cooperation, 43
Spain: Guyanese settlements; Carib war,
    18; colonialism, 13, 15, 21
stereotyping, racist, 130
structural adjustment, 2, 4, 38, 40-1, 98,
    101, 107, 144
Sucre, Brian, 70, 72, 86
sugar: industry strike, 34; political
    economy, 14, 25-6, 28, 32-3, 36-7,

39, 41
Suriname, 13-14, 16, 21, 26, 75; territorial dispute, 59-60
Surinamese Liberation Front, 88
Survival International, 53, 83

tailings dams, 79-81, 84-5
Tan, Vincent, 116
Taruma people, 9
Thomas, Isolina, 122
Thomas, Benson, 150
trade unions, 30
Treaty of Utrecht, 1713, 14
tuberculosis, 67, 137

United Force (UF), 32, 49, 134
United Nations, Food and Agriculture Organization, 99
Union of Soviet Socialist Republics (USSR), 34
United States of America, 29, 31, 32, 74
University of Guyana, 53, 149; Amerindian Research Unit, 55, 83, 97, 121, 123, 129, 152, 156

vaqueiros, 47
venereal disease, 67, 120, 137
Venezuela, 25, 50, 152; gold mining, 91; road network, 58; territorial disputes, 31, 59, 62, 77; Wars of Independence, 21, 30

Wai Wai people, 9, 126, 136, 150
Wapishana people, 9, 16, 45, 48, 51, 138
Warao people, 7, 12-14, 20, 123, 136
West India Company, 14
Westoby, Jack, 99
Whitehead, Neil, 18
Williams, Toni, 111
Williams, Wilfred, 73
Working People's Alliance (WPA), 33, 38
World Bank, 2, 38-9, 55-6, 58, 70, 72, 77-8, 83, 85, 98, 102, 144-6, 150, 153; development model, 43; export strategy, 41; Forest Policy, 115; International Development Corporation, 106; Recovery programme, 75; schizophrenia, 146
World Commssion on Forests and Sustainable Development, 111
World Conservation Union, 119
World Council of Churches, 89
World Rainforest Movement, 2, 55, 82-3, 85, 99, 113, 121, 148
World Rainforest Programme, 147
World Resources Institute, 118

Ye' kuana people, 16

171

Other Books from the Latin America Bureau

GREEN GUERRILLAS
Environmental conflicts in Latin America - A Reader
Helen Collinson (ed)

'This is a book about heroes and villains, more to do with sheer survival than good causes... While warning of the dire consequences of the present unsustainable rate of degradation of natural resources in Latin America and the Caribbean, it also shows that when people directly affected by environmental change - the villagers, slum-dwellers, Indians, fishermen and city residents - are given a chance, their proposals to do things differently can work.' *Times Literary Supplement*

Brings together leading environmental writers from both sides of the Atlantic, including Latin America. Vivid reports from the grassroots are combined with concise, hardhitting analysis of the continental movements in the 1990s.

250 pages, index, 1996
ISBN 1 899365 04 4 pbk
Distributed in the USA by Monthly Review Press

RETURN OF THE INDIAN
Conquest and Revival in the Americas
Phillip Wearne
Foreword by Rigoberta Menchú

'The ambitious scope of **Return of the Indian** in documenting the experiences of the indigenous nationals of the Americas, both North and South, makes this volume a welcome addition to recent work published on the subject.

Phillip Wearne covers the continent from Alaska to Tierra del Fuego, distilling the past 500 years to one enduring theme: dispossession. Although the manner and context may differ according to the colonial and post-colonial power, the outcome has been the same - disenfranchisement and resettlement in the push to extend the land under cultivation or extraction. Human rights, land and the environment emerge as inextricable, making up an unholy alliance in the Indian nations of the Americas...

Return of the Indian is an optimistic account. These are nations poised to regain lost ground, and there has been a renaissance in indigenous activism. This is a meticulously researched book which is also accessible.'
Times Literary Supplement

240 pages, 16 colour plates, black and white photos, index, 1996
ISBN 0 304 334588 pbk
Published in the USA by Temple University Press

For a free copy of the Latin America Bureau's latest books catalogue write to:
Latin America Bureau, Dept GFF, 1 Amwell Street, London EC1R 1UL
Tel: 0171 278 2829   Fax: 0171 278 0165   E.mail lab@gn.apc.org

172